SHAHHAT

An Egyptian

CONTEMPORARY ISSUES IN THE MIDDLE EAST

Shahhat

SHAHHAT

An Egyptian

RICHARD CRITCHFIELD

Syracuse University Press

I wish to thank the Ford Foundation for its grant support and the editors of *The Christian Science Monitor, The Economist* (London), the *Los Angeles Times, The Washington Star,* and *The New Republic* for publishing articles on Egypt which helped finance a year's stay in an Upper Nile village. As is evident, I owe a great debt to my interpreter, Nubi el Hagag, of Luxor.

RC

Library of Congress Cataloging in Publication Data

Critchfield, Richard.
  Shahhat, an Egyptian.

  (Contemporary issues in the Middle East)
  1. Egypt—Social life and customs. 2. Peasantry—
Egypt. 3. Shahhat. I. Title. II. Series.
DT70.C74   301.29′62   78-11945
ISBN 0-8156-0151-4/CRSEP

Manufactured in the United States of America

In memory of their help and enthusiasm
and our happy days beside that wonderful river, the Nile,
I dedicate this book to
Margery and Samuel Bunker.

Richard Critchfield is a special correspondent for *The Economist* (London) and contributor to *The Christian Science Monitor*. He has written about peasant life in the Third World since 1959 and is the author of numerous articles and books on the subject, including *The Long Charade* and *The Golden Bowl Be Broken: Peasant Life in Four Cultures*. Critchfield is currently studying rural cultural change in Asia, Africa, and Latin America under a Rockefeller Foundation Humanities Fellowship.

CONTENTS

FOREWORD

HAT ARE VILLAGERS in India, in Egypt, in Mexico really like? How are they organized in social units—in families, work groups, and communities—that are viable and self-perpetuating? What are the structural and behavioral characteristics of these units? How do villagers perceive life, its opportunities, its limitations? How do they see their relationships with their fellows? When, how, and with whom do they quarrel? Make peace? Love? Hate?

For nearly fifty years anthropologists (by no means to the exclusion of others) have searched for answers to questions like these, living with villagers in order to question them and to observe their behavior, describing their findings in books and articles. Following the lead of Robert Redfield, anthropologists initially described their research as the study of "folk" societies, in contrast to the study of the more isolated tribal societies that had previously been the focus of anthropological interest. After World War II, however, anthropologists—Redfield included—came to realize that "peasant" is a more appropriate term, and thus was born the new subfield of "peasant studies."

From about 1950 to the early 1970s investigations of peasant society dominated anthropology; it is quite possible that more than half of all research anthropologists carried out during this period concerned peasants. It was an enormously productive period, in description and in theory-building. Peasant societies were defined and described, their principal characteristics were noted, and a number of significant theories and concepts emerged to explain peasant social structure, economies, and behavior. Anthropologists quickly realized that peasant communities are, and have been throughout history, much more closely tied to cities and nation-states than have been the tribal societies they had previously studied. Recognizing this, most anthropologists accept some variant of

Kroeber's definition of peasants: part-societies with part-cultures, class segments of larger populations that include market towns and sometimes metropolitan centers.

Consciously and subconsciously post–World War II anthropologists have envisaged peasant communities against the backdrop of, and in contrast to, the tribal groups of the so-called primitive world of North and South America, Africa, and Oceania. The similarities to, and the differences between, these two broad categories of communities structured research and hypothesizing, determining decisions as to what constitutes "data" and what does not, that is, what is or is not important, unique or not unique, in peasant societies. Perhaps the first significant thing noted was that the village rather than the clan or lineage is the basic social unit, and that the bilateral principle more often than not takes precedence over the unilinear principal in determining kinship. Since peasant communities tend to lack strong extended families, lineages, and clans, anthropologists have sometimes felt they are more centrifugal, more atomistic, less tightly integrated than tribal societies. But in attempting to explain how they functioned in the absence of these extended kin groups, anthropologists came to see that contractual ties can work just as effectively as kinship ties in glueing a society together. Achieved relationships that include friendship, reciprocity bonds, patron-client ties, and fictive kinship (in Latin America the *compadrazgo* godparenthood institution) are highly effective devices to knit together individuals, families, and social classes.

Peasant personality and character have also attracted the attention of anthropologists, and most, following Oscar Lewis, have concluded that the idyllic picture portrayed by Robert Redfield is erroneous. Peasant life has its satisfying side, but frequently it also has its darker side, as Richard Critchfield's *Shahhat* makes clear: gossip, witchcraft, fear or envy, distrust of neighbors, family quarrels, and the like. Today, to say such a thing is no longer viewed as equivalent to an attack on motherhood, as it was when Lewis first took issue with Redfield; we now realize that such behavior, in the context of the poverty and limited opportunity of traditional peasant life, is highly adaptive. Under similar conditions we would all do the same thing.

Concern with peasant behavior also has led anthropologists to the concept of world view, the cognitive orientation of peasants, their view of the world around them that determines their life strategies. We have found that traditional world views, and particularly a zero-sum game outlook—the belief that all good things in life are limited, so that one person's success is at the expense of others—often make it difficult for peasants to take advantage of the new opportunities increasingly available to them. Happily, a traditional world view is proving to be, in times of rapid change and new opportunity, no more than a holding action, a delaying operation, for with real change, and the growth to adulthood of a new generation, these views give way to new outlooks more adaptive to contemporary reality.

It is against this historical background of peasant studies that *Shahhat: An Egyptian* is best read. *Shahhat* is not, as its author makes clear, an anthropological study in the narrow sense of the word. But although Richard Critchfield is a journalist, he looks at villagers through the eyes of anthropology: he correctly understands culture to be what "provides human beings with a design for living, with a ready-made set of solutions to problems so that individuals in each new generation do not have to start from scratch." He also knows that culture is an adaptive device, that it and those who follow its dictates are strained, sometimes to the breaking point, when change comes too rapidly for adjustment. Interestingly, although Mr. Critchfield emphasizes his credentials as a journalist, in one way he sees himself as more anthropological than anthropologists themselves. Certainly, to live for a year in a small village, in intimate association with a single family, and its friends and enemies, is anthropology and not journalism. Yet when Mr. Critchfield suggests that this year was characterized by a "deep personal engagement" that is "of course very different from that of the anthropologist," I must disagree with him. Personal engagement is the hallmark of anthropologists, for some deeper than for others, but almost always present in some degree. Mr. Critchfield's engagement obviously is deep, but it is no deeper than that of many anthropologists I have known, including the late Oscar Lewis, after whom he models his own work. The research of Lewis, whom I knew well, certainly was marked by deep personal attachment to his informants, in Mexico City and Tepoztlán, and concern for their well-being. In my own case, after nearly thirty-five years of continuing research in a Mexican village, including twenty years of residence in the home of the same family, I claim some degree of "deep personal engagement" with the community and its inhabitants. Anthropologists are less coldly scientific and more warmly human, I believe, than Mr. Critchfield imagines.

xi

Nevertheless, in emphasizing his feelings of deep personal attachment in contrast to the "scientific" approach of the anthropologist, Mr. Critchfield is making an important point about his work: it is neither scientific nor theoretical. It is, in his own words, "verbal portraiture," and it represents the work of an artist of very great talent. To note that *Shahhat* is neither scientific nor theoretical is no more a criticism than to say that a great painting is neither scientific nor theoretical. Both science and art communicate important points, in a different language and in a different way. It would be a mistake to assume that a nonscientific, nontheoretical account of village life cannot speak to the more theoretically minded reader. Quite the contrary. The remarkable thing about *Shahhat* is the extent to which it illuminates and confirms the points anthropologists have made about peasant society. Who, after reading of the violence, drunkenness, cursing, fear of the evil eye, bad feelings between families, and broken relationships between mother and son in Berat, can continue to believe in the stereotype of idyllic village life? Mr. Critchfield correctly notes that "misery does not unite people, as one might imagine, but divides them." But not inevitably, or all of the time. What anthropologist cannot read of Shahhat's zest for life, his love of the land, his appreciation of his friends, without feeling, "This is a man I, too, have known and loved."

In our quest to know how others live, many paths lead to understanding. For anthropologists, comprehension of peasant society has been deepened by the accounts of novelists, poets, historians, political scientists, sociologists, psychologists—and now by that of a journalist. Richard Critchfield has given us one of the most absorbing accounts of peasant life I have ever read. He writes with the skills of a novelist, and he paints with the brush of an artist. No one who reads *Shahhat* will forget the book's principal protagonist. Shahhat the man speaks for and to us; in him we see something of ourselves. And in so doing we gain deeper understanding of ourselves, and of the ties that bind us to others.

University of California, Berkeley   George M. Foster
Spring 1978

AUTHOR'S NOTE

THIS IS THE STORY of how a deeply traditional Egyptian, when faced with sudden changes in his way of life, tries to master his condition and communicate with those around him. He belongs to the oldest people in the world, yet like most of his countrymen he is very young. It is the story of how he comes of age.

The setting is a village called Berat, high on the Nile. As in any story set in the Third World today, particularly the Arab world, it enters the difficult ground of cultural, and psychological, turbulence. In the traditional anthropological view, culture is what provides human beings with a design for living, with a ready-made set of solutions to problems so that individuals in each new generation do not have to start again from scratch. That is, the successful core of culture is its adaptive function. Culture breaks down when it is too traditional and when change comes too fast.

In the remote and isolated upper Nile valley, the teachings of medieval Islam overlay early Christian influences and pharaonic customs and values going back at least 6,000 years. Foreign conquerers have come and gone—the Persians, Greeks, Romans, Byzantines, Arabs, Turks, French and English. As Henry Habib Ayrout once observed, while the Upper Egyptian villagers changed their masters and their religion, their language and their crops, they never changed their way of life. The reason for this extraordinary continuity was that village values are determined by agricultural tasks, and theirs were based upon the age-old annual flood of the river. The Nile's last flood came in the mid-1960s, after the new High Dam at Aswan began storing water. This increase in scientific and material power, instead of diminishing cultural turbulence, left the people of Upper Egypt far more vulnerable to it.

The purpose of this book is to show, through the life of one Egyptian peasant, or *fellah,* how such disruptions affect the way people

xiii

think and feel. The situation is a universal one in the Third World today, but in few other places do the old and new collide quite so emphatically.

Shahhat, the central figure in the story, with his Arab Bedouin blood, may be a little closer to the dark springs of life than the average *fellah*. Yet the Saidis who inhabit the middle Nile valley up to Aswan are known for their conservatism, hot blood, and quick tempers. Shahhat is typical of the great mass of poor Egyptians in his emotionalism and search for explanations to natural phenomena, not in modern logic, but in the sacred and profane supernatural. A mother driven by rising expectations, an uncle who accepts modernization and its values, and a sharecropper who hedonistically exploits them—all represent people found in the rural Third World today. For these reasons I found Shahhat and his problems exemplary.

At the request of those in the story themselves real names and their photographs have been used. No attempt has been made to preserve anonymity, with two minor exceptions—Hasan and Suleyman, which are not their real names. Most of the villagers were as interested as I was in trying to make themselves and their way of life more familiar to Western readers.

The time span, after a look at Shahhat's early years, mostly covers a single year, from August, the month of the Nile's old annual flood, to another August twelve months later. My interpreter and I tried not to influence developments by our presence; I feel, in the main, we succeeded.

The word *fellah* is the intensive adjective of the Arabic verb *falaha,* which means to till the soil. In Egypt it also implies a peculiarly organic relationship to the land beside the Nile, one's native village, and its very old way of life. Since money figures frequently in the story, a reader might note from the outset that although rates of exchange keep changing, the purchasing power of an Egyptian pound is about that of two American dollars. There are a hundred piastres in a pound.

The setting—the Theban plain near the present town of Luxor—was chosen as being in Upper Egypt's most traditional region. The story is not intended to portray all *fellaheen* life. Six out of ten rural Egyptians live in the triangular Nile Delta north of Cairo to the Mediterranean. Here modernization has come gradually since the river was tamed by a series of dams near Cairo and agriculture shifted from the old flood to year-round irrigation a century ago.

It is only along the remote upper Nile, isolated by the desert, that pharaonic influences are still strong. The hundreds of statues and busts in the Cairo Museum suggest the facial and physical appearance of the villagers on the Theban Plain have not changed much in the past thirty or forty centuries; unlike in Cairo or the Delta, there is little Arab, Turk, or Greek blood. The painted friezes in the tombs of nobles and officials of the 18th and 19th Dynasties, which honeycomb the hills on the west bank from Luxor, indicate many methods of cultivation have hardly changed at all. Since the introduction of diesel irrigation pumps this past decade, many *saqias* or cow-drawn water wheels dating from the Ptolemaic period (332 to 30 B.C.) have been abandoned (though not, because of a higher water level, in the Delta). But still in use in Upper Egypt are the *shaduf* or well sweep, the *norag* or threshing sledge, the *midraya* or wooden winnowing fork, and the basic tool of the *fellaheen,* the *fass* or short-handled hoe. All these go back to early pharaonic times. (The calendar was introduced in Egypt in 4241 B.C. and the first dynasty of Menes began in 3400 B.C. Recent archeological discoveries provide evidence Upper Egypt has been settled since the Stone Age and wheat was cultivated along the Nile as early as 13,000 B.C., the earliest known date man has farmed.)

In Upper Egypt today village death rites, though prayer performances by Moslem sheikhs, are in conformity to pharaonic, not Islamic, tradition, as is the wailing of mourning women. Saidi women use *kohl* to blacken their eyelashes and outline their eyes and henna to redden their hair, just as Nefertiti did. Both men and women shave off their body hair, a practice that goes back to antiquity. The occurrence of adultery, fornication, and sodomy, despite severe Moslem penalties, seems an assertion of pagan sensuality absent elsewhere in Egypt. Such discoveries as the complete archives of a village scribe named Meches—who recorded the day to day activities of Kerkeosiris village in 120–111 B.C.—reveal that the size of land holdings (average two acres), the cropping of wheat, barley, and lentils, their very yields, the raising of pigeons, and the deeding of land to ex-soldiers, have changed little. The control of irrigation water is much the same and Meches' descriptions of village disputes and banditry could be contemporary.

Nile agriculture is unique and is based totally upon irrigation in a virtually rainless climate. In Egypt the river cuts its northward path through bare desert for 750 miles—the irrigated valley is a sharply delineated strip of green seldom more than five to ten miles wide south of Cairo. It is actually a trench cut deep into the desert floor so that from the valley the cliffs on either side resemble mountains. Its bottom is filled with twenty to thirty feet of silt carried down over tens of thousands of years from the Ethiopian plateau, and to a lesser extent, the mountains and lakes of present-day Uganda and Tanzania.

The Nile provided water and the necessity for irrigation since little grew on its banks without it. This in turn led to a centralized authority to control its flow and the rise of a socially differentiated and eventually civilized state. As it flooded its banks each August, the mineral-rich silt perpetually renewed the soil. The leaching of the flood waters also rescued Egypt from the curse of salination which led to the early disappearance of the other two first river valley civilizations, in Mesopotamia and the Indus Valley. As Herodotus wrote, "Egypt is an acquired country, the gift of the river."

The Nile's changing flow created a rhythmic cycle of life for a people who, perpetually reminded of eternity and the brevity of human life by the desert and the colossal pharaonic monuments, developed a distinct mentality: they preserved and repeated, but did not originate, create, or change. Each August the Nile, fed by distant snowfall and rains in Africa, rose to overflow its banks. For weeks the *fellaheen* dammed it back, then allowed the water to flood their fields from September to November. Drained back into the Nile again, the water left behind its fresh, fertile level of silt. The *fellaheen* had little to do but sow their wheat, barley, and lentils—the age-old crops of Egypt—and wait for the April harvest. Only one major crop was grown each year and summer was a time of rest.

One can only guess how long this went on; at least for 240 generations and perhaps twice that many, a staggering continuity when one considers Jesus lived only 80 generations ago and the United States has been a nation for only eight. Then, just a decade ago, it suddenly came to an end.

Population pressures caught up with Egypt, as elsewhere, in the latter half of the twentieth century. Egypt's people, who numbered no more than 7 million in pharaonic times, but may have reached 20 million during the six centuries Egypt was a Christian country ruled by Rome, were reduced by war and disease to 2.5 million by the early 19th century. Since then the number has risen steadily. It is 40 million now, half of it concentrated in cities, and is projected to reach 74 million by the year 2000.

In recent times anyone seeking to govern Egypt has been forced to put prime importance upon feeding such large and growing numbers of people. This can only be done if there is an assured year-round water supply to grow two or three crops a year, instead of one as before, on the same amount of land and getting extremely high per acre yields, as Egypt has done. Political necessity led to the construction of the High Dam at Aswan, an earth-filled structure two miles long and a mile wide at the base and seventeen times bigger than the biggest pyramid.

The idea of taming the Nile was not new since some years the flood was excessive. From Imhotep, who designed the first pyramid, to the modern British, who built the first Aswan Dam in 1902, raising it higher in 1914 and 1936, no one had much success. After a destructive flood in 1938, plans were drawn up for a much higher dam south of Aswan. After delays caused by World War II, the revolution led by Gamal Abdel Nasser in 1952, and his disputes with the World Bank and the United States, the dam was finally begun in 1960, under Russian guidance and finance. By then providing enough water to expand irrigation, not flood control, had become its main purpose. It began storing water in 1964, generating electricity in 1970, and was finally completed in 1971, one of the four or five biggest dams on earth.

At first universally recognized as being a success, it soon became evident that many of the dam's economic benefits were being undermined by unpredicted ecological backlash, although the outcry from Western environmentalists tended to ignore Egypt's need to feed its people. In 1975 Egyptian and American scientists began the most ambitious study of a lake and river ecosystem ever attempted to "measure the Nile" and determine the chemical, biological, and geological factors involved in the composition and movement of its waters. The preliminary finding of this study, to be completed in 1980, was that while the dam had helped to almost double Egypt's food supply (improved agricultural technology also figured in), a steady rise in the underground water table of the Nile valley threatened large areas with salinity, alkalinity, and water logging. Massive drainage and leaching projects have been undertaken. Other negative environmental effects include the loss of silt, the erosion of the Nile's riverbed, and the spread of such aquatic weeds as water hyacinth and the snails which carry the dangerous schistosomiasis parasite known as bilharzia in Egypt. These too are being combatted, with mixed success.

The last Nile flood in the region of the Theban Plain, the setting of our story, came in 1966–67 upon completion of an elaborate new network of irrigation canals bringing water from Aswan. From then on, continuous crops were grown, two to three each year. Chemical fertilizer, *Nitrokima,* artificially manufactured at Aswan, was applied heavily. New high-yielding grain varieties were introduced, as were such cash crops as sugar cane. Ancient water wheels and well sweeps started to be replaced by small diesel pumps. Field work became constant and year round. This transformation began only in the late 1960s and is not yet complete. This shift from flood to perennial irrigation took place in the more populous Delta in the mid-19th century, and there the *fellaheen* have had over a hundred years to culturally adapt. They have successfully substituted animal manure, plus some chemical fertilizer, for the Nile's lost silt and in many places ended the threat of salinity with underground tile drainage. Crop yields have steadily risen and continue to rise. Part of an entire younger generation is literate, and so much importance is placed on education even the poorest *fellaheen* families somehow manage to send at least one son or daughter to a technical college; the need to educate and export surplus family members to seek jobs in Cairo or abroad is generally accepted. An agricultural revolution, given a century's time, has created new cultural values.

This is barely beginning to happen in Upper Egypt. Crop yields have steadily fallen the past ten years. The *fellaheen* are unaccustomed to year-round pump irrigation and few understand that too much water raises the underground level; when it reaches four feet below the surface, it stifles roots and plants turn yellow. This is mistaken for the failure of chemical fertilizer to replace the Nile's silt. Dung continues to be used as cooking fuel. Illiteracy is high and few villagers grasp the importance of educating their children. Spending patterns remain traditional with large sums going for feasts, all-night prayer performances, and weddings rather than investment in agriculture or education. Sizeable amounts of small family budgets go for cigarettes, liquor, and hashish.

In the Delta a typical family possesses the national average of two acres of land, a buffalo or two cows, a donkey, and a few sheep. Chickens, pigeons, and rabbits are raised for family consumption. Egyptian clover is grown to feed the livestock and wheat, maize, and vegetables for the family's diet. Cash income of $1,200 a year comes from sales of surplus maize and wheat ($400), butter ($240), sheep ($200), and a cash crop of cotton or something new like seed potatoes ($560). Average monthly expenditures are $8 for meat (one kilo every Thursday night is a Moslem custom), $10 for cloth and sandals, $6 for tobacco, 20 cents for matches, $3 for sugar, $3 for tea, $1 for kerosene, and $1.30 for soap, for a total of $32.50 (really poor landless laborers' families may go down to $25 or so a month, but not much lower). In contrast, an Upper Egyptian family with the same land, livestock, and cash income may spend almost twice that much, the difference coming in cigarettes, meat, and sugar and tea (to serve friends and neighbors in traditional hospitality). The Delta family may spend as much as $20 a month on education, the Upper Egyptian very little. Daily field wages range from 70 cents to $1 in Upper Egypt; in the Delta they are twice this as more jobs exist in the nearby towns.

Upper Egypt seems destined to follow the Delta cultural pattern given time, as do new settlements on land irrigated and reclaimed from the desert. Whatever its drawbacks, and aside from allowing continuous land use, the Aswan Dam by the late 1970s made it possible to reclaim 900,000 acres of desert land, two-thirds of which has been brought under the plough. Yet so much land had been lost to urban sprawl and salinity, Egypt still had only 5.6 million irrigated and cultivated acres, just about what it had when the dam was built. Egypt's only real hope for the future, given the density and growth rate of its population, lies in irrigating more land.

In a talk this writer had with Anwar Sadat in the summer of 1976, the Egyptian President spoke of trying to double the amount of irrigated land by the year 2000. He planned to pursue a development strategy of investing heavily in agri-industry and gradually shifting the Nile valley out of fodder and grain production and into high-value cash crops like fruit, vegetables, dairy, and poultry for export. In this way, he felt, Egypt could feed its projected population by buying wheat to feed its cities from abroad. He believed such a strategy made more sense than rapid industrialization in Egypt given its low level of literacy and its strong agricultural traditions. Sadat is Egypt's first ruler of truly *fellaheen* origins; he worked in the fields in his youth, and he still retains close ties with his native village in the Delta. He was deeply concerned about the disruptive cultural effect of rapid change as raised in this story, especially in the villages, and said he told those who wanted to modernize too fast to "look to our community, our people, and our heritage." He was worried about the emergence of a spiritually rootless society, especially among the young, and said, "Egypt should return to the main principles of our heritage. I don't want the new generation to be a lost generation."

Readers can locate Berat village from Luxor, which lies two miles east of it across the Nile and figures in the story. Luxor, whose name comes from the Arabic *el uksur,* or "the palaces," is, of course, famous the world over as the site of ancient Thebes and the greatest assembly of pharaonic tombs and temples in Egypt. It was from Thebes, after the

Shahhat's hamlet of Lohlah, one of eleven which make up Berat village, lies just outside the gates of Medinet Habu, the mortuary temple of Ramses III, and the last and southernmost ruin of what was the necropolis of ancient Thebes. This view eastward from atop a temple pylon shows the fields of Lohlah and Berat's ten other hamlets, which are scattered from the desert to the Nile's western bank. The present-day Egyptian town of Luxor lies just across the river, two miles east.

capital was moved from Memphis about 3,600 years ago to escape the tomb robbers who plundered the royal graves in the great pyramids, that Egypt conquered much of the known world and pharaonic civilization came to full flower. The Theban rulers included such famed pharaohs as Thutmose, Amenhotep, the heretic Ikhnaton, Tutankhamon, Ramses II and Ramses III, and Merneptah, the pharaoh at the time of Moses and the Exodus.

The view northward from a temple pylon; a temple guardian is in the foreground. In the background is Gurnet Marai, Berat's only hamlet above the irrigated plain, and the cliffs of the Libyan Desert, where the great Sahara begins.

Luxor is a small town today 450 river miles up the Nile from Cairo, though it is less than an hour's flight by jet. A visitor is pleasantly surprised to find so many of the ancient granite courts and pylons, columns and colossal statues of the Luxor and Karnak temples still either intact or reconstructed during the past century. They rise remarkably well preserved over the noisy, squalid streets and river wharves of the modern town. Even now Luxor is a place of horse-drawn carriages and flowing

Looking southward, Berat's only Christian hamlet of Basili lies on the edge of the irrigated fields; a walled white church in the arid, lifeless desert beyond has been continuously used for worship since Roman times.

tunics with few cars and little modern dress. This and the gigantic temples give it a timeless air; one does not feel back in antiquity, but one does not feel quite in the late twentieth century either.

Across from the town, on the western bank of the Nile, in desert foothills two miles inland over a flat green plain, can be found almost a dozen separate assemblies of enormous mortuary temples and more than four hundred excavated tombs—what was once the Theban City of the Dead. The furthest reach of this, two more miles inland along a steep, twisting road through soaring limestone cliffs in the Libyan Desert, is the desolate Valley of the Kings, where the pharaohs had their secret tombs. The mile-wide necropolis falls mostly within the present-day village of

The pylons of the temple of Ramses III and the cliffs of the Libyan Desert rise above the mudbrick houses and palm trees of Lohlah as Shahhat (left) cultivates his fields of onion and Egyptian clover.

Qurna, inhabited by the descendants of Horobat warriors, who arrived to settle there in the thirteenth century as tomb robbers, an occupation many still follow.

Just to the south of Qurna and extending from the Nile to the desert's edge, is Berat village. It covers about four square miles of wheat, maize, cane, and clover fields and is almost entirely inhabited by ancient *fellaheen* stock. The soil itself is composed of the dust and debris of towns and palaces lost to time. The ploughs of the villagers uncover potsherds, fragments of jewelry and glass, bits of bone, and crumbling pieces of linen, ancient mummy wrappings. Continuously inhabited as long as anywhere

The canal path behind Shahhat's house and his remaining fields of ancestral land. The path passes the family's walled garden of date palms and grapes, Suniya's house, the land tilled by El Azap, and the house and land of Hagg Abd el Mantaleb, the rich miser.

on earth, it is hard to imagine how many people have lived, died, and been buried here.

Berat's seven thousand people live in eleven distinct hamlets, each a cluster of mudbrick houses shaded by date palm, acacia, and Egyptian sycamore, with a minaret rising here and there. There is only one pharaonic ruin standing in Berat, and this is a large and splendid temple on its northwestern edge built more than three thousand years ago by Ramses III. It is known today by an early Christian designation as Medinet Habu and is one of the two or three most perfectly preserved temples in Egypt, even to the still-bright colors on some of its ceilings and walls.

Medinet Habu is the last and southernmost temple in the Theban necropolis. With its gigantic granite battlements, pylons, and pillared courts, and nothing but desert to the south, it suggests the decline of our most enduring civilization and the end of a long line of imperial pharaohs, of whom Ramses III was indeed the last.

Huddled between the high temple walls and a new irrigation channel from Aswan, named after its setting as the Ramses Canal, are some forty houses, one of Berat's smallest hamlets. So obscure it barely has a name, it is known by the local *fellaheen* merely as the place of Lohlah, after the great-grandfather of some of the present inhabitants. Beside the temple, it seems scarcely worth a glance. But the villagers have preserved something more precious than stone. In the thirty-two centuries the temple has stood silent and dead in the rainless desert air, successive generations in the humble mudhuts have kept a way of life alive. It is one that in a few more years will probably be lost forever.

To the traveler the hamlet of Lohlah looks like every other Egyptian village. There are the same cows circling the waterwheels, the same pigeon-lofts on the roofs, the same dark, curious Egyptian faces swathed in black or white. There is the familiar whiff of cooking smoke, dried cow dung, Turkish coffee, and sweet and heavy scents. If you peer down its mud-walled lanes, but for the flies, dust, and squalor, it might be picturesque. But no one would dream of wanting to live there. It is down one of these lanes that Shahhat's house lies and where our story begins.

SHAHHAT
An Egyptian

PART ONE

To resist him that is set in authority is evil.

> The Instruction of Ptahhotep
> (*circa* 2675 B.C., Thebes)

The Nile floods have fallen, the spring grazing is good. Go out with Allah's blessing and enjoy the land, its milk, its flocks, and its herds. And take good care of your neighbors.

> Amr, the Moslem conquerer of Egypt, who swept out of Arabia with 3,500 cavalrymen in A.D. 633. He was speaking to his victorious warriors after defeating the Romans and seizing Cairo.

A Prayer to Ammon-Ra

O H, MY GOD! I demand from you an invitation to Mecca! In any way, by money justly earned, before I die!"

Shahhat listened to his mother's passionate cry with a wry grin, knowing what would come next.

"But I would need to take Shahhat."

"Me? I wouldn't go. Even if it cost nothing."

The grin grew wider. When he was amused, Shahhat had an unusually broad, kind, and gentle grin like that of a small boy, one of those infectious grins to which it is difficult not to respond with one in return.

He laughed, seeing his mother assume the haughty dignity she always wore when someone tried to bring her down to earth.

"If you went to Mecca," he teased her, "you would come back a very pious Moslem. There would be no more drinking or cursing in the house. You would keep us to a narrow path. Who could live with you? Go to Mecca! *Yah salaam!*"

That is how they would go on in the old days. In Ommohamed's presence Shahhat was always humorously combative. She made her demands, arms upraised, luminous eyes flashing in her theatrical way; Shahhat resisted them. She told him, "It is important to dress well, even if you have to go hungry." He habitually went about in the same faded black tunic, so full of holes his hairy chest or brown muscular arms showed through, the same old gray wool scarf wound about his skullcap, his bare, bony feet kicking up the dust; he looked like a beggar.

It is said Egyptian peasant women are old at thirty. In the harsh desert dryness and heat a woman quickly grows thin and plain, and beauty and smiles give way to a resigned, sad expression. Ommohamed was in her mid-forties and still beautiful. It was true her face had begun to

3

Ommohamed, Shahhat's mother, keeps her fierce pride and romantic hunger for the future despite her harsh and often tragic life.

wrinkle around the eyes when she was amused. And disappointment had etched faint lines about her mouth. Yet she had that strong-boned kind of face that holds its looks no matter what life brings. She had the peculiarly straight nose, oval face, fair complexion, and large lustrous eyes familiar from ancient Egyptian statues and paintings. Strangers were surprised to learn she had borne twenty children, only to see fourteen of them sicken and die. By the time she entered middle age, Ommohamed had suffered many tragic losses; not only were all but six of her children dead, but her parents and grandparents had been carried off in a malaria epidemic—all her family but two brothers were gone.

These losses had taught Ommohamed to be fatalistic; yet she kept, which was part of her fatalism, an unquenched hunger for the future, for

4

hunger for the future was what kept her going. Most of her hopes were pinned upon Shahhat, the oldest of her three surviving sons and the first to reach manhood.

He did not resemble her. One of the grandfathers of Ommohamed's husband, Abd el Baset, came not from the ancient stock of the Nile *fellaheen*, but was an Arabian Bedouin, from fierce and wild horsemen who lived out on the sands and rock far east of the Nile, surviving by herding, carrying goods in camel caravans, and, in lean times, by plunder and killing. There were ancient race hatreds between the *fellaheen*, as "diggers of the soil," and these desert marauders. But Khalifa, Shahhat's great-grandfather, after a bloody falling-out with his tribe, had come to the valley with a string of camels, sold them for land, married, and settled down. He eventually prospered and bought ten acres, one of which Abd el Baset had inherited from his father.

Khalifa's Bedouin blood had come out in Shahhat. Once fully grown he stood well over six feet with a strong, muscular build, straight as a stick, brown skinned, and slightly hooknosed. Except for his curly black hair, with its hint of African negro blood, he looked more Arabian than Egyptian; most of the young men in his village of Berat were shorter, more heavily built, and had strong cheekbones, thick noses, and heavy jaws. Among their rugged faces, Shahhat's stood out as singularly sensitive and expressive. His finer, more Semitic features and more excitable temperament, his sense of vengeance that was not without its cruel side, and his love of the desert which most *fellaheen* regarded with horror, marked Shahhat as one with the blood of tent dwellers and herdsmen.

Such Arab blood is not uncommon among the Saidis, the taller, sturdier, darker-skinned race of Egyptians who inhabit the middle Nile Valley up to Aswan, although many are of pure pharaonic stock. Yet Ommohamed never knew quite what to make of him. Her two younger sons and three daughters resembled her own family in their quieter character and facial appearance. After one of Shahhat's hot-blooded outbursts of temper, she would pray, "Oh, Allah, make my son calm and quiet."

As she grew older Ommohamed held on to the romantic imagination of her girlhood, even as a middle-aged woman beaten down by loss and misfortune. She never asked for pity and dismissed it with withering sarcasm. But she did want it to be accepted by all her neighbors that life had not dealt with her in a fitting fashion; that she was not intended to stay among the poor and humble forever. And with her fierce imagina-

Shahhat, whose name is the Arabic word for "beggar," but also means "he who demands of God." His Semitic looks, excitable temperament, and love of the desert reveal his Arab Bedouin blood.

tion—despite the poverty she never escaped—she clung to the belief that if she could only kiss the black stone of Mecca and journey to Mount Arafat to secure Allah's blessing, there was still time for her fortunes to change.

A year before Shahhat was born Ommohamed had once broken the most inviolate principle of Islam: that there is no god but Allah. Since then she had become very pious, strictly following Koranic ritual and observing the moral laws of prayer, almsgiving, and fasting. She feared Shahhat's hot blood and quick temper was Allah's way of punishing her and was secretly obsessed with the belief that only a pilgrimage to Mecca would bring her absolution. What had the good woman done?

She had prayed to be blessed with a son strong enough to survive to manhood—not to Allah, but to the ancient pharaonic god, Ammon-Ra.

Even twenty years later Ommohamed shuddered to think about it. It was blurred in her memory with the malaria epidemic when she was twelve years old and the sudden terrible fevers that brought death so quickly to so many the men piled the bodies onto carts and dumped them into common pits in the graveyard—no one even had a burial shroud; and her marriage a year later to Abd el Baset, a soldier just home from the army, with black curly hair and broad shoulders, who had to pay for her dowry himself—her nearest surviving relative, an uncle near the Nile, refused to part with more than a humiliating four pounds.

She remembered how her extreme youth, proud ways, and affection for her brothers—especially Ahmed, orphaned at the age of four—right from the first put her on bad terms with Abd el Baset's family, so that he had to build them a separate mudbrick house down on the plain.

How happy the first ten years of marriage had been until her two sons, Jahalan and El Azap, eight and nine, fell ill, and after terrible delirium, died. No one could explain to her why. She herself came to believe that demons sent by Satan had strangled them. She also had two daughters, who were spared, but when she gave birth to two more male babies and they both died the same way, she became terrified that Abd el Baset would divorce her.

She was frantic. She sacrificed sheep at the holiest of shrines. She bought amulets and magic written charms, that, burned in a pot of incense, were said to make a wish reality. She consulted sorcerers and *sufis* and the most revered old sheikhs. She prayed incessantly to Allah. She even sought the help of Christian Coptic priests, for her whole position as a woman, wife, and mother was at stake.

At last, when all else failed, she crept late one night into the walled grounds of the great stone mortuary temple of Ramses III to appeal to the ancient god.

She was frightened. It was August, the time of year when a howling wind rose each night from the Libyan Desert. The date palms crackled, and men passing the temple walls on their camels and donkeys had covered their faces to avoid swirling dust and sand; familiar neighbors became mysterious, shrouded strangers. High on a temple pylon a watchman's lantern swayed and flickered, casting quivering shadows on the soaring stone walls. Ommohamed waited until he moved out of sight, his robe catching the wind and billowing furiously out behind him as he made his nightly rounds. It was past midnight, the time, Ommohamed thought, when all manner of demons and evil genii were about. She had also heard the temple grounds swarmed with deadly vipers and scorpions after dark.

The house Abd el Baset had built on the land given him by his father lay just outside the temple's high, eastern walls where a Roman fortress and enormous ceremonial gate built by Ramses III to Syrian design faced the village. Ommohamed, like many of her neighbors, had not been far inside the temple grounds before, and now she realized how vast they were. The entire assembly of great, granite buildings, colossal in their proportions, stretched far into the desert. Looming up across a large open space and dwarfing all else, was the mortuary temple of Ramses III with its soaring pylons, court after court, complex of towers and battlements, and the ruins of an imperial palace to one side. This assembly was properly known as Medinet Habu, a designation given by early Christians who built a church inside its high walls in the days of Roman persecution and tried to efface the eroticism of its stone reliefs. The villagers merely called it "the city" and paid it little attention. Save for the occasional busload of foreign tourists, the grounds were deserted except for thousands of pigeons which roosted in the cool shade of its stone walls and circled to darken the sky whenever a hawk appeared.

Few villagers set foot inside the temple grounds by day, let alone at night. It was not just that they feared accusations of theft and a police beating and torture, though Ommohamed had heard the men speak of it.

8

Nor that the many huge stone idols with heads of cats, jackals, and falcons offended their Islamic sensibilities, though she had heard that, too. Deep in everyone's heart was the feeling there was something deeply, supernaturally, troubling about the temple grounds. Seeing the glow of the watchman's lantern had gone far away, Ommohamed stealthily moved along the shadows of the high walls. She saw they were adorned with symbols of life and procreation, just as Sheikha Daiyi, the village sorceress, had told her. Some were obscene—one entire wall seemed devoted to portraying a procession led by the god of the penis—as if in the ancients' religion the sacred and obscene lay very close together. There were enormous reliefs depicting the pharaoh's victories in war; she saw tongue cuttings, prisoners being crushed beneath chariots, mass decapitations and castrations, with heaps of genitals carved in stone. She saw what neighbors had whispered: in all the temple's homage to death, as the cradle of life, there was a lustful power, a vicious attraction, and Ommohamed remembered gossip that villagers engaged as watchmen soon felt drawn toward it and themselves became filled with lust, just as if this power emanated from the dead stone itself.

In Ommohamed the temple inspired different feelings. She was terrified. The lantern no longer in sight, she left the shadows and hurried through the coarse high grass, dew soaking her skirts and long black cloak. She reached her destination, the sacred pool of Ammon-Ra, which was set deep into the ground within grassy banks and a series of steep stone steps. Looking about to see she was unobserved, Ommohamed slipped down the bank and went about the pool seven times. She remembered not to hurry but to move in the slow measured steps of a ritual recaptured from the ancient friezes in the temple itself, just as Sheikha Daiyi had instructed her.

She moved and swayed, quivering from throat to ankles, now begging Allah to forgive her, now fervently calling upon Ammon-Ra, the Unknown, to help her conceive a son so endowed with the force of life that he would not die as her other sons but would live on to manhood. Round and round she moved, hypnotized by her own whispered invocations, at last collapsing in a panting, trembling heap. Then, fighting back revulsion, she dipped her hands in the slimy black water and drank of it.

She told no one what she had done. When Shahhat was born, in contrition she named him Mohammed, after the holy prophet himself. Then, fearing anything that might attract the Evil Eye of the envious, she began to call him Shahhat.

9

Shahhat is the Arabic word for *beggar*. In her fear, Ommohamed left him unwashed and shabbily clad. The baby's eyes were extremely filthy, and half a dozen flies were usually buzzing about each eye, unheeded and unmolested. He appeared utterly neglected as his mother tried to conceal from the neighbors and evil genii that her whole life now revolved about him. Even as a small child he was half-angel, half-devil, forever trodding in the dough if she tried to bake bread, thrusting his little hands into the cooking fire or crawling after beetles, scorpions, and snakes. In terror he would be fatally stung, Ommohamed paid Sheikha Daiyi to provide the boy with supernatural protection against creeping, crawling creatures; from that day on he could even put a live scorpion on his bare arm and let it move about and nothing would happen. Anxious he be as healthy as possible, Ommohamed did not wean him until he was three.

The word *shahhat* has a second meaning: "he who demands of God." It was fitting.

By sixteen Shahhat was almost fully grown, a muscular strapping youth who could do the work of two men. He was remarkably quick of comprehension, yet neither of his parents thought to send him to the government primary school in the neighboring hamlet of El Kom, open since the 1952 revolution, which had taken place the year Shahhat was born. Few boys from the village attended, and in the experience of Ommohamed and Abd el Baset, Shahhat's six years at the *kuttab,* the traditional Moslem school in El Kom, where he learned to read, write, add, subtract, and memorize the Koran, were enough for a boy who would spend his life tilling the soil. As soon as Shahhat was big enough, his father sent him to the fields. Shahhat did not mind; he was proud to do a man's work and accepted it as Allah's will.

Abd el Baset, now in his late forties, gradually turned all the cultivation of the land over to Shahhat. He himself opened a small shop by the temple walls where men gathered to play cards and dominoes. There he came to devote his days to drinking and gambling. No longer handsome, Abd el Baset had become a fat, genial man with a large black moustache and a heavy drinker's flushed and bloated face. He was starting to begin each day with a glass or two of date wine and kept steadily put-

Shahhat, the Nile, and the temple of Luxor.

ting it away until nightfall. He was affable and easygoing, and perhaps the most popular man in the village, with a knack for attracting and keeping friends. When his luck held, he made much money at cards. He was a kind and gentle husband and father at home whose sudden bursts of temper—the only evidence of the Bedouin blood he had passed on to Shahhat—ended as quickly as they flared up.

When his luck failed, as it sometimes did, Ommohamed, who had come to love her husband with a fierce, possessive passion, would swallow her considerable pride and send Shahhat into the Luxor market for onions and tomatoes which they would peddle from door to door. Shahhat looked forward to these predawn excursions by donkey to the river and then crossing its swirling waters by ferry just as the wharves of the town began to stir. The heavy, clumsy ferry would leave the bank

11

and heave through the water so slowly that it was only by the bank receding that Shahhat could tell the ferry was moving. He would hang over the side, watching the river mist rise, shrouded in his scarf and tunic, as most of the passengers were, hunched against the morning chill. These men said little. Scarves wrapped about their faces, their heads sunk forward on their chests, they habitually seemed lost in sleep or meditation. In the dim gray light it seemed to Shahhat as if they were all sitting on some strange aquatic animal, swimming out to a cold, dismal, nightmare country. Then the ferry would swing out to midstream and all too soon was bumping heavily against the landing stage. Shahhat could never get his fill of the dark, cold Nile, murmuring and lapping its banks in the mists of dawn, moving along to he knew not where.

When he returned home, he and Ommohamed would go about the village, crying in long sobbing wails, "Come if you like green onions! Come, people, for Allah, but tomatoes!" Since Ommohamed found this humiliating, Shahhat more often went alone, the onions and tomatoes loaded on his donkey, and then he would speak and laugh with everyone. He was so talkative, light-hearted, and cheerful he was welcomed everywhere, and the women liked to tease him. They would disdainfully handle his vegetables, squawking with mock indignation, "Why so expensive, Shahhat? You are no good!" He in turn, with his wide, infectious grin, would wink and reply in such a loud voice everyone could hear, *"Taiyib billil?* Okay tonight after dark?" When they reddened, abashed, he would burst into his deep, hoarse laughter; if Shahhat thought something was funny he could go into convulsions until the tears came. He was irreverent, forever parodying the customary salutations so that "good morning" became "black morning" and "If God wills, tomorrow" became in his words, "If God wills tomorrow we are dead."

His neighbors grew used to Shahhat's hot temper. There is a saying that the Saidi *fellah* of Upper Egypt is like a volcano which will erupt when least expected. If someone should be disrespectful of his parents or bully and abuse poor men or children, he could suddenly turn on them, his eyes full of fury and his face and neck crimson with all the muscles strained. Shahhat's anger could be told by his trembling, passionate voice, the fire in his eyes, and the movement of his long, thin hands as he clenched his fists. Yet if he was quick to anger, he was at once affable and good-natured again. If Shahhat felt depressed and sat about as if paralyzed, pensively gazing into space and hardly hearing anybody, all the neighbors would feel gloomy too as if something lively,

12

Ahmed, Ommohamed's stern younger brother, is Shahhat's idol of what a man should be but also his chief rival for his mother's respect and affection.

avid, and intense were missing from their day. Like Ommohamed, Shahhat loved to gossip; the characters of his fellow villagers fascinated him, and to describe some daily episode he threw himself into attitudes, changing the expression of his face and his voice. Like his mother he went into great detail, quoting from memory whole descriptions and conversations. As he spoke, his hands, with their long Bedouin fingers, were never at rest; he waved them back and forth, shook a finger in the air,

13

Faruk, Shahhat's sharecropper, is something of a drunkard and voluptuary with his own idea of morality.

clenched a fist and beat it against some surface. His neighbors often found it more entertaining to hear Shahhat describe some event than witness it themselves.

After his father, the two men who most influenced Shahhat were his mother's brother, Ahmed, and Abd el Baset's sharecropper, Faruk. They could not have been more unlike.

In spite of his youth—he was still in his late twenties—Ahmed was stern and cold, a humorless, serious man who went his way and disdained idle gossip. He looked remarkably handsome and of great strength, and around him Shahhat's face took on an expression of servile admiration. His whole being at such times seemed to express guilt and confusion as if, in the presence of such a heroic figure, he was ashamed of his own uncouth, garrulous ways. He was also a bit jealous of Ahmed, for Om-mohamed was fiercely maternal toward her younger brother, having raised him from childhood. She would always defend him: "Ahmed never had a chance to play or be a real child. Right from the first he had to be hard and aggressive and take everything by force. He almost never laughed."

Faruk was the opposite; he had a good deal of humor. He was in his mid-forties, a husky, thickset man of medium height whose puffy face, pitted purple cheeks, bloodshot eyes, and wet, open lips gave him away as a confirmed drunkard and voluptuary. Faruk was one of Abd el Baset's favorite drinking cronies, and many a night the two of them would come staggering up to the house, arm in arm, both drunk, and bumping into each other. With one or two more friends they would sit downstairs for hours, passing a bottle around, all talking at once, and loudly interrupting each other. "Oh, my God, what will wine do to a man?" Faruk would moan, pouring himself another glass.

Faruk's association with the family had become close. A year earlier, when Shahhat was fifteen, the last August flood of the Nile had come. The new High Dam at Aswan had stored enough water in Lake Nasser so that the valley could be permanently enclosed with dikes. Water became available the year round for the first time, and three crops a year, as well as such new crops as sugar cane, could be grown. The land of an old feudal estate, Sombat, which had been seized after the 1952 revolution, was finally redistributed. Abd el Baset, as a former soldier, was eligible, and his many cronies among the petty government officials saw to it that his name was put on the list. He was given title to two and a quarter acres in two separate fields at Sombat, a mile from the family's house on the other side of El Kom. This distance made it necessary to form a partnership with someone from El Kom who lived beside the land and could protect the crops.

The land was not given outright. The government retained the power to tell the new owners what and when to plant. It provided water—not always enough or in time, they soon discovered—and credit for seeds, fertilizer, and labor. The government bought a fixed quota of each harvest at a low price. This meant constant dealings with the village agricultural inspector and so much delay, favoritism, and bribery that most of Abd el Baset's neighbors found it profitable to make sharecrop-

15

ping arrangements. A system was worked out whereby a man in El Kom protected the crops, dealt with the inspector, and helped with the ploughing, sowing, watering, weeding, and harvesting in return for a third of each harvest.

At first Abd el Baset cultivated with Taiyar, one of his two sons-in-law, and a shopkeeper and *fellah* from El Kom of some standing. But when his daughter divorced Taiyar and married another man, Abd el Baset replaced Taiyar with Faruk.

Faruk made such sharecropping contracts with seven other *fellaheen* and suddenly found himself prospering. He had been a serf on the Sombat estate in his youth and was long accustomed to the utmost poverty. Now he found himself with money for the first time in his life. At first he worked hard, but soon he was hiring other men to look after the crops and deal with the inspector while he himself plunged into every sort of debauchery, drinking heavily, smoking hashish, chasing women, and spending long hours gambling with Abd el Baset. Ommohamed said he looked like the village headman, riding about his donkey and wearing a clean white tunic every day when he should have been out in the fields.

Ommohamed was mortified by the association as Faruk's dissolute character was well known. She preferred to cultivate with Taiyar, who was plump, pompous, always went to the mosque on Fridays, and was eminently respectable. When she complained that Faruk might cheat them, Abd el Baset—who was not above striking Ommohamed if he felt it was justified—angrily told her to be still. He himself was satisfied and paid no attention to village gossip as his own reputation for drinking was worse than Faruk's.

Shahhat was grieved to see the Nile's last flood. From the first he distrusted *Nitrokima,* the new chemical fertilizer artificially manufactured at Aswan to replace the Nile's lost mineral-rich silt. Until now only land susceptible to the annual flooding and the natural refertilization it brought could be cultivated. Once the high water came in August and the fields were inundated, there was little to do but sow one's wheat, barley, lentils, or maize in November and wait for the April harvest. Now three crops were to be grown each year, even in the scorching summer heat, the field work was unending, and chemical fertilizer had to be used for the first time in the Nile valley.

Shahhat felt frustrated. Left to himself to cultivate his father's acre of ancestral land beside his house, he was content. He used the

16

methods handed down from the time of the pharaohs, and everything he put his hand to turned out well. On the government-deeded land at Sombat it was different. He had to depend upon Faruk or the inspector for almost everything, and things seldom went as promised. He longed to be independent of anyone.

Then, ever since he had reached puberty, Shahhat found himself with a growing sexual hunger. He was torn between pride in his masculinity and seeing this as a curse, as the village afforded little way of finding satisfaction and relief. Faruk and the men in the fields good-naturedly called him El Tor, "the bull," joked about the size of his penis, and claimed only a donkey would satisfy him. It was a common dilemma among the young men. Few girls were available, and even if they were willing, the social risk of going with one was high. The Koran decreed that a detected adulteress was to be put to death by stoning. Even fornication was punishable by scourging with a hundred lashes. Sodomy also drew the death penalty.

In fact, everything went on, if very secretly. Islamic law required the burden of proof; a charge of adultery needed at least four eye-witnesses. Naturally, detection was rare. The last incident of proven adultery in the village had taken place a few years earlier. The woman's husband, father, and brothers had taken her out into the desert, slit her throat, and left her body to the jackals rather than face a public trial and execution.

The village men took fierce pride in their strength, masculinity, and solidarity; the severe penalty given a woman caught in adultery assuaged this pride, as did some men's treatment of their wives, never addressing them as more than *"Yah mara!* Woman!" and forever putting them down. This same pride led to a drive to reduce competing males to lesser status through domination, sadism, and even sodomy; dominance was everything. Sodomy with another male or an animal was treated as a mere peccadillo.

Shahhat was anguished when some small boys one night came upon himself and a friend, El Azap, out in a tall maize field competing to "see who was the strongest" with a female donkey. Faruk and the others, when they heard about it, roared with laughter and took it as proof of Shahhat's sexual prowess. The prevalence of sodomy deeply mortified the village women. Ommohamed, prepared to think the worst of Faruk, would not have been surprised if copulation with boys or animals numbered among his other follies; she told Abd el Baset he was a bad influence on her son. In truth Faruk had several times taken Shah-

17

hat with him to the house of an old widow with two daughters who engaged in prostitution, where Shahhat had his first woman. But, though he had no fear of death, Shahhat had an exaggerated terror of all illness, and when he learned how many men went to this house, he was afraid to go back.

On most matters of sex the village women spoke as openly and unblushingly as the men. Ommohamed and her friends discussed the most intimate details of their married lives with each other. Young girls grew up with a knowledge of everything and experience of nothing. This atmosphere of pagan sensuality combined with the threat of severe Islamic punishment created a peculiar air of tolerance mixed with tension in the village. Everything went provided it was done discreetly; whispered gossip provided a welcome distraction and entertainment, but public exposure demanded the harshest condemnation.

If Abd el Baset, Ahmed, and Faruk, each in different ways, suggested to Shahhat how a man might live, his mother peopled his world with villains. These were the relatives of Abd el Baset—his older sister, Fatnah, and two cousins, Sobhy and Hagg Ali. Down through the years Ommohamed had never been able to visit them nor speak of them without a note of anger or injury.

As Shahhat had grown up, he had become accustomed to hearing her tell of their endless intrigues against herself and his father. In middle age Ommohamed took to smoking a water pipe in the evenings, and then she would let her romantic imagination portray her husband's family in the most dramatic shades of black and white. In her version Fatnah was selfish and grasping, and even when Ommohamed had been a young bride, had objected if she took food home to Ahmed. But the worst villains came to be Sobhy and Hagg Ali, who were pictured as little more than robbers of widows and orphans. Their villainy consisted of countless plots to cheat or humiliate herself and Abd el Baset.

She never succeeded in making the details clear, and Shahhat did not know the truth of it. Ommohamed believed her stories implicitly, and she was an honest woman, honest in her temptation to dramatize everything that had happened to her. Even Faruk became a paragon of virtue compared to the cousins. Evidently Faruk liked Ommohamed,

18

Old Yusef, the village bore, peddles limes and lemons to tourists in front of the Habu Hotel. Shahhat's house is nearby, reached by a narrow lane behind the hotel.

as he behaved freely in her presence and even shared a water pipe with her. For all her complaints, Ommohamed could forgive Faruk his follies; just as he, she had a good deal of humor.

The cousins were another matter. It was certainly true that both of them had grown mysteriously rich in a short time, and it was whispered about that the money had come from robbing pharaonic tombs; but nothing had ever been proved, and indeed, both of them were on familiar terms with the police inspector.

Sobhy, the youngest of the two who was still in his thirties, had been a fishmonger. Overnight he had found the money to build the village inn, which was situated not far from Abd el Baset's house across from the great entrance gate of Medinet Habu, the assembly of temples. Even Ommohamed would admit that Sobhy had not been a bad lot in the days he sold fish. But soon his inn, which he called the Habu Hotel, was attracting the worst scoundrels and swindlers on the Nile's west bank. Once an innkeeper, Sobhy grew inordinately fat and bad-tempered. He gave free liquor to the police inspector and was not above informing on his neighbors out of spite. He seemed to go out of his way to make enemies; he boasted that he never went outside without a revolver in his pocket. At the inn he was surrounded from morning to night by a crowd of toadies and flatterers; idlers whom he fed and gave free drinks or cigarettes to now and then. These always hastened to light his cigarettes with a show of servility and to agree with all he said.

Hagg Ali was sometimes part of this unwholesome entourage, but he traveled a great deal to Cairo, hatching up some nefarious scheme or other. He was a man of about fifty with cunning, calculating eyes, a hawk nose, wrinkled face, and an ingratiating, obsequious manner. He always had a watchful look as if he were perpetually reconnoitering and spying; he was as resourceful as a fox and knew how to use people at their expense.

During thirty years of quarrels with Fatnah, Sobhy, and Hagg Ali, Ommohamed sometimes tried to make peace, partly out of calculation, for all of them had money, but really because she did not feel it right for Shahhat and his two younger brothers to live unreconciled with their blood relations. Sobhy and Hagg Ali, at least—for Ommohamed had not seen Fatnah for many years—seemed to share this feeling and at times the quarrels would be formally healed for a while, before erupting again over a new issue. Abd el Baset, in his affable way, preserved his peace at home by always siding with his wife.

Indeed their house had been built to get away from his family, a move frustrated when Sobhy had opened his inn practically next door. This house, reached by a short twisting lane from the temple road, Abd el Baset himself had made of unbaked mud bricks; it stood two stories high and was roofed with palm branches and palm leaves and possessed a large pigeon-loft of crude brick, mud and pottery jars on the roof; with its high walls slightly inclining inward in the ancient Egyptian style, this dovecote gave the house the look of a fortress, just as it would have had in pharaonic times.

A heavy wooden door opened directly into a cool and light front room, as far as strangers ever went. Air was admitted through two small

20

apertures high on the walls which, like the ceilings, were plastered with gray mud and chopped straw. The tattered remains of scraps of newspapers hung about, as Ommohamed had once pasted some up instead of pictures. Aside from a large wooden bench where Shahhat slept at night, some rolled-up sleeping mats, a few earthen vessels, and Ommohamed's handmill to grind maize, this room was bare—visitors sat either on the bench or the bare ground. Behind was a second room for women, a stable, storeroom, open courtyard, and kitchen; a large oven occupied the kitchen's whole width and was black with soot and flies which buzzed about, annoying and persistent, in spring and fall. An outdoor stairway led to an upstairs room and an open rooftop terrace where the family gathered for its evening meal. This upper room, which housed the family's most prized possessions and where Ommohamed and Abd el Baset slept, was where most family life went on. Two sides were occupied by large sleeping benches covered with clean white counterpanes, a third by a wardrobe with a cracked mirror and a wooden chest of drawers, piled high with a mountain of every conceivable article of clothing or cooking pot.

The upper room had two large windows, one facing the lane and the temple walls and the other looking out over the Ramses Canal and the family's fields behind. Someone was always moving along the leafy canal banks: black-shrouded women or men in white or pastel turbans and tunics, on foot or astride donkeys, schoolboys, herds of sheep, processions of camels, buffaloes going to water, or men coming from the fields with hoes and sickles. To the west the pink, granite, temple ramparts rose above the rooftops and tall swaying palm trees; from here the village looked peaceful and picturesque.

A stranger might find this room shabby and scarred, but to Ommohamed it held shadows as well as substance. For years Shahhat did not know how the mirror on the wardrobe, part of his mother's dowry, had been cracked. At last Ommohamed told him. She remembered the date clearly as it happened the day Shahhat was weaned. Abd el Baset brought home a plump, fourteen-year-old girl and introduced her as Hasaniya, whom he had just taken as his second wife. In fury Ommohamed had screamed, "No! Choose me or the other! I'll stay with you no more!" and she had hurled a pot of tea at him, breaking the mirror.

Of all her disappointments in life this rankled the most, and Ommohamed hated to even think of it. She had rushed to Sheikha Daiyi who told her, "Do not be afraid. I shall arrange that Abd el Baset is for

21

you only. Not for the two." The old sorceress had prepared a magic charm, but Ommohamed had not needed it. Abd el Baset caught his young wife stealing money and divorced her and sent her away within eleven days. Years later Ommohamed was coming from the Nile with him when they passed Hasaniya, long since married to another man and living far away. Abd el Baset had asked, "Who is that?" having failed to recognize her. It was the only satisfaction Ommohamed could find from an episode that had wounded her vanity as nothing ever had. Abd el Baset had never been unfaithful, much les considered another marriage, since, though by Islamic custom he was allowed four wives.

Proud in all ways, Ommohamed tried to conceal her superstitious side, but Shahhat knew she favored the bed on the northern wall for here she always had her dreams. She was a great believer in them. Once when he had been ill with fever as a child, she had dreamed she was sailing on the Nile in a *felluca* when she saw Shahhat standing on the western bank. A voice called to her, *"Maas salaam,* go with peace," and Shahhat had come flying through the air and into her arms. When she awoke, he had recovered. Another time she had dreamed she was again sailing on the Nile when the *felluca* landed on the eastern bank near the tomb of a saint named Nubi. When Ommohamed later found such a tomb actually existed, not far from the great temple of Karnak, she prayed to Allah, promising that if she would give birth to another son, she would name him Nubi. When Shahhat's younger brother was born, she took him to the tomb and sacrificed a sheep. Ever since Ommohamed had great faith in dreams, especially if green, the color of the Nile, figured in them.

Midway through his sixteenth year, Shahhat started getting into trouble. Strangers would come to the house to complain to Ommohamed, "Shahhat made a fight with my son. Your boy is crazy," or "Shahhat bit my hand. I'll have to go to the doctor for treatment and who is to pay?"

Then she caught him taking eggs from the storeroom. She discovered some grain was also gone. She did not know the village boys all did this, exchanging it for hashish, which they secretly smoked in the fields.

Abd el Baset was at a loss what to do. He had never had to punish his son. As a boy Shahhat would sometimes take meat set aside for his father and give it to his friends. Ommohamed might shriek, "*Yah wahid!* Oh, my God, now Abd el Baset will divorce me and you will be the cause!" but his father would only laugh and tell her, "If Shahhat eats meat, my belly is full." Ommohamed later told Shahhat, "When you were a small boy, I never saw your father angry with you. He never laid a hand on you. Perhaps it was a mistake." In turn, Shahhat was fiercely loyal to his father. When he sold onions and tomatoes he refused to turn all his earnings over to Ommohamed, but saved some amount for Abd el Baset despite her protests, "Please don't give it to him. You know your father spends easily."

Then Abd el Baset caught Shahhat red-handed trying to carry away a full sack of grain. Forced to punish him at last, Abd el Baset tied his son in the stable and left him there for a day, saying, "If you are going to act like a donkey you can share the same stall." When her husband left the house, Ommohamed secretly brought Shahhat food and tea.

They suspected he was also drinking but had no proof until one night Shahhat and his friend, El Azap, went across the river to Luxor and bought a large bottle of "French brandy," downing it between them. They staggered drunkenly about the town, insulting everyone they met, challenging strangers to fights, and creating such a nuisance they were chased by the police. El Azap was caught, slapped about, and thrown into the police station's stable to sober up overnight. Shahhat escaped into the darkness of the trees beside the Luxor temple but fell into an open sewer. He washed himself and his clothes in the Nile. But when he presented himself at the door of his uncle Ahmed's house on the western bank, still drunk, soaking wet, and reeking of the sewer, a foolish grin on his face, Ahmed cursed him, slapped his face and sent him home in a clean tunic of his own.

When Abd el Baset heard about this escapade, he went to fetch a heavy stick. Shahhat fled the house and caught a ride in a horsecart; he slept off the liquor's effect and woke up to find himself in Dandara, a river town some sixty kilometers away. Hungry, without money, and stubbornly defiant, he walked home all the way, taking two days and eating dates and drinking water from canals. He arrived home with his feet so badly swollen and with such a pathetic, exhausted expression on his face, Abd el Baset saw he had punished himself enough and had not the heart to do more.

23

Ommohamed secretly feared that Shahhat's growing wildness was Allah's way of punishing her for praying to the ancient god and drinking from the pharaoh's sacred pool so long ago. She tried to persuade herself that the temples were only stone and had no power, that the past was dead. But in her superstitious heart she was frightened it would obtrude itself into the present and was not entirely to be ejected.

Suniya

ONE DAY SHAHHAT came home to announce he planned to marry Suniya, a pretty girl who lived just down the canal. Ommohamed and Abd el Baset were stunned. It was not just that they felt Shahhat at sixteen was too young, though most youths waited to marry in their twenties. Their real objection was that Suniya belonged to the despised Jamasah tribe, the traditional water carriers of Upper Egypt. The Jamasahs, thirteen hundred years before, had once come late to a gathering called by the Prophet Mohammed. According to Upper Egyptian belief, he had condemned them so harshly that, ever since, their descendants had suffered discrimination and social ostracism from orthodox Moslems along the Upper Nile.

Her son's marriage to a Jamasah was unthinkable to Ommohamed. When Shahhat declared his intention, she threw up her hands and cried, "No, no, my son! Suniya is from a bad family. The Jamasahs publicly scorned the holy Prophet. They are crafty and dishonest. How could we hold up our heads?"

Ommohamed had nothing against Suniya herself and indeed was fond of her. The girl and Shahhat had grown up side by side, often play-

24

ing together as children. Now fourteen, Suniya was a gentle little being, delicate but sturdy, with pretty, soft features and a skin tanned by constant exposure to the sun. The expressions of her eyes were still those of a child, trusting and inquisitive, and she always smiled in a sad, timid way. She was quite young—a girl with an undeveloped figure—yet of a marriageable age. She was decidedly pleasing, and had she been from any other family, Ommohamed would have quickly given her consent and blessing. She was aware that Shahhat had matured early and might settle down if he had a wife.

Instead she pressed Abd el Baset to forbid the marriage. "It would be terrible for our family to take anyone from the Jamasah as a wife," she told her husband. "Shahhat is very young. He does not understand such things."

One of the village *ghaffirs* or constables, a man named Salem, had married a Jamasah. Salem was a direct descendant of their hamlet's namesake, Lohlah, yet he and his family were now virtual outcasts. He cultivated five acres just south of the temple grounds, and, in a house on the edge of the desert, he and his wife and six children lived far from their neighbors. Neither the Jamasahs nor the other villagers had much to do with them. Salem, now nearing fifty, was a taciturn, lonely man. Ommohamed did not want such a fate for her son.

Abd el Baset agreed with his wife, and they determined to break up the romance. Everyone was told to try and persuade Shahhat marriage with a Jamasah could only lead to a lifetime of regret.

By now Shahhat was cultivating the acre of land Abd el Baset had inherited from his father by himself; it lay just between the row of walled houses and gardens in Lohlah hamlet and the new canal. Shahhat was endowed with considerable strength, and when he ploughed, leaning heavily on the shaft with his large hands and calling *"Ha!"* and *"Hoosh!"* to direct his pair of cows, for he used no bridle, he seemed to cut open the soil by the sheer force of his will. When he mowed clover, bending from the waist and not squatting as did the weaker men, he swiftly flashed his sickle without stopping a minute, the firm muscles of his shoulders rising and falling like levers.

Shahhat watered this land with an ancient well sweep, called a *shaduf;* a broad, copper bucket was suspended from one end while a large lump of dried mud served as a counter-poise at the other. This was an extremely laborious task, demanding that he dip, lift, and pour thousands of buckets each day. It needed strong rhythm, arms and thighs like iron,

Shahhat labors at a *shaduf,* an ancient wellsweep used for almost six thousand years along the Nile to lift water up from canals into fields.

and the most stubborn stamina. Stripped down to his undershorts, Shahhat sang with an unwearying voice as he worked which gave a solemn and melancholy dignity to his labor.

Sometimes, if the canal water was low, he would water with a *saqia* or big horizontal wooden water wheel which Abd el Baset's grandfather, Khalifa, had built. This was drawn counterclockwise by two cows; its crude, wooden cogs engaged a second, vertical wheel which carried a belt of earthen water jugs into the water to fill. These moved mouth downward into the deep well, splashed into the water, and then came up to the top of the wheel to pour their contents into an irrigation channel. Both the well sweep and water wheel were as old as antiquity, as were the sorrowful songs, more like weeping, which Shahhat wailed as he worked at them.

Suniya's house overlooked Abd el Baset's land, which was divided into clover and onion fields and a walled garden where Shahhat's father had planted grapes and eighty date palm trees. Often as Shahhat worked, Suniya would lean out of her upstairs window, looking extremely pretty with her pale round face with its small fine nose and bright black eyes; Shahhat would gaze up at her and notice how moist and timid her eyes looked and the way her hair tumbled down on her bent neck. And he would burst into song as he lifted and splashed out the copper buckets. He sang with a genuine deep passion, youthfulness and strength, and with a sort of careless, mournful grief; his whole face would be transfigured and his eyes particularly shone with emotion.

Soon he was hiding in the acacia trees below Suniya's window at night and calling her in a hoarse whisper to come outside. Her mother, thinking a dog was prowling, would stick her head out the door and cry "Get away!" and the two of them would stifle their amusement. Suniya's father was away, working as a construction laborer on the Aswan Dam, and he sent home much money. Her mother, who was in ill health, seldom came outdoors, and Suniya was very free to come and go.

Sometimes, if no one was in sight, they would hastily snatch a kiss, and Suniya would tell him in a soft, caressing voice how much she missed him when they were apart. Once she brought a bottle of cognac hidden inside a basket of onions; they crept inside Abd el Baset's garden and, hidden by the high mudbrick wall and seated beside Suniya on the grass, Shahhat got drunk. Instead of becoming foolish or quarrelsome or sick as he usually did, Shahhat experienced a sense of release, and he spoke for hours telling Suniya all that was haunting him. She watched him with her dark, intent eyes and greedily drank in every word.

After that the garden became their private world; the air was fragrant and warm, there was a scent of henna, and breezes would crackle the palm leaves. To Shahhat these times were an ecstasy of enchantment as if the blue sky and the shafts of light through the date plams and the sun-dappled grass had been created just for them. If Suniya brought brandy or cognac and he drank a little, he forgot himself and spoke more eloquently than ever before, just as if his spirit had become something immensely vast, as if a desert opened before him, stretching away in boundless distance. Suniya spoke little but listened and gazed at his face or the ground in such a tender, gentle way it seemed to Shahhat as if he had stolen her heart and mind, and that she was bewitched, under his spell. As time wore on he spoke less, for lovers understand each other best when they are silent, and Shahhat no longer felt the need for words.

These meetings did not pass unnoticed. Abd el Baset took to watching from the upstairs window, and one day, after he saw Shahhat picking onions for Suniya, he shouted when Shahhat came home, "You son of a dog! How can you give our things to a Jamasah?" Ommohamed quickly came between them, crying, "No, no, my husband. Shahhat is just a boy. He is young. You are to blame. Always you have given him his way, right from the first."

Ommohamed's pride was threatened. Shahhat's marriage to a Jamasah would mean disgrace. Yet she feared losing his affection and calmly tried to reason with him.

"To marry for love, Shahhat, that is for children," she told him. "Marriage means you are establishing a household. You must become a real man who looks to the needs of the house and the land, a man who fathers many children and raises them. It means to prosper and lead a decent life so that everyone must respect you." Ommohamed described the kind of marriage she had expected—expected as by right—as a small girl: a husband who would give her love and comfort and an expected place. She knew from hard-earned experience that a villager's freedom and dignity depended upon observing the time-honored codes. The ideal of every *fellah* was to own land and a buffalo, marry, father children—especially sons—and prosper. Ommohamed knew young men like Shahhat were ardent, sensual, and romantic, but that the heat of such passion cooled all too soon; after thirty or so it was the children, the household, the needs of the land, and the family's social position within the village that bound a husband and wife together. In her eyes men were kept in place less by their own virtue than by Islamic law and village social pressure.

To Ommohamed family, property, and social position were everything; the family's task was to uphold such values and work the land, producing children as helpers and eventual replacements in a task that would go on forever. The institutions of family and property had been strengthened by time and tradition, and anyone who lightly violated the customs that supported them would be severely punished and ostracized. As vain and proud as she was, Ommohamed was also shrewd and realistic. While with a minimum of inspiration she could paint wonderful pictures of how her life might be changed, she had to possess a hard core of realism if her fantasies were to keep her going.

She implored her son. "This marriage you want is without thinking or experience. You want to heedlessly rush into something you will regret all your life." She never raised her voice, yet she knew her own future was at stake.

Ommohamed's brother, Ahmed, was outraged when he heard the news. Elegantly dressed and remarkably handsome, Ahmed was tall, staid, and important looking. He had the appearance of great physical strength, and in build, in his cold, humorless manner, and in the expression of his whole person, he resembled a warrior depicted in the pharaonic stone friezes. He was married, lived near the Nile, and earned a good living as chief night watchman at the largest hotel in Luxor. At first glance one would perceive he must be in charge of other men; he had the look of a stern, hard master who might strike his inferiors in the face. This was evident from his superior manner of standing, from the way he sometimes spoke from the side of his mouth, exposing the glint of white, perfect teeth, and from the harsh, aloof expression he wore, such as is found on people who are accustomed to thinking soberly and in solitude. Ommohamed felt deep affection for him, and acted more as if she were his mother than his sister; she knew she always had Ahmed as her ultimate reserve, if it ever came to that, in the long run.

Hearing Shahhat wanted to marry a Jamasah, Ahmed came to the house, burst inside, and seized his nephew by the shoulders. Ahmed shouted in Shahhat's face, he was so angry. "If you marry her, Shahhat, I shall disown you, by my God, Allah, I will! You will be no nephew of mine! I would rather kill you than see our family so disgraced! Marriage to a Jamasah would destroy us!"

In Shahhat's sixteen-year-old eyes, Ahmed—so handsome, manly, and commanding—was a heroic figure. Shahhat deeply loved his father, but Abd el Baset, with his love of drink and gambling, was a soft, fluid character; affable, easy-going, thriftless, generous, kind, and warm but in the end, weak and irresponsible. Ahmed was none of these things. Abd el Baset did not care much for money, power, or respectability; he used to say a *fellah* had no time to go to the mosque which was attended by a lot of pious hypocrites anyway. He would not have said his prayers or kept the fasts had not Ommohamed kept after him. His creed was that the moment was to be enjoyed; one was soon dead. Abd el Baset was all too human; only Ahmed could be cast in the heroic mold Shahhat's young imagination required.

Ahmed's opposition planted the first seeds of doubt in Shahhat's mind. Some weeks before, when he had proposed marriage, Suniya had agreed at once, with cheerful and almost submissive readiness. They both feared her father might soon marry her to someone else. Shahhat knew marriage to a Jamasah meant social ostracism, but he did not care. Salem's sons, Sayeed and Jamal, were among his friends, even if Salem himself always seemed to work on the far side of the fields or stay in the house when Shahhat was around. No one had asked for his eldest daughter's hand. At twenty she was a spinster with no prospects.

Now, for the first time, Shahhat began to consider the marriage in practical terms. He told Suniya, "If my parents won't give their consent, we must elope to Cairo. Any money we took from here would be quickly spent. How would we live? How shall I work in a strange place if I cannot find a job or a house to live?"

Hearing him, Suniya turned pale, her eyes wide open and her lips trembling, for she had been fearing this. "I have gold," she said in a hollow, frightened voice. "We can take it. In Cairo we can do anything to live. You are strong and can do the work of two men. I can work also." She paused, desperately searching for arguments for she had learned how fiercely Shahhat's family was against their marriage. "Oh, Shahhat, even if you are the poorest street beggar, I would be happy. We don't have to eat much. Because I love you and you love me. Nothing else will matter."

At last Shahhat realized that if he married Suniya he would have to leave home. He was miserable. For days he went about absorbed in

31

thought, and when his work was done he would stay in the garden, his head sunk on his chest, staring at the ground as the sun's last rays penetrated the date palms and threw light on the trunks of the trees. Allah made man that he should be alive, that he should have happiness, grief, and joy, and live to the full each of his days, Shahhat thought. He could not understand why Suniya should suffer for what had happened so long ago. Yet he also thought that if his life could have been represented in a picture then his parents, his house, his fields, even Ahmed and Faruk, would have been true, while his love for Suniya and his dream of marriage to her would have stood out from the whole as something different, as out of the drawing. And he thought, too, that it was too late for him to dream of such happiness, that his life had been written from the day he was born, and that he would have to go back to the life Allah had given him, that it was impossible to devise some new special sort of life with Suniya alone.

Resigned to his fate, he no longer saw her every day. He found excuses to avoid work in the field beside her house. Soon two or three days would pass before they met. Then word came that Suniya had fallen ill; for a week she did not leave her house at all. An old Jamasah woman secretly brought messages to Shahhat. "Suniya wants you," she would whisper to him on the canal path. "Suniya sends for you. Quick, take these two pounds from Suniya." Then, at last, "Suniya is very sick. Come to her."

Tormented, bewildered, Shahhat decided to run away to Cairo. He stole some grain from the house and sold it to El Got, a shopkeeper, to pay his expenses. Perhaps he would find work in Cairo and discover how they might make a life there—then he would send for Suniya. El Got, an ex-convict just out of prison who ran a shop along the cart road to El Kom, paid cash for stolen grain to village youths who obtained pocket money this way, taking small amounts from their houses or the fields of rich men like Hagg Abd el Mantaleb, the village miser.

The night he left Shahhat went and stood for a long time below Suniya's window. When she appeared he told her he was going. All in the village slept; there was not a light anywhere, and it seemed to Shahhat as he spoke to her from the darkness of the field that he was standing in the deepest abyss and could not reach her. Suniya's face was paler than he had ever seen it, and she gazed down at him in such a tender way, her eyes brimming with such love and hurt, it came to him that in her quiet, timid way, Suniya had resigned herself too and accepted everything.

Sadness, mingled with relief, took hold of Shahhat. Suddenly he wanted to cry, passionately, as he had once desired Suniya for his wife. Moisture came out of his eyes and a lump rose in his throat, but the tears did not flow. He wanted to shout, seize Suniya, run away with her, and defy them all. Then she called softly to him, "*Maas salaam,* go with peace, Shahhat."

"Oh, my God, Suniya, I want to weep. . . . " he cried, but the moment for weeping had been lost. She left the window, and he stood there stupefied for some minutes then turned and stumbled across the fields toward the Nile.

But the time was September 1967, Egypt went to war, and Cairo was no place for an ignorant peasant boy of sixteen; not even the army would take him. He was gone but a few weeks, but it was long enough. On his return he learned Suniya's betrothal to a cousin, a soldier serving in the Sinai Desert, had been announced. He did not speak to her, but when they passed in the road or Shahhat would look up from his work and see her watching him from her window, he would always see that same look of love and hurt in her eyes. He did not go to the marriage. From his field he watched the young girls going down the road, singing and clapping their hands, and then Suniya herself, hidden in white and red silk veils, riding a camel as men fired pistol shots into the air and women made their shrill tremolo cries of joy. The singing and dancing went on late into the night, and when Shahhat's younger brothers brought home colored sweets, he angrily seized them and threw them out a window.

For days Shahhat was agitated. Everyone avoided him. Abd el Baset went away to Cairo with Hagg Ali. The cousin had managed to get himself engaged as a foreman with an archeological excavation near ancient Memphis. In what he portrayed as a conciliatory gesture, Hagg Ali offered to make Abd el Baset his deputy. The cunning cousin calculated a relative might prove more pliable in exploiting whatever opportunities for pilferage or payoffs came his way. They were to be gone three months.

The day after Abd el Baset left Shahhat quarreled so violently with Ommohamed she fled the house. As soon as she was gone, he broke into her strongbox and took a gold necklace Abd el Baset had given her on their wedding day. He sold it to a Luxor goldsmith for a fraction of its worth, then used the money to get wildly drunk, smoking hashish and seeking to forget Suniya with prostitutes. When Ommohamed discovered the necklace was missing and heard reports about what Shahhat was doing in Luxor, she appealed to Ahmed. He in turn reported the theft to the

33

village headman who sent four constables or *ghaffirs* to Luxor to seize Shahhat.

They brought him back—bound, unshaven, unwashed, and haggard—by ferry and donkey cart and threw him into a cell at the headman's jail in El Kom. Salem, one of the *ghaffirs,* and aware of Shahhat's story, kept apart. But the other three, after they untied Shahhat and he fought with them, knocking one down, began to beat him with sadistic pleasure. They tied him on his back to a wooden bench, his bare feet in the air, and began taking turns beating the soles with switches, in the not uncommon Mediterranean punishment of *bastinado*. Shahhat spat at them, screamed abuse, and threatened to kill each one. The worst— a small, vicious *ghaffir* with sunken cheeks and small, beady eyes—seized Shahhat's hair, lit a match, and set a handful on fire. Terrified, Shahhat screamed for mercy and the others emptied a bucket of water over his head. Then they left him alone, without food or water, for three days.

On the fourth morning, Salem opened the cell and passed a loaf of bread to Shahhat, who crouched in one corner like a wild animal, snarled, and threw the bread back in his face. When the headman heard of this, he ordered Shahhat's feet beaten again. The sadist among them took up a switch, and with mounting excitement, a frenzied pleasure on his face, he beat Shahhat until his feet were raw and bloody. Shahhat was pale and vomiting with pain when they stopped him; water gushed from his eyes, and his feet and ankles were soon so livid and swollen he could not stand. The headman, evidently feeling guilty, released him, and Salem gave Shahhat his donkey to ride home.

Ommohamed cried out with horror when she saw him. Shahhat staggered into the house, his face pale and beady with sweat, unable to hold the lids open over his bloodshot eyes. Ommohamed bathed him, brought clean clothing, helped him to bed, and would not leave his side. Neither of them spoke of Suniya or the necklace. Then Ahmed came and righteously began to lecture Shahhat. "Now you have learned your lesson and will not steal again . . . " he began, but before he could say more, Shahhat leaped from the bed, seized a wooden stave, and raised it to strike his uncle. Ommohamed screamed and threw herself between them, taking the full force of the blow on her side. In pain, weeping, hysterical, she was carried upstairs to bed. When Ahmed returned to Shahhat, he brought some neighbors with him, and they tied his hands and feet and remorselessly began hitting his injured feet again with switches. Hearing Shahhat's screams of pain, Ommohamed staggered downstairs again,

34

panting, almost falling, and cried to Ahmed to stop. She cradled Shahhat's head in her arms and begged him to forgive her. Then she shrieked at Ahmed in rage, "Go! Go! Let us finish with this!" It ended there. When Abd el Baset returned home, Ommohamed said nothing about the necklace, and when he learned the story, neither did he.

Shahhat recovered and went back to work in the fields. But he stayed away from home in the evenings, drinking and carousing with other young men at Abdullahi's place in El Kom.

This was a low, dark hovel, rank-smelling from the fumes of stale liquor and hashish, where the most notorious wastrels in the village gathered at night; it was usually crowded with dirty, drunken and abusive men, who shouted at one another in rough voices and found pleasure only in liquor, gambling, whoring, and brawling.

A dim oil lamp, hung over a low circular table in one corner where men sitting on straw mats played cards, was the only light and seemed unable to dispel the habitual darkness of the place. All the objects in it were dimly illuminated, their outlines blurred; when someone new would enter and squat down to sit crosslegged against a wall, it was hard to see who it was. Even the most innocent face took on a demoniac look in the faint, shadowy light. Sin hung over the air of Abdullahi's like a fog.

Abdullahi himself was usually to be found sitting like a sack in front of the fire, his legs tucked under his heavyset body as he brewed tea, put fresh coals into someone's hashish pipe, opened bottles, took money, and muttered grunted commands to his wife. This forlorn creature, the only woman ever there, ran about filling and taking orders, black-shrouded, scraggly-haired, and shrill-voiced.

Abdullahi was full of sharp practice and deviltry. He was a man in his forties, hideously pock-marked, with frizzy hair like a negro's and a look of an aging wrestler; he habitually dressed in a sooty tunic with his vest unbuttoned, displaying a chest covered with the same frizzy black hair. He kept a phlegmatic silence for the most part unless someone related to him the latest village gossip. When the story was finished he would invariably strike his fist on the ground and exclaim, *"Yah ragil!"* mutter an obscenity or two, and turn away to spit confidently. Aside from liquor and hashish, his place was known for its secret and clandestine sale of opium which Abdullahi daily indulged in himself as could be detected from his manner and voice.

Shahhat could never afford anything but the cheapest bottle of *zabeeb,* a concoction from dates so potent the men liked to drop matches

35

El Azap, Shahhat's friend, has the rugged looks and patient ways of those Upper Egyptian *fellaheen* of ancient, non-Arab, pharaonic stock.

in the empty bottles to see the fumes explode. It was seldom long before he and his friends were completely intoxicated, so that they sat about grinning stupidly with bleary eyes, stupified by the bad liquor and the noisy uproar of coarse laughter, jingling bottles, and foul-mouthed oaths from the card players. The clientele of Abdullahi's warmly welcomed Shahhat, telling him, "Your father is a powerful man! He has done many bad things in his life!" And then, as if this were not compliment enough, they would add, "Always he pays for the drinks!" Mornings Shahhat would curse the loss of his money and vow never again to wallow in the mire of Abdullahi's. But, unwilling to spend evenings home with his parents, he often went back.

One night as he staggered home drunk he met El Azap on the canal path. His friend, coming late from the fields and carrying a sack of clover and a sickle, was singing loudly as he feared meeting genii in the darkness. "Why do you sing in such a loud, ugly voice?" Shahhat demanded. Seeing Shahhat was drunk, El Azap replied, "No one in the village can fool my eyes, Shahhat. You go to Abdullahi's; I shall do as I like." Seizing on this as an excuse for a fight, Shahhat swung and hit El Azap on the mouth. Infuriated, El Azap swung his sickle and caught Shahhat in the arm. Staring dumbly at it for a moment, as it had sunk into the flesh, Shahhat pulled it out and threw the sickle into the canal. El Azap lunged to retrieve it, Shahhat went after him, and the two of them wrestled in the half-dried mud of the bank. Men came running to pull them apart, shouting, "Are you crazy, Shahhat?" "Leave him. What can he do, this drunken boy?"

The two youths soon made the fight a jest, but Shahhat kept his arm covered with the long sleeve of his tunic so his parents would not see the wound. It festered and did not heal. When Abd el Baset heard about the fight some days later, he demanded to see Shahhat's arm. When he saw how bad the infection was, he cursed his son. "You son of a dog! You hide such a wound from me? Do you think me a boy? Why, my son, have you said nothing? You keep silent all these days! Do you want to lose your arm?"

Despite Shahhat's protests, Abd el Baset took him to the hospital in Luxor for treatment. Afterward Shahhat complained to Ommohamed, "I'm ashamed we went to the doctor. Now all the village will see the bandage and say, 'Shahhat has a bad wound and El Azap nothing. See who is the better man.' "

Nights of the Genii

By THE TIME he was twenty-one Shahhat seemed to have forgotten Suniya and settled down. Rural, gregarious, stay-at-home, he had made his unadventurous choice and chosen the village, his security in past and present. With his love for the soil, his feel for physical labor and nature's rhythms, his taste for songs, stories, and gossip, his mind was governed by the senses and stayed close to things done and felt; life to him was a succession of todays. But if he was resigned and fatalistic, he could also be unyielding. When his parents decided to build a small house in Abd el Baset's walled garden and move there, Shahhat stubbornly refused to go. He said he would keep the livestock in the old house and stay to protect them at night; in truth, the memory of his days in the garden with Suniya was strong.

The move was prompted by Ommohamed's desire to get further away from Sobhy's inn. Though it stood some distance away, separated by several houses along a narrow, walled lane, a drunken uproar could often be heard at night. Sobhy and his customers argued in such loud discordant voices and swore so much Ommohamed would sigh, "Oh, my God, what is the matter now?" Those who kept swearing also shouted the loudest and the most continually. The language was obscene in the utmost, but this did not upset Ommohamed. The village women and children listened to foul words and the most licentious talk without being perturbed; they had grown accustomed to it. What bothered Ommohamed was that she sometimes imagined the voices were insulting Abd el Baset and herself.

The idea to move was not a sound one. The garden was infested with vipers and scorpions, and the house was never finished. The family moved home again within some weeks. Yet it was time enough for Ommohamed to become fast friends with a woman called Bahiya, the wife of Hagg Abd el Mantaleb, the rich village miser, whose house was just on the other side of the garden. She appeared the first day they arrived with a large basket full of bread, tomatoes, sugar, tea, two rabbits, and four pairs of pigeons and declared in a loud voice, "Because you are our neighbor now, Ommohamed, I must welcome you." Soon Ommohamed

Bahiya, the wife of Hagg Abd el Mantaleb, the village miser, is Ommohamed's confidante, friend, and fellow gossip.

took an even more generous basket filled with food to Bahiya's house. It was not long before Shahhat, returning home from the fields, would find his mother and Bahiya sitting together on the floor, sharing a water pipe and sipping tea. They often looked embarassed to see him, and from their whispers and glances of understanding Shahhat could guess they were telling about the most intimate relations with their husbands. Bahiya had strong opinions on all subjects and believed in speaking the truth, particularly if it was unpleasant.

Scarcely a day passed in the village without some mention of Bahiya's husband, Hagg Abd el Mantaleb. Once a serf, he was a fanatically industrious man who now owned ten acres, a village shop, bought and sold grain, held half-shares in a dozen diesel pumps, and was engaged in so many money-making enterprises he seemed unable to keep track of them.

Everyone was in his debt. He was the first man in the village to arise each day, was tilling his fields at dawn, opened his shop at nine, was forever riding here and there on his donkey, and staged out in his fields after dark. He expected his family to slave just as hard, and Bahiya was the only woman in the village who daily went to the fields to cut fodder.

His stinginess was such that only the elderly, disabled, or feeble-minded would harvest for his low wages, and it was said Bahiya had to feed the family on maize bread, onions, beans, and cheese. Hagg affected great piety and was as respectable as Sobhy was disreputable. He had built the village mosque, although his generous impulse had not lasted long enough to complete it with a minaret. He discouraged frivolous talk and gossip. So grave and preoccupied with urgent important business was his manner and so great his wealth said to be, everyone stood in awe of him and found his company intimidating.

In recent days Hagg had won the government franchise to sell such rationed goods as tea, sugar, matches, salt, flour, cooking oil, and kerosene. Since no one could go without them and he kept his shop open only a few hours each morning, everyone was forced to queue and crowd as he measured out each dollop of sugar and salt. Once he became rich, Hagg Abd el Mantaleb rode apart, his shoulders hunched, his head thrust forward, and his lips moving so furiously Shahhat said he must be counting his money. Hagg seemed to endeavor to show everyone and everything how busy, grave, and sensible he was.

It seemed curious to Shahhat that Bahiya and his mother should become friends. Both had strong wills; otherwise they were unlike in

40

every way. His mother's eyes were bold, handsome, and shrewd. Bahiya's were dull and squinty. Ommohamed was romantic, extravagent, sharp-tongued, generous, and intensely proud. Bahiya was quite unself-conscious, a busybody, insensitive, impervious to criticism of Hagg or herself, bossy, and yet surprised and hurt if she met resistance. Ommohamed was poor and Bahiya rich; yet it was his mother who spent her days in comparative leisure, seldom missing a marriage or funeral, dressing and eating better, and appearing the grand lady, while Bahiya toiled hours in the field each day like the poorest laborer. Yet once the friendship was made they seldom kept long apart.

This friendship survived many trials. Bahiya's oldest daughter, Zeyneb, became infatuated with Shahhat's friend, El Azap, and started stealing cloth from her father's shop to sell it to give him presents. When she brought some to their house, Abd el Baset became angry and told her, "Your father is good to us. If I need a sack of flour or two sacks of flour, your father will give it to me whether I have money in my pocket or not. I eat bread and salt with that man. How can anyone face Allah who takes such things? Go, girl!"

To Ommohamed's embarrassment, Zeyneb found she could sell her stolen goods through Su'ad, a niece of Abd el Baset who lived next door to their old house. Su'ad, a plump, lazy woman whose husband had run off to Cairo and was badly in need of money, taunted Ommohamed, "Your stomach becomes sick when you see Zeyneb coming to visit me all the time."

One day Ommohamed's old side injury, where she had taken the blow Shahhat meant for Ahmed, pained her badly. When she asked Abd el Baset to go and collect some money Hagg Ali owed him for their ex-cavation work so she could see a doctor, her husband replied, "You go. If I ask Hagg Ali and he says no, either I'll kill him or he'll kill me. That son of a dog is all lies and false promises. It is better, my wife, if you go."

Hagg Ali, seeing Ommohamed coming, told his wife to say he was not at home. She taunted Ommohamed, saying, "Why doesn't Bahiya help you if you need money? If she's such a fine friend, why does she spit in your face?"

"Who says so?"

"Su'ad. She has told everybody. All our family."

Thirty years of feuding with Abd el Baset's relations had not taught Ommohamed to ignore their gossip. When she got home, she told her husband, "If Bahiya spits in my face, I can separate her head from

41

her body. Yes, Hagg Abd el Mantaleb is rich there days, but I know his days when he sold onions along the road."

"You pay attention to such gossipmongers?" Abd el Baset exclaimed. "You must go to Bahiya now. Before you change your clothes. Right away."

"I'll take my rest, my husband."

"No, now!"

Ommohamed arrived at Bahiya's house looking so proud and haughty, her friend clutched her breast and demanded, "Why are you trembling so? Your face is black." Soon the two women were in tears as Ommohamed, demanding Zeyneb stay and listen, told what she knew about Su'ad and the stolen cloth. Then, her anger spent, she was comforting Bahiya, "There, there. Be calm. We can thank Allah the evil is only in Zeyneb's light fingers."

The next day Bahiya invited Su'ad to her house on a pretext, held out a copy of the Koran, and demanded the frightened woman swear she had never taken stolen goods from Zeyneb. Taken by surprise, Su'ad swore she was innocent. Returning home along the canal path she became dizzy and fell into the water. When Shahhat came running from his well sweep and pulled her out she was frothing at the mouth and trembling all over. Everyone said that Su'ad had been possessed by a devil. Three sheikhs were fetched from El Kom to exorcise it.

To Ommohamed, swearing falsely on the Koran was not to be taken lightly. Especially since it was Su'ad who had done so. Her fat neighbor, whose sly, viperish eyes always looked as if they could see through everyone and everything, was forever eavesdropping from her house next door and spreading all she heard throughout the village. Seeing Su'ad and her pretty daughter, Batah, leave their house one day in dresses made from the stolen cloth, Ommohamed could not resist taunting her. "Oh, now the thieves are known by all," she told Abd el Baset in a voice loud enough so Su'ad could hear. "Well, Allah punishes everything in his own good time. *He* never forgets." Her husband laughed and replied, "Speak as you like. If any of these dogs opens his jaws, I'll close them fast enough."

Zeyneb was soon married to the village headman in El Kom. When he divorced her within a month it was rumored he had caught her stealing and that she still secretly met El Azap. Hagg Abd el Mantaleb quickly married her off again, this time to a prosperous *fellah* from El Tot, a hamlet on the far side of the village. Hagg hired a dozen taxis to taken the bridal party to El Tot. What happened was never clearly established because Hagg would never speak of it. But it was said that when he went to load the bride's possessions, he found large quantities of hidden cloth, tea, and sugar stolen from his storeroom. As the story went, he began to wail and carry on so loudly Bahiya ran to silence him, crying, "My husband, stop that! You forget our guests!" Whatever happened, though Bahiya sometimes visited her married daughter, Hagg never spoke of her again.

It was while the family briefly stayed in the garden and Shahhat was sleeping alone in the old house that he first began to be troubled by genii. Shahhat was now of an age when he could take a wife, but in the five years since they had forbidden his marriage to Suniya, his parents had found no one they could agree upon, both Abd el Baset and Ommohamed wanting a girl from their own side of the family. The first genie appeared to Shahhat while he slept, taking the form of a beautiful woman. No one was surprised. Many village men had been visited by such genii in their sleep, and it was not unknown for a man to even take one for a wife. One sorcerer in El Kom had done so and had been forced to stop sleeping with his real wife altogether because his genie warned she would kill him if his wife conceived a child.

Shahhat's genie tormented him. Night after night she appeared in his dreams and demanded he make love to her. She was so insatiable he found himself exhausted each morning; he lost weight and had little strength when he worked in the fields. At last he confided in Ommohamed, saying, "She is very, very beautiful and wants me to marry her and not an earthly bride."

Horrified, Ommohamed took Shahhat to Sheikha Daiyi, her blind sorceress in El Kom. The old woman warned him, "Oh, my boy, if she wants to marry you, it is very dangerous. You must refuse. If you already had a human wife you could accept. But because you are still unmarried, even though genii can give you all you desire, they can put you completely in their power."

Shahhat asked what he could do.

"Ah, go to Sheikh el Hufni in Luxor. He has been to Mecca many times and possesses many ancient books and knowledge about genii.

43

He will make you a magic charm and put it into a box of iron to free you from this devil."

Sheikh el Hufni, a bent, ematiated, toothless old man with a snowy white beard, demanded seven pounds in advance and eight more if his exorcism succeeded. "If it fails," he told them in a high-pitched, quavering voice, "you need pay no money at all. I will return your seven pounds." It was a lot of money, as much as the family spent for food each month, but Ommohamed said she would sell two sheep. The old sheikh burned incense, recited some Koranic verses, and prepared a *hegab,* a magic written charm. He took an irregularly shaped piece of white paper, wrote some secret, unintelligible words upon it in a red blood-like substance, and folded it and refolded it until it was a tiny triangle. Then he threaded a piece of string through one corner and told Shahhat to wear it about his neck when he went to bed. "Ah, now if the genie comes," the old man said, "you must call *'Allahu Akbar,* God is most Great!' and hold up some iron, for the genii have a great fear of that metal."

Shahhat still slept alone in the house, and that night the genie came as always, this time riding up on a white horse. In the golden haze in which he always saw her, Shahhat watched as she dismounted and advanced toward him, her red, silk robes billowing around her and her golden necklaces and bracelets flashing blindingly in the strange brilliant light. She drew so near he could smell the sweetness of her perfume; she had never seemed so beautiful. He stopped breathing and his heart ceased to beat as he clutched the small *hegab* at his neck with his fist and held out a piece of iron. His fear overcoming his desire, he whispered, *"Allahu Akbar!"* No sooner had he uttered these words than the perfume became a stinking sulfurous ordor, the golden haze dissolved into black smoke and flames, and the genie's features changed before his eyes into the hideous face of a black horned devil. Shahhat could feel the hot poisonous fumes of the devil's breath and saw a blur of twisted open mouth and dilated yellow eyes. *"Aoozoo belah min el Shaitan rajun!"* he shrieked. "Oh, Allah, protect me from Satan!" He squeezed his eyes shut as tightly as he could, clung to the iron and charm for dear life, and tried to call out. But from his throat came only a hoarse, hollow gasp. In terror as he squirmed to get away, he felt hot, moist, scaly hands seize his shoulders and neck, dragging him from the bench and across the floor. He shuddered convulsively, gasping for Allah to save him, and fainted away. In the early morning, Ommohamed found him lying asleep in the lane just

44

outside their door. When she awoke him, he told her what had happened, saying "She wanted to kill me, but I held onto the *hegab*." Ommohamed decided not to let him sleep alone in the house again.

For nights she sat by his side, but he slept so fitfully and moaned so loudly, Ommohamed would shake him awake. Both of them feared the genie would return, and before going to bed each night Shahhat would chant the Koran, begging Allah to protect him from Satan so the genie would leave him in peace.

Then one night as he returned from Abdullahi's on his donkey after drinking much *zabeeb,* he was loudly singing to keep his spirits up when his donkey suddenly balked and would not move. The air about him grew icy cold, just as if the temperature had dropped. Shahhat feared to look into the darkness ahead, and when he did he cried out in alarm. There was the genie, this time turning somersaults, black, horned and with a hideous grin on his face. In panic, Shahhat pulled out his knife, thrashed wildly about in the air in front of him, and stabbed the donkey. The animal, though only slightly cut, toppled forward and fell, throwing Shahhat to the ground. Shahhat scrambled the other direction on all fours and some dogs, hearing the commotion, began to loudly bark. When he reached home he told Ommohamed the dogs had saved him.

Nothing happened for some time. The family moved home again, and Shahhat swore he would not stir outside the house after dark. But when El Azap made fun of him and demanded they go to Abdullahi's one night, Shahhat agreed, and so it was that he again found himself returning from El Kom by donkey alone, for El Azap dropped off at his house.

Suddenly Shahhat found himself in a desert whirlwind. One moment there was nothing; the air was still. The next, without warning, a furious wind was roaring all about him, dragging him off the donkey, twirling him about, ripping off his turban, tearing at his clothes, and whipping him around and around. In his ears was a furious whistling roar, and Shahhat went cold with fright as he realized that this time the genie had taken the form of a dreaded *marid,* the most terrible of all genii or demons, who comes from the blood of a dead killer and appears as a whirlwind to suffocate its victims. As he fought for breath, it howled in his ears, tore at his clothes, beat against his face, and spun him round and round; he clutched at his throat with his hands, trying to get air. He couldn't breathe; the roar howled and howled relentlessly and dragged him choking into its black vortex.

45

Some neighbors found him at dawn, lying unconscious in the road. His donkey stood nearby munching grass. They carried Shahhat to the house of El Azap's father, which was near, and El Azap put crushed onion up his nostrils and splashed cold water on his face. Someone ran to fetch an old man with a saintly reputation, and he came and held a Koran over Shahhat's head. When Shahhat regained consciousness they carried him home where he told his mother, "I have seen genii before but not like this. I was certain I was going to die." He was ill for days, too weak and exhausted to rise from the bed. When he did get up he experienced a sharp, stabbing pain in his chest. Ommohamed brought Sheikha Daiyi from El Kom and Shahhat told her, "This thing tried to wrap itself around me and smother me."

"Yes," she exclaimed, "it was a *marid,* Shahhat. It wanted to carry you into the desert to die or perhaps down to the Nile to drown. The *marid* always tries to kill human beings. You should have called, '*Allahu Akbar!*' as Sheikh el Hufni told you, and held out some iron, for even *marids* have a great dread of it, and cried, '*Hadeed ya mashroom!* Iron, thou unlucky one!' A *marid* is the most powerful of all evil genii. You are lucky to have survived."

Sheikha Daiyi left precise instructions for Shahhat's cure. Certain magic charms were to be burned by his side each sunset at the time of Magreb prayers. Each morning, noon, and evening Ommohamed was to burn incense, swinging the silver pot of smoking incense over Shahhat's head seven times. One amulet was to be put in the center of the front room, and this Shahhat was to step over seven times each day. After fifteen days he was to bring a china bowl to her house, and she would write secret words in ink on the inside. On the night of the full moon he was to wash out the words with water, then swallow the water in three gulps. After that, Sheikha Daiyi promised, he would feel no more pain in his chest and be strong again.

Shahhat faithfully did what she said, but the pain did not go away. Abd el Baset, less superstitious than his wife, finally took Shahhat to the Luxor hospital. He was given an x-ray and the doctor, an elderly Christian, found evidence of a rheumatic heart. He told Shahhat he was to avoid tobacco, spicy foods, alcohol, and strenuous physical labor. When Shahhat scoffed at this diagnosis, Abd el Baset took him to a Moslem doctor who agreed with the first and told Shahhat sternly, "If you don't take care of yourself you will be dead in one or two years." This so frightened Shahhat and his father, Abd el Baset took him to a third doctor, a heart specialist in the nearest large town of Qena, who found nothing wrong with Shahhat. He was left not knowing what to believe. He told Abd el Baset, "All these things the doctors say are lies. Everything is from Allah. The death of a man is written by Allah from the day he is born. Nothing these doctors do or say can change it." In time the chest pain went away, and Shahhat soon smoked, drank, ate, and worked as he always had. Nor was he again troubled by genii.

Abd el Baset seized upon Shahhat's recovered health and spirits as justification for throwing a big *hafla* or evening party. He would hire a band of musicians, some popular storyteller, and perhaps even dancing girls. The hafla would last for seven days. It would cost a small fortune, but all those invited would help to pay by tipping the musicians and providing their own liquor, beer, and hashish. He said he would slaughter two sheep to provide feasts for all on the first and last nights.

Ommohamed was astonished but pleased; never content with doing "as well as the neighbors" she could be as extravagant as he. If either of them felt luxuries were required to feed a guest—and Ommohamed was justly famed as the best cook in the village—pigeons, beef, mutton, or chicken was bought, even if it meant the family ate nothing but bread and beans for a week. Anxious to outdo everyone in hospitality, Ommohamed might serve twenty to thirty glasses of tea in a single day, which meant she spent more on sugar and tea alone than most village families did for food. The precarious income from the crops seldom came to more than four or five hundred pounds a year. But if Abd el Baset's luck at gambling held, there was always money enough.

Then, in the midst of their preparations for the *hafla,* Abd el Baset confessed to his wife that he had sold half of the acre inherited from his father to Hagg Abd el Mantaleb to pay off his gambling debts. Ommohamed was enraged and protested so violently Abd el Baset slapped her, and when she persisted, raised a hoe and might have hit her with it had not Shahhat caught his arm. He was at once contrite and begged her forgiveness. Shahhat was so angry his father had sold the land, he did not trust himself to speak to him and went to Abdullah's each night to keep out of his way. To Shahhat a man who sold his land had lost part of his manhood, and he was deeply humiliated and ashamed for his father.

Abd el Baset's main concern was Ommohamed. He was aware of what property and social position meant to her; guilty at reducing the first, he threw himself into enhancing the second. By God, he'd give a party the village would not quickly forget! He would slaughter not two sheep, but four. What was life for, he told her, but to eat, drink, and be merry for no one knew what would happen tomorrow, and it was but a short way to the grave. Shahhat was healthy again; what better cause for celebration? If one was generous to others, would not Allah provide? In his heart, abashed and guilty for squandering some of his sons' patrimony, Abd el Baset had to show them all.

Come Fill the Cup

THE FIRST NIGHT of the *hafla* arrived; it was a cool, pleasant May evening. For two days Ommohamed, her two married daughters, Samah, and the neighbor women had been cooking, preparing a repast consisting of boiled chicken, stuffed pigeon, grape leaves stuffed with rice, all kinds of spiced vegetables, salads of leeks, tomatoes, and lettuce, great heaps of wheat and maize bread, four kinds of cheese, and a variety of sweets. Abd el Baset had brought cases of date liquor, anise, beer, and something called "French brandy" from a Greek merchant in Luxor which Shahhat and El Azap were to sell later in the evening. There was the smell of a sheep being roasted over a spit in the courtyard. Ommohamed was in constant request; with a harassed, flushed look, and breathless, she hurried about the kitchen where fires had been going since dawn.

Abd el Baset, clean shaven and moustache trimmed, his face ruddy and glistening from a hot soapy bath, flew about in a clean white *gallabiya,* supervising neighbors who set out wooden and palm-stalk benches for the village notables and straw mats for the other men, counting the bottles of liquor, and worrying that the storyteller, who had to come four hours by train, would not arrive in time. His sweating face gleamed in the lamps strung about, not only in the yard and the lane, but extending across the road to the temple walls, for later there would be dancing. He had already drunk one bottle of anise and was ready for another. A few early arrivals stood about, passing around cigarettes and smoking them with an expectant air; there was rough laughter, and it was all getting very noisy. Strangers passing along the road would look about from their donkeys wondering what unusual was astir.

"The old sheikh is on his way from the railway station," was the rumor. Once Abd el Baset began planning for the *hafla* he had settled for nothing but the best, and the storyteller he had engaged was a very old and famous one. The sonorous voice of Amr, the *mueddin,* could be heard calling the faithful to the last prayers of the day, then the sound of his high-pitched cry faded away.

Around eight o'clock everyone started to assemble, and soon the open yard before the house and the lane were crowded. Men filled up all the benches and mats, women swarmed into the house to find places in the doorway and windows, and children scrambled to crouch breathless in any space they could find until someone shooed them off again. Abd el Baset, Shahhat, Ahmed, El Azap, and other relatives and neighbors went about in a genial manner, serving small glasses of tea, bringing fresh coals for the water pipes, and passing around cheap Cleopatra cigarettes, which they lighted with great ceremony. One of them moved about with a silver perfuming vessel in which frankincense was burning; this, hung from a chain, was swung about each man's head, wreathing him in a gray haze of sweet-smelling smoke.

Everyone came. Faruk arrived with Bahiya's brother, Fatih, who was also another of Abd el Baset's drinking cronies. Fatih, an excitable, red-faced, handsome man, was one of the shrewdest cattle dealers about. From the way he and Faruk eagerly greeted everyone, slapping their shoulders and bursting into deep hoarse laughter, it was evident they had drunk a drop too many already. Faruk was rough and affable and got along with everyone. Ommohamed noticed her husband's sharecropper could not resist casting his bloodshot eyes in the direction of the women. Faruk could scarcely open his mouth without uttering some loud curse, confirming her low opinion of him.

Salem was there, standing aloof and taciturn with his *ghaffir*'s rifle, for the headman had sent him to see order was maintained. Lamei, the biggest landlord in the village, arrived with several men and they went respectfully up to the front bench, the previous occupants hastily

Fatih (left), a shrewd cattle trader suspected of possessing the Evil Eye, and Lamei (right), with two hundred acres the richest landlord in Berat, are two of the village's favorite subjects of gossip.

finding seats elsewhere. Old Yusef, a neighbor, sixtyish, bent, toothless, and garrulous, talked without pausing for breath to anyone who would listen to him. Only Hagg Abd el Mantaleb was missing, having sent word he would be late; he had little time to spare for such frivolity. The house was filled with women; Su'ad's pretty young daughter, Batah, leaned out an upstairs window, laughing vivaciously as if she hoped to catch someone's eye. Shahhat's younger sister, Samah, torn between modesty and curiosity, stood behind her, her veil half covering her face. Sheikha Daiyi sat in a row of other old women on the door stoop, and above the uproar in the kitchen, Bahiya's loud, assertive voice could be heard. There was a stir as Sobhy and Hagg Ali came together and warmly shook hands with Abd el Baset as if to show everyone thirty years of feuding among blood relatives was of little account. There was a series of sharp honks from the road and a bustle as Abd el Baset rushed out to great someone; the storyteller had arrived.

Soon Abd el Baset led him through the crowd, a blind old man with a pale face like wrinkled wax above a sparse, white beard. He took a seat on an upraised, wooden platform Abd el Baset had built against the house, which was festooned with blindingly bright, naked lightbulbs. The sheikh held a single-stringed violin in his lap as did a second old man, who sat down beside him. As the roar of the crowd heightened in expectant exclamations, the two old men began plunking their violins, testing them, the first making a high piercing chord and the second one of a slightly lower pitch. There was a commotion as the band of musicians arrived, carrying their bagpipes, drums, a mandolin, a flute, and cymbals; they took places in the rear for they would not play until the night's storytelling was over.

The village audience all knew the story to be told. It was to be the favorite romance of Abu Zeyd, a black-skinned Arab of the Hilalee tribe of long ago. After an unruly childhood in which he killed his schoolmaster in a burst of temper but somehow mastered all the sciences, Abu Zeyd set out at the age of eleven to slay his father, in the mistaken belief the intended victim was his father's murderer instead. Shahhat stood at the back of the crowd, waiting for the old man to utter the opening hymn of praise to Allah. When he did in a quavering voice worn with age, but still melodious, the audience fell hushed and still; there was nothing feigned in the villagers' adoring attention. They loved such performances. Faruk licked his full, wet lips and leaned forward eagerly, as if to take the phrases upon his own mouth. Lamei lowered his head and closed his eyes as if at Friday prayers at the mosque.

The old storyteller sat with his long, spidery fingers on the violin and strummed the opening chord; then, as complete silence fell all

51

around, he uttered the first verses, full of the soft warmth of familiar understanding. His voice was a little shaky to start with but it gathered power and assurance from the attentive audience as he went on.

He had a magnificent speaking voice, although the tone was yet monotonous. Gradually his whole being began to course like a stream through the familiar verses, filling them with his own feeling; Shahhat could see the men around him tremble and respond. Someone sighed, "Allah!" and soon there were many such exclamations from the crowd. "Allah! Allah!" would come at each newly remembered turn of phrasing, and these gasps and cries of "Your voice is sweet!" and "You are famous!" increased the confidence of the old voice with its sweet high register.

> One day to a spring, with some friends I went,
> When the chiefs had gathered at a banquet of state . . .

The recitation was a dramatic one and quite varied in style. The storyteller changed his tone to suit the substance, now threatening, now pleading, now declaiming, now admonishing.

> To Allah I cried—"O Compassionate!
> Through living! Eternal! I pray, for the shake
> Of the Excellent Prophet, they delegate . . ."

It was no surprise that he should be word perfect; in the villages the blind storytellers and Moslem teachers had a faculty for memorization that was celebrated; even Shahhat as a boy had once known almost the entire Koran by heart. Now he listened with admiration, staring over the heads of the men as gray wisps of smoke wafted about from the pipes; he was half entranced by the ebb and flow of the poetry which completely absorbed his attention.

> God assist thee to take our blood revenge,
> An the tents of Hilal to desolate . . .

Between each verse there were a few moments of silence in which nobody stirred or uttered a word but contemplated that which had gone before. The old storyteller then sank his chin on his chest as if to regain his strength and softly linked his fingers. Abd el Baset hastened to bring him a glass of tea or iced water, and then once more the old man would look upward toward the sightless light and declaim, and once more Shahhat felt the tension of his words as they entered the minds of his listeners.

It was almost midnight when the reading was complete; it would continue in nightly installments the six more nights of the *hafla* until, as everyone already knew, Abu Zeyd and his mother would be happily reunited with the father, and they would all set off in search of new pasture and more adventures in Africa. The men roared in applause as Abd el Baset led the old man into the house to be fed. Tears welled up in Shahhat's eyes; like his father he had been drinking steadily from the large stock of liquor, and he was passionately moved by the storyteller.

The crowd relaxed, and as benches and mats were pushed back, the musicians came forward to take their places and play. Shahhat and El Azap carried their cases of bottles from the house and at once were surrounded by men, who pressed about so frantically and shouted their orders so loudly Shahhat thought his head would split. Everyone was suddenly active, the young men passing around the wine and liquor, the old men smoking their water pipes; children ran about this way and that to retell parts of the recitation with excited cries and there were bursts of raucous laughter. After another go at the wine, everyone sat down to eat as Abd el Baset and other men hurried from the house with heaping platters of food. The musicians kept playing, men talked and shouted back and forth, women called from the house, and children cried in such a wild medley of sound, it made a terrifying din.

Abd el Baset was everywhere at once, turning this way and that, greeting one friend after another, pouring more wine for somebody, lighting somebody else's cigarette, having a quick drink himself, calling to Ommohamed to fetch more of this or that dish, jostling everyone with his big heavy body, and beaming with joy. "*El hamdu li-llah!* Praise be to God!" he kept saying. "Shahhat is good again, and I must celebrate the health of my son!"

Some of the men, quite drunk, leered at the dishes Ommohamed had prepared and seized all that came within their reach like birds of prey. A few even filled their pockets for Ommohamed's reputation for succulent spices and sauces was richly deserved. The food eaten, the yard was cleared and the men formed a large circle which extended through the lane and out into the road. Then, one by one, each man got up to

53

dance. He would start slowly, waving his wooden stave about his head in slow, graceful sweeps and taking long, gliding steps. After some minutes of this, someone would step into the circle with him and tie a cloth around his hips. At once the musicians would sharply quicken the tempo, the bagpipes whine, the flute screech, and the cymbals crash as the dancer would begin to rapidly jerk his hips from side to side and forward and backward in a vibrating, sensual fashion. "Allah! Allah!" the men would start to shout, excitedly cheering the dancer on. Some of the men danced together, fighting mock battles with their wooden staves. Abd el Baset, quite drunk, stood beaming, waving a bottle of "French brandy" to the beat of the drums. This distasteful drink, made of only God knows what, numbed the brains of all who drank it, just as if they were suffering from concussion.

The young girls, shedding their black veils to reveal sequined dresses of the brightest oranges and reds, whirled and stamped their feet in the front room of the house. One of Shahhat's friends, a brown-skinned, muscular youth called Snake, stood looking in and teased the girls, "Oh, my God, I'm going to marry this and this and this! I'll get a new one every week!"

"You'll have no success with us," the pretty Batah taunted him as she whirled past. "We have other boy friends. We have no time for you!"

Weary and confused, Ommohamed went quickly about, supervising the women in the kitchen but was apparently satisfied that there was so much and such food that none of the neighbors could find fault. Since no strangers from outside the village were present, Abd el Baset called upon the girls to come outside and dance. A few of the more daring ones like Batah accepted and entered the circle demurely covering themselves again with their black veils but with their faces showing in coquettish smiles. Soon they were whirling about in fast, rhythmic steps, and when Abd el Baset insisted Ommohamed join them she pulled her veil across her face, danced awkwardly for a moment and then, in a burst of embarrassed laughter, fled to the house.

The night deepened and the old storyteller was put to bed, but nobody wanted to go home. The men no longer knew what they ate or what they drank. No one could hear distinctly what was said. Only at intervals when the music softened could women's voices be heard calling from the kitchen.

Faruk entered the dancing circle with a bottle in each hand and a third clenched in his teeth, and this added to the general hilarity. Then Faruk dragged Abd el Baset into the circle and tied a cloth about his waist. Through the yard and into the house went the acclamation, "Abd el Baset himself will dance!" Shahhat watched his father, a foolish, drunken smile on his face, twist his heavy body this way and that, swiveling his hips back and forth and tapping his heels; he saw Ommohamed looking on from the house, her face radiant. Some of the men leaned on each other and went into ecstacies, laughing and cheering him on. "Allah! Allah! Oh, my God, Abd el Baset!"

Shahhat blinked. He had been snatching drinks whenever he could, and now he was reeling and saw his father double. His head was swimming, and he barely understood when someone thrust a red face before him to say that Abd el Baset was taking Ommohamed to Sobhy and Hagg Ali for a formal reconciliation. In a burst of good feeling, Shahhat grinned foolishly, swaying back and forth. Someone seized his shoulder. It was Ahmed and Shahhat tried to focus his eyes on his handsome uncle, seeing his face was contorted with anger.

"If you speak with these people, I don't know what I shall do with you, Shahhat!" roared Ahmed, who was evidently drunk himself. "If anyone dares speak to you, you tell me! I'll stand beside you!"

Shahhat was jostled and almost fell over, no longer being steady on his feet. It was old Yusef, not staggering, but pausing on each foot with the other high in the air. He was stopping everyone who passed him to seize their tunics and shout in their faces, "This party cost more than fifty pounds!"

Then Hagg Ali was before him, a wide grin on his cunning face. "Why, Shahhat, don't you come and speak with your uncles? There has been a reconciliation between us and your father and mother!"

Shahhat grinned, belched loudly, and tried to focus his bleary eyes on Hagg Ali. But his eyelids were like lead, and he could barely keep them open. He felt dizzy and then saw Ahmed standing just behind Hagg Ali and furiously shaking his head.

"No!" Shahhat bellowed, more loudly than he had intended so that men turned to look.

Hagg Ali's face twisted into an angry, purple fury, and Shahhat could see the veins swelling on his forehead. All affability gone, he stepped back, swung his arm, and slapped Shahhat hard across the face. Stunned by the blow, Shahhat fell backward, stumbling against some cases of empty wine bottles. There was a crash of breaking glass. Recovering his balance, he rubbed his cheek, weaved back and forth, and said, his head hanging low, "Thank you, my uncle."

"Why do you not speak?" Hagg Ali sputtered. "I tell you, go speak with your uncle Sobhy!" Benumbed by the liquor, Shahhat opened his mouth, closed it, and opened it again. Infuriated, Hagg Ali swung and slapped him again. At this, sparks exploded inside Shahhat's head; he reached about and grabbed the first thing at hand, a wine bottle, and was about to raise it to bring down on Hagg Ali's head when someone seized his arm—he saw it was Ahmed. Men crowded about, exclaiming in excited voices, the musicians stopped playing, and Abd el Baset burst through. "You stupid boy!" he shouted in Shahhat's face. "Do you want to kill Hagg Ali?" He thrust Shahhat from him, and Shahhat lost his footing and fell. Then he crawled to his knees, seized a handful of stones, and looking around as if he dared anyone to stop him, he broke past his father and ran out into the road. He wanted to find Ahmed, but his uncle was not in sight. There were shouts behind him, and Shahhat ran down the road into the plaza, past the temple gate and the inn, down a row of houses, and around the corner to the mosque and canal bridge. Dogs started barking all over the village, and when Shahhat reached a maize field just beyond Hagg Abd el Mantaleb's house, he plunged into it, panting and sobbing for breath. He heard the shouts come closer and then become fainter and less frequent. The men must have gone back to the party for he drowsed, and after a long time passed, he could hear Faruk's voice calling, "We hope every year you give such a party, Abd el Baset! Oh, nights of pleasure! Oh, nights of joy!" Breathing heavily and feeling sick, Shahhat put his head down on the rough soil, closed his eyes, and at once fell into a deep sleep.

When he awoke the sun was beating down on his face. El Azap found him and said his father had spent the whole night searching for him. It was said Ommohamed had cried all night and fought with his father.

Together the two friends went to the village cafe to drink tea. Some small boys, seeing Shahhat, ran to tell Abd el Baset, who came at once. He spoke very gently, telling Shahhat everything would be all right if he would go to Hagg Ali and apologize. Shahhat refused. He told his father what had happened and said in an accusing tone, "Ahmed is a real man. If he tells me to do anything, I must follow him." In his shame at selling some of his land, Abd el Baset said nothing more about Hagg

56

Ali. "Just give us this week to finish the *hafla* without further trouble," he begged his son.

Ommohamed could scarcely conceal her delight that Shahhat had sided with Ahmed against the two cousins; she had been humiliated when Abd el Baset dragged her off to shake hands with them the night before.

The rest of the *hafla* was a great success. The old storyteller, warming to his audience, was magnificent, and his performance was talked about in the village for years afterward. Ahmed did not return until the last night, and, when he did he wore his usual stern business look. When he saw Shahhat, this cold expression left his face, he flushed a little, laughed in an awkward fashion, and went to grasp Shahhat's hand. But Shahhat pulled it away.

"Yes, I made the quarrel, but where were you?" Shahhat demanded. "I did not find you beside me. What do you want, Ahmed? Do you want me to go to prison?" For a long time afterward uncle and nephew did not speak.

A Father, and Kind

SHAHHAT'S WILD AND UNRULY WAYS did him no harm with his friends; all of them had reputations for deviltry. Aside from El Azap, these included El Got, the ex-convict; Abd er Rahman, a big raw-boned, hard working youth with a fondness for rough jokes and horseplay; and Snake, who came from the Horobat tribe of tomb robbers who lived amid the pharaonic tombs in Qurna.

Snake (left) and Abd er Rahman (right), wild and unruly youths, are two of Shahhat's closest friends.

Like Shahhat and El Azap, Abd er Rahman and Snake were strong and muscular; in all their movements one detected the athletic and devil-may-care attitude of youths well aware of their merits. All four had a certain swing of the shoulders, spoke and laughed louder than anyone else, and always looked as if they were on the point of performing some feat that would astonish everybody. When they were together they seemed to habitually be seeking something to fight or some-

58

thing to laugh at. They feared no one and were ashamed of nothing. Abd
er Rahman had Shahhat's Bedouin look, while in Snake's dark brown
skin, curly hair, thick lips, and strong cheekbones, there was something
plainly African. The four were inseparable; each might come and go for
days or weeks, marry, have children, chase women, quarrel with their
parents, and feud with other villagers, but among themselves they were
always light-hearted, affable, and high spirited and found everything
amusing.

All were in their early twenties except El Got; he was well past thirty and of an age most village men stayed home at night, settled around the fire with their wife and children. In truth, El Got was constantly on the lookout for a new bride. His name, El Got Gargetan, was not his real one, but meant "the cat from Gargetan," his native village. He had been in prison for killing a neighbor in a blood feud and upon his release had come to Berat and settled down.

El Got's attraction was the subject of much ribald speculation for he was a slight, weaselly, pale little man with a creased, homely face and round shoulders that were always hunched forward as if he were cold and had earned him the nickname of "the cat." Yet he had been married and divorced four times; all of his wives had been big, plump, comely women who were said to have wept copiously when he divorced them and sent them away. El Got was decidedly undersized when he went about with the four tall, strapping youths except for his exceptionally large hands which hung from his sides like giant paws.

Not long after the *hafla,* Shahhat, El Azap, Abd er Rahman, Snake, and El Got set out for Qurna one evening to attend a Jamasah wedding. Abd el Baset and Ommohamed had been invited but were ashamed to go. Everyone knew they had prevented Shahhat from marrying Suniya because she was a Jamasah.

Yet Abd el Baset decided the family must be represented if it were not to look like a calculated insult. "Shahhat must go," he declared. "We must send someone." He gave Shahhat two pounds, telling him one was to give the musicians and the second he was to spend himself. Abd el Baset was always generous with Shahhat, even allowing his son to smoke in his presence—something no other village father did.

With the others' encouragement, Shahhat spent both pounds on date wine, and by midnight the five of them were drunk. The wedding had been a peaceful one, but when the time came for the traditional departure of the bride for the house of the groom, Salem, who was the bride's uncle, stood up and gestured the large company into silence. He apologized that instead of the traditional camel or horse, the bride would go in a taxi and since only one was available, no one but the bride's immediate family should ride along. "Nobody else try to get into the taxi, please!" Salem declared. "I know that most of you are drunkards, but everyone has some self-respect. We want to finish this wedding day in peace!"

Several pistols were fired into the air, and men in the crowd applauded or jeered. Shahhat's friends took Salem's words as an insult directed at them, and they pushed Shahhat to his feet to protest for them. Shahhat stood there reeling, not knowing what to say, and everyone in the crowd turned to look at him.

"You are a man without manners, Salem!" he called. "You are a Jamasah!" His friends whispered and pushed him from behind, urging him on. "People must respect one another. Did you not send us an invitation to this wedding or did we come by ourselves? Your words insult us!" Thinking he had gone far enough, Shahhat sat down. His small group applauded, but everyone else sat stiff and silent; Shahhat's romance with Suniya was commonly known.

Salem apparently did not intend to let such a show of bad manners go unanswered. He turned on Shahhat angrily, "Why do you speak such bad words? Who are you to speak anyway? Who are your father and mother? Are they so fine they refuse to attend a wedding of Jamasahs?" Salem's frustration after long years of being ostracized for marrying a Jamasah now boiled to the surface. Trembling, unable to control himself, he shouted at Shahhat, "Your father is the biggest drunkard in the village! Everyone knows him! He would sell his moustache to gamble at cards! The drunkard has even sold some of his land!"

A shocked silence swept the crowd. Shahhat was on his feet again, though this time his friends were trying to hold him back. "Yes, thank you, Salem," he roared. "You are the same as my father. If my father is no good, you are no good. If he is good, you are good. Now you can finish your party." He turned and left the wedding, followed by his four companions.

Once out in the road they told Shahhat he must not stomach such an insult. Snake and El Got cursed Salem in the foulest language, and Abd er Rahman suggested blocking the road with rocks. Soon, drunk, red-faced, and breathing heavily, the five of them carried the largest rocks they could lift into the center of the road. When headlights appeared in the distance, they scrambled down in a ditch to hide, gathering up handfuls of stones. When the taxi was forced to stop, they pelted it with their stones, and the bride's brother, who had gone to fetch it and was beside the driver, was hit in the forehead; Shahhat saw a trickle of blood on his face and shouted to the others to stop. Men from the wedding, aroused by the commotion, came running—pistols, wooden staves, or whatever they could find in their hands—and Shahhat and his friends fled across the dark fields.

When they reached the village, they sat down on the edge of the road beside the temple wall and for an hour talked over what had happened in excited voices. When the headlights of a car approached and they recognized it as the same taxi, everyone but Shahhat ran off; he sat there stubbornly waiting, seeing what would happen. When Salem, who was being driven home with his sons, saw Shahhat, he had the taxi stop and jumped out, carrying his *ghaffir*'s rifle. "Where is the son of Abd el Baset, the drunkard?" he called, and Shahhat, standing, replied, "Here I am. What do you want?" Shahhat did not move and Salem came up to him and shoved the butt of his rifle into Shahhat's chest. "You dirty son of a dog!" Salem cursed him. "You spoke bad words at our marriage party. Who do you think you are, Shahhat? A small boy still? Such boys dig a pit for themselves, and then their parents fall into it."

Shahhat was afraid but not yet sober. He lunged for the rifle, Salem held on to it, and they grappled for it. Salem's grown sons, Sayeed and Jamal, watching from the taxi, now jumped out and came to their father's aid. Someone hit Shahhat a hard blow on the back, and as he went forward, another punched him in the stomach, knocking his breath out. "*Yah wahid!* Help!" he gasped as he went down under a rain of blows. He was kicked in the ribs just as Salem, furiously shouting and trying to shove his sons away, finally managed to herd everyone back to the taxi. Then he came back, dragged Shahhat to the side of the road, and drove away.

Shahhat's face was bruised and swollen the next morning. He gave his parents such a dramatic account, putting himself and his friends in such a favorable light, that Abd el Baset felt his honor was at stake and vowed to kill Salem.

Just then Salem, without knocking or the customary greeting, burst into the house. "I come in peace. I do not want further fighting," he hurriedly told Abd el Baset, his hands before him. He then told Shahhat's parents how their son had first insulted the Jamasahs present at the wedding.

Abd el Baset was at once apologetic. He told Salem, "All your possessions are on my head. I carry all your burdens. Anything you order, I can do to my son." Salem, who had prepared for the confrontation, went outside to fetch the village headman and Sheikh Nubi, a respected elderly neighbor, whom he had left waiting outside on the road. Ommohamed hastened to prepare tea as the four of them discussed the trouble, deciding

62

Abd el Baset must pay any medical expenses to the bride's brother. Shahhat and his four friends were in turn to reimburse him.

This settled it as far as the headman was concerned. But Sheikh Nubi felt village decorum demanded that Shahhat come to kiss the top of Salem's turban, the traditional gesture of apology. Shahhat was brooding upstairs, and when Abd el Baset went to fetch him and he refused to come, the father exploded, "You son of a dog! You want to shame me in front of these men? They say I am a drunkard and a gambler who has sold some of my father's land and am not a man. You must kiss the head of Salem!" When Shahhat refused to budge, Abd el Baset slapped him hard across the face.

Fighting back tears, his cheek stinging from the blow, Shahhat went down and did as his father had ordered him. Only Sheikh Nubi saw that Shahhat deliberately kept a distance between his lips and Salem's turban. But as the headman seemed satisfied and was anxious to go, he said nothing. Salem on his part, as soon as he saw Shahhat was prepared to make the traditional gesture of apology, pulled his head away, protesting in a fatherly manner, "No, no, Shahhat! You are a young boy. I told you the boys make a pit and their parents fall into it. Our grandfathers lived peacefully in this village with your grandfathers. I just hope in the future you will not drink so much as you did last night. Your father could drink all the Nile and not be changed. He is a man who can hold his liquor. But drink makes you young men lose your senses."

Both his father and Salem had disregarded the vengeful Bedouin streak in Shahhat's blood. Shahhat felt to the core of his bones that his father's public humiliation could not go unanswered. He could accept his drinking and gambling, but anyone who sold land was to Shahhat's mind not a man. He felt Abd el Baset had been disgraced and it was up to him to avenge him.

Shahhat was plowing one of his fields at Sombat, a mile from their house, a few days later when he saw Salem's son, Jamal, passing on the canal road. "Where's your father?" he hailed him.

"Who wants him? He's in Luxor."

"Come and drink tea!"

Jamal followed Shahhat to the small shed made of cane stalks at Faruk's threshing ground. Between harvests it stood empty and deserted. As soon as Jamal went inside, Shahhat overpowered him, wrestled him to the ground, and bound his ankles and hands, gagging him with a piece

63

Jamal

of cloth. "Don't try to escape or call anyone," Shahhat told him. "I won't harm you." Shahhat went home, took food from the house, filled a water jug, left word he would spend the night in El Kom, and returned to the shed. He stayed beside his captive the rest of the day, telling Jamal, "Let your father suffer for a day or so."

When Jamal did not return home that night, Salem's wife became worried and urged her husband to report it to the headman. She knew about the trouble and feared Shahhat might be capable of doing anything. "Hold your tongue," Salem ordered her, "and say nothing to anybody." Salem went to Abd el Baset and told him what had happened. Abd el Baset listened solemnly and then told him, "Say no more. This afternoon Jamal will be home. It will be all right." Salem agreed to return to his house and wait.

Abd el Baset sat down and drank a full bottle of anise. Then he drank a second bottle. He said nothing to Ommohamed but bathed, dressed in a clean white *gallabiya* and turban, and went back to sit on the bench in the front room and stare at the wall. When Ommohamed demanded to know what was wrong, he merely muttered, "If we divorce, your son will be the cause."

He knew there could be only two or three places where Shahhat and Jamal could be if they were not out on the desert. He reached the shed at the threshing ground last of all and was very drunk, having stopped at Abdullahi's to drink two more bottles.

He found Shahhat asleep and Jamal bound and gagged beside him. He untied Jamal, told him to wait outside, and turned back to his son. Shahhat was awake, his eyes riveted on his father's face. Abd el Baset put his foot on Shahhat's neck. "You make me as small as the sesame seed. So small I can no longer show myself before the world."

He spoke with great weariness and finality. "I will kill you, Shahhat."

Abd el Baset turned away, not knowing he had just uttered the last words he would ever speak to his son. He took Jamal home where Salem, his eyes moist with tears, embraced him. The tears were not for Jamal but for Abd el Baset himself; he looked like a ghost. When he went back to Sombat, Shahhat was gone.

For days no one knew what had happened to him or where he had gone. They did not know that, like a man possessed, he was wandering about the desert without food or water. Just before dawn two days later, Samah came downstairs to light the fire and had to stifle a scream as she came upon Shahhat crouched on the floor of the storeroom. He was pouring grain into a sack. His face was filthy, coated with dust, and his eyes bloodshot and hollow. He looked imploringly into his sister's eyes and whispered fiercely, "Say nothing. You do not see the camel."

"Nor the camel driver," whispered Samah, fighting back her tears.

"Bring the sheep. If anyone asks you, tell them the sheep broke in here during the night and ate the grain." He embraced her. "Goodbye, my sister." Then he gathered up the sack and was gone.

When Ommohamed woke up and came downstairs she was not deceived by Samah's story. *"Yah wahid!"* she began to cry. "I can't take any more!" She cried to Abd el Baset to come as Shahhat had stolen some grain. "My husband," she sobbed, "it is me or Shahhat in this house! He is my son no longer!"

Disbelieving, Abd el Baset cursed her. "Daughter of a dog! Shahhat would not steal from his parents!" Then he saw it must be true. He turned furiously on his wife, "You are the cause! You have given in to him all his life. How can Shahhat survive in the city? How will he get money? How will he get food?"

Abd el Baset was distraught, blaming himself. He found a neighbor who was going to Cairo and gave him fifteen pounds, begging him to search for Shahhat and give him the money to come home. There was a small cafe frequented by the Qurna and Berat men when they traveled to Cairo; perhaps Shahhat would turn up there. But the days passed and there was no news of him.

One morning when he went to shave, Abd el Baset found his hand could not easily grasp the razor. When he went to tell Ommohamed about it, his words slurred, and she could barely understand him. She wanted to send for a doctor, but he soon felt better and harshly told her he was all right.

He went out of the house, headed for the road, but found he was stumbling and could not move his legs normally. He turned back to the house, thinking to call Ommohamed for help. Then the second stroke came, tearing through his body; he breathed fiercely, fighting for air, staggered, and fell. Samah saw him from the house and screamed.

They carried him into the bench in the front room. He recovered consciousness but could barely speak and could not move his left side at all. Sheikha Daiyi was sent for, and other revered sheikhs from El Kom, and they recited chapters from the Koran all that day and through the next morning. Ommohamed prayed as she had never done before. In the afternoon they took him to the ferry and across the Nile to the hospital. After an examination, the doctor said there was little to be done. Abd el Baset tried to smile at his wife, but with half his face paralyzed it was only a twisted grimace. "I am dying," he told her calmly. "*El hamdu li-llah,* God be praised." He asked that they take him home where he was washed and dressed in clean clothing, and then said his prayers. Right at the end he asked for a drink of Nile water. Neighbor men gathered below could be heard exclaiming, "Allah! There is no strength nor power but in Allah. God have mercy upon him!" Women on the stairway began to raise cries of lamentation; Ommohamed turned him round to place his face toward Mecca, she closed his eyes, and his lips formed the final prayers, "To God we belong; and to Him we must return. There is no God but Allah and Mohammed is his Prophet." Then he was gone.

Ommohamed screamed and screamed; no one would have thought such a slight woman could have uttered such screams. It was a terrible sound and all the village heard it. By the time others reached her, she was tearing at her face, her breasts, her own flesh, in utter abandon. Moving swiftly up the stairs more and more women poured into the room, uttering as they came the most piercing shrieks, that swift thrilling Arab ululation which is called the *zagreet,* their tongues rippling on their palates to produce an ear-splitting sound.

The house echoed to their shrieks, but above them Ommohamed's blood-curdling screams could be heard. Bahiya had to use all her strength to hold her and prevent her from hurting herself; she fought and twisted to get away, her dress ripped to shreds and her face smeared with ashes. The women encircled Abd el Baset's silent corpse, never stopping their fierce quivering shrieks. Some struck their breasts and howled, "Alas for him! Alas for him!" Others moved and swayed, beating their own faces and quivering all over their bodies as they twisted and turned and called upon the dead man to rise.

They changed his clothes and covered him with a sheet. Ommohamed, her arms outstretched toward his body as other women struggled to hold her back, began to call, "Rise, my golden one! Rise, my master, my camel, my protector! Rise, my life!" Her cries and the women's lamentations affected the whole village. Hearing them, Hagg Abd el Mantaleb slammed close the shutters of his shop. Men hastily rose from tables at the inn, shattering glasses and bottles to the floor. El Azap, sweating and wet at his well sweep, pulled his tunic over his head and ran toward the sound, barefoot, just as he was. Everywhere men in the fields dropped their work and came running. They gathered in the yard to stand about sobbing and muttering, *"Malesh.* Let it be forgiven." Fatih was there, ashen-faced and stricken. "May God have mercy upon him," he kept repeating. Faruk came and quickly went—later he was found lying face down in a field, dead drunk. The cousins, Sobhy and Hagg Ali, were demonstrative in their grief as if loud mourning would wipe away the many years of quarreling. Ahmed, his handsome face lacerated with pain as he heard his sister's screams, came last to stand alone against a wall, dazed, seeing nothing around him.

Some of the women were early overcome with exhaustion; Abd el Baset's elderly sister, Fatnah, nearly blind, fainted with hysteria and had to be carried out. In the early morning the washers of the dead came— two old men from El Kom who would claim the dead man's clothes in payment. Hagg Ali brought a new white linen shroud, and whenever the men seemed overcome by the women's grief or Ommohamed's long, terrible bursts of screams, he would go about, passing around cigarettes.

Samah could not bear the sight upstairs—her mother's sightless gaze, the flickering oil lamp, the swish of sponges in hot soapy water, the

67

scratch of a razor. She herded the two small boys, Nubi and Ahmed, away from this morbid spectacle, but even downstairs she could hear the sound of trickling water and the thump of the body as they turned it over on the stripped wooden bed. She covered her ears and squeezed her eyes as tightly shut as she could.

Abd el Baset, at last washed and sprinkled with camphor and perfumed with rosewater, cotton stuffed in his nostrils and ears, his ankles bound and his hands placed across his breast, lay in peace in the new white shroud, and it remained only to wait for morning to bury him. Ommohamed, all passion spent—a ghastly sight in her rent clothing, blackened face, and torn hair—whimpered in Bahiya's arms. The quavering voices of the old sheikhs rose from below in Koranic verses praising God. There was no flush of dawn, but in the east the sky was growing light. Everything became visible, though dimly.

There was a commotion on the road. The sound of chanting, the dirges, and the moaning were stifled as in one collective breath.

They led him in, half-dragging, half-carrying him as if he were sightless and unable to walk. No one could look at his face—so tortured, exhausted, twisted in pain—the very picture of human failure. They took him upstairs where he stopped for a moment to look down upon his father's face; then he sagged to his knees and into his now gently weeping mother's outstretched arms.

PART TWO

Hast thou resolved upon strangling me,
O Allah?
Loosen the noose!

Sung by Nile *fellaheen* while laboring

Ordinary Life Goes On

L IFE, LIKE THE WATERS OF THE NILE, can begin in young and rushing
mountain freshets, find its tortured way through desert hills and
sand, ease round the cataracts and stubborn stone, and settle, placid, on its
unobstructed course down a fertile valley to the sea.

Shahhat, driven by Abd el Baset's memory, Ommohamed's grief,
Ahmed's censure, the neighbors' expectations, and his own surgent hopes,
set out to become the man his father was. In the first weeks of mourning,
like a sinner seeking redemption, he lost himself in hard, physical labor.
He rose before dawn each day, went by donkey to the Nile, crossed by
ferry to the Luxor market to buy vegetables, date wine, and sweets to sell
in his father's shop, and was home tilling his fields by eight o'clock. Afternoons he spent cooking *kunafeh,* a sweet vermicelli popular in the Moslem
holy month of Ramadan, at an open oven in the broiling sun. Dusk
found him back in the fields gathering fodder. He neither drank, nor
smoked, nor joked, nor even spoke much. In these weeks he was a sober,
lonely figure in his black tunic of mourning, working barefoot, unshaven,
growing thin and hollow-cheeked. When he kept to his course through
the month-long fast, when the villagers could not eat nor even swallow
water from the first break of dawn to sunset, everyone was amazed and
said to themselves that Shahhat had become a real man at last.

He and his mother seldom spoke. To Ommohamed life seemed
over. All she desired was to visit Mecca and die. She went nowhere,
wailed in a loud, sorrowful voice each morning, and concerned herself
with little but preparations for Abd el Baset's death rites. These cere-
monies, to be held the seventh, fortieth, and hundredth day after the
death, to be followed by a final, much larger ritual on the first anniversary
of his departure, were in accordance with pharaonic custom but took the
form of Islamic *zikrs,* or prayer performances. The cost was enormous,

71

Shahhat making *kunafeh*, a sweet vermicelli, during the holy month of Ramadan while still in mourning for his father.

Shahhat and his younger brother, Nubi, stand at sunset before the temple of Ramses III.

and since the government-deeded land at Sombat was left in her name, Ommohamed borrowed three hundred pounds on future sugar cane harvests—a sum equivalent to a normal year's spending—plunging the family deeply into debt.

At each *zikr,* forty sheikhs, darweeshes, and *munshids*—most of them elderly bearded men from El Kom—gathered before the house to chant prayers for Abd el Baset's soul all evening and well into the night. Hour by hour, on and on, the men prayed aloud, rapidly, in a hum of incantation, sometimes in a low bass drone and sometimes rising to a shouted hysteria. Such *zikrs* can be held for any religious occasion such as a departure or return from a pilgrimage to Mecca, but most often as a rite for the dead.

"Oh, Allah, bless our lord Mohammed among the former generations; and bless our lord Mohammed among the latter generations; and bless our lord Mohammed in every time and period; and bless our lord Mohammed among the most exalted princes, onto the Day of Judgment. . . . "

As the night deepened the words would speed up, and the sheikhs would rise and begin rocking back and forth, their heads and shoulders pulsating up and down to the rhythm of their prayers. "*La ilaha illa-llah, la ilaha illa-llah.* . . . There is no God but Allah, there is no God but Allah. . . . " Sometimes one of the younger sheikhs would move to the center of two facing lines of men, and the others would begin turning their heads very quickly to the right and left, in time to each rapid repetition of *La ilaha illa-llah;* the man in the center would throw his arms about, turn his head in every way, now to the ground, now to the sky, reaching an ecstasy of religious passion. His face became red, his skin beaded with sweat, and his neck muscles stood out like ropes as he suddenly exclaimed in a very high pitch and with such vehemence it became a piercing scream, "*Allah! Allah! Allah! Allah! Allah! la la la la la la la la la la la la la la la lah!*" Then he would cry the phrase, "*Ya'amee, Ya'amee, Ya'amee, Ya'amee!*" repeating over and over, "Oh, my uncle!" until his voice would slowly become faint and he swayed and started to fall. Another sheikh would then rush out to catch him as he began to foam at the mouth, his eyes closed and his arms twitching. Aroused and excited, all the sheikhs began ejaculating with greater rapidity, violently turning their heads back and forth. Joining them, Shahhat would be swept into the emotional frenzy, and thrusting his head and shoulders to each side, sweating, his loose tunic flapping about and his whole being one with the chanting sheikhs, he would imagine his father being sped across El-Sirat—the bridge that extends over the midst of Hell and is finer than a hair and sharper than a sword. Sinners like Shahhat himself might slip and fall into the fire and ice, there to pray amidst beatings and torture until their sins were forgiven; a good man like his father might enter Paradise at once.

Shahhat, schooled only in the beliefs of medieval Islam, pictured Paradise in shimmering golden lights; he imagined glittering fountains and streams, glassy green fruits, and girls with eyes black as gazelles. The

74

Koran promised even the lowliest man eight thousand servants and seventy-two beautiful wives or *houris,* tents of pearls, jacinths and emeralds, goblets of the finest gold, and songs from the angel Israfeel. For the most blessed there was the highest spiritual pleasure of beholding, morning and evening, the dazzling, unseeable presence of Allah Himself, of such blinding radiance it was like looking into the sun.

Shahhat believed he himself would be beaten down to the seventh hell by the retributive angels, Munkar and Nekeer, and he accepted this. But his father was such a good man that, for all his sins of gambling and drinking, if enough *zikrs* were performed, he had at least a chance at Paradise. Neither Shahhat nor Ommohamed would have denied Abd el Baset this, even if it took everything they possessed.

Their intense mourning impressed everyone. Abd el Baset's cousin Sobhy, the innkeeper, feeling contrite, offered to buy Ommohamed a young female buffalo. "You take the milk at night and the calves when they come," he told her, "and I'll take the milk in the morning for my family and the inn." He promised that if Shahhat would feed the buffalo for a year, half of it would belong to her. Since a buffalo lives for thirty years and can bear twenty or more calves, nothing was said about its eventual sale.

Ommohamed, haggard and hollow-eyed, a ghost of her former self, was shocked. "But what will people say about us?"

"Nothing," Sobhy replied. "You are not dancing and beating tambourines." The children, Samah, Nubi, and Ahmed, were delighted at the prospect of milk every day; their mother hushed them, demanding, "How can you laugh in front of the neighbors? What will they say about us? Is it not your father who is dead?"

Shahhat was furious. "I will never give fodder to it! Let it die! I take no charity from anybody!"

"It is not good," his mother agreed. "The father dies and the family gets a buffalo." But her shrewd practicality won out, and when Sobhy brought the buffalo to the house, she begged Shahhat to say nothing. "Please, my son, Sobhy is like a lighted candle, proud and happy. He wants to do this in memory of your father."

Sobhy's generous impulse had barely lasted as far as the marketplace, and he bought the cheapest buffalo to be had. Seeing Ommohamed's disappointment, Sobhy shrugged and told her, "Well, keep it in your house. Use its dung for your oven. If it dies, I'll throw it in the desert."

Hagg Ali suffered no such penitence; soon he was demanding

75

Ommohamed repay him for the burial shroud and cigarettes he had given out to the mourners the day Abd el Baset died. When she reminded him he still owed the family seventy pounds for grain her husband had given him, Hagg Ali said not to think of it, that he would help her get a government widow's pension worth ten times the amount. Ommohamed was not deceived. "Hagg Ali is as cunning as a snake," she told Shahhat. But her romantic imagination needed only a minimum of encouragement. She seized upon the notion of a widow's pension as a means of solving all her cares and enabling her to make her pilgrimage to Mecca.

As time went by and Hagg Ali said nothing more about the pension, one day she pressed him about it. He flared up in annoyance, telling her, "A woman must keep her tongue in her mouth! Not speak!"

"I do not care about the money," Ommohamed told him with quiet anger. "But now that Abd el Baset is gone, you are our father, Hagg Ali. To whom do I have to look to help my two small sons, Nubi and Ahmed? If they need food, I shall send them to your house to catch your sleeve, my cousin."

"No!" Hagg Ali exploded. "I am not going to be a father to anyone! I do not know you, woman! Do just as you like!"

Ommohamed was ashamed she had trusted him. She told Shahhat, "I knew from the first Hagg Ali is the son of a dog. But I did not want to believe it. Who else do I have to turn to?"

The family in time became isolated in its mourning. Ordinary life went on in the village, and it began to relentlessly draw them back into its affairs.

Two months after Abd el Baset's death in June, there was a sensation. Faruk was found at his threshing ground one morning beaten insensible. They took him to the hospital in Luxor, but for days no one was allowed to see him. Shahhat was known to have been at the threshing ground the afternoon before. It was whispered about that perhaps Shahhat had tried to kill Faruk in an outburst of temper, that perhaps Faruk had cursed Shahhat's father in his harmless way. Even Ommohamed felt compelled to ask her son, "Did you beat Faruk?" Such suspicions infuriated Shahhat, since he had left the threshing ground early and the beating was as much a mystery to him as anyone else. He sullenly refused to discuss the matter with anyone. As soon as Faruk could speak, the village headman went to see him. At the sight of Faruk's bruised and livid face, the headman demanded, "Who did this to you? Because we can kill him. Was it Shahhat?"

"No, no, not Shahhat." But beyond that Faruk would not go. He stayed in the hospital ten days, and Shahhat often went to see him, determined to learn the true story. At last Faruk told him. What had happened was this.

That night, after Shahhat went home, Faruk stayed on at the threshing ground, smoking hashish. It was a bright, moonlit night, and he had secretly arranged to meet a certain woman from the neighboring village of Lagulta there. A big woman, homely enough in the daytime, she had been deserted by her husband and yet was still as agile as a young girl. Although not a common prostitute, she sometimes went with village men like Faruk for a price. When she came across the fields just before midnight, Faruk looked about to make sure she had not been followed, then took her into his shed. He had smoked too much hashish and he staggered about, fumbling, when they heard a loud, prolonged, drunken shout coming across the fields.

"Fa-aruk!"

Faruk muttered an oath and he and the woman fell silent, listening. Again after a little while came the same shout, harsh and long-drawn-out, as though it was coming from the earth.

"Fa-aruk!" Then they heard a second man's voice calling, as drunken and harsh-sounding as the first.

The woman, recognizing the voices and certain who had followed her, shrank against the back of the shed, pulling her black cloak about her, and it was strange to see the look of terror on such a strong-looking village woman's face. Faruk swore as she broke into a loud sob. "What's the matter with you, woman! Be silent and they'll pass by!" The voices sounded familiar to Faruk also and made him uneasy. They could belong to two men from El Kom who often drank at Abdullahi's. Every time they got too drunk and smoked hashish afterward, they forgot everything, abused everybody, created an uproar, and had beaten up some of their neighbors so badly they had been jailed.

"Fa-aruk! Fa-aruk!" The shouts sounded close to the shed.

Frightened, Faruk looked about for a wooden stave or some other weapon but the woman got in his way, clinging to his arm and sputtering, "Protect me, for the love of Allah!" He thought to look outside, but before he had time, a drunken cough was heard and into the shed came a man. He was so tall he had to stoop under the door, so long-legged, long-armed, and long-nosed everything about him looked long except his neck, which was so short that he seemed almost hump-backed. He wore an old, grimy tunic, and his turban had slipped to one side revealing a glistening bald crown; because his face could not be clearly seen in the dim shadows of the shed, he looked terrifying. Over his shoulder peeped the barrel of a rifle, which was also long. Behind him was a second man, shorter and thickset. They reeked of liquor and hashish fumes. Faruk saw they were the two he feared—coarse, filthy, dishonest, and drunken men. They beat their wives, were in continual quarrels, and when they drank too much at Abdullahi's they insulted, despoiled, and terrorized everyone.

They stopped just inside and the tall man looked about, then saw what he was after. He went up to the woman, swung his arm, and struck her in the face with his fist. He laughed and the other joined in, cruelly and stupidly. Stunned by the blow, the woman did not utter a sound but only cowered, and instantly her nose began to bleed.

"Sons of dogs! Bastards!" Faruk cursed, but they were upon him at once, pounding his head and stomach with their fists. The breath knocked out of him, he sagged to his knees, gasping for air, and they tied his hands with twine. In a moment he was hunched on the ground, struggling helplessly.

Obviously aware of the terror they aroused and pleased by it, the two drunkards seized the woman and dragged her outside. They started undressing her, snarling like animals all the while. As Faruk watched from the shed, they stripped off everything until she was stark naked. The woman shuddered with fright, her teeth chattering, and in the bright moonlight she looked very strange, pale, and beautiful. The shadows that fell upon her, her long black hair, her firm full breasts, and the luster of her skin stood out vividly. Then they pushed her to the ground and crouched over her so that Faruk could no longer see.

Suddenly the woman howled a loud, terrified cry. But she quickly controlled herself and only an occasional moan could be heard above the animal sounds of the men. From time to time Faruk could hear dogs barking in El Kom, the cries of children, and the sound of distant voices.

"Hurry!" he heard one of the men whisper urgently.

The thickset man finished first and stood about with a bottle, holding it up to his throat from time to time to swallow long draughts of liquor. Then he moved off, and Faruk could see the woman's arms were now locked around the tall man's shoulders in a passionate embrace and that her plump legs, white and lustrous in the moonlight, were wrapped tightly around the man's dark exposed thighs. Faruk could not tear his eyes away as he listened to the woman's moans. Then he felt a hand on his neck and saw only a few inches from his own the mocking face of the other man—a blur of black unshaven chin, bloodshot eyes, and an open fleshy mouth exposing broken, tobacco-stained teeth; the liquor and hashish fumes were overpowering. The man suddenly yanked up Faruk's tunic and burst into a deep, hoarse laugh. "Wah!" he shouted to his companion. "Faruk wants his turn! As true as God!" Seeing the man was breathing heavily, and judging by his stupid, grinning expression, was inclined to continue his tricks, Faruk broke away, rolled to one side and cursed him, "Son of a dog, I'll kill you! Pig! Donkey!" Then as if this were insufficient to express his anger, he went on, "Son of a whore! You burn your religion!" A rebuked expression crossing his drunken face, the man backed away and went outside.

Once the two men had satisfied themselves, they evidently felt guilty, and without heeding the woman, lazily untied Faruk, apologizing and making jokes. The woman demanded money, to which they paid no attention, and snatching up her clothes and cursing them, she disappeared into the fields. The tall one took up his rifle and gruffly ordered the other to follow. It might have ended there if Faruk, raining curses upon them, had not staggered after them. The tall man turned him back and struck him on the shoulder with his rifle butt. He struck him again and Faruk fell and tried to crawl away on all fours, causing the two of them to laugh loudly. Then, excited and eager as if they were beating some wild beast, they both began pounding and kicking him until he lost his senses.

Faruk told Shahhat he saw both men at Abdullahi's almost every night. He said he wanted to avoid a blood feud, such as were not uncommon along the Upper Nile, with members of one family killing off those of another in an unending cycle of revenge. Faruk's own older brother had been killed in such a drunken quarrel. A blood feud was prevented only after the sobered assailant came to Faruk's house carrying his burial shroud. He told Faruk he would sleep on the floor that night, saying, "Now if you want revenge you can take it." The man was serving a three-year sentence for unpremeditated murder.

Faruk refused to name his assailants or the woman to Shahhat and never did. Life in the village was lived in the present. What happened yesterday, especially if it could be blamed on liquor and hashish, was finished and forgotten. Faruk continued to drink with the same two drunkards at Abdullahi's and meet women at his threshing shed. Life went on as before.

79

Most village feuds were over water, especially since the end of the Nile's yearly flood and the introduction of perennial irrigation and diesel pumps seven years before. These pumps were the first machines ever used in Berat. They were usually too expensive for one man to own and run, and the cooperation required in partnership and selling water to others was outside village tradition. Yet once pumps were available, all but a few fiercely traditional *fellaheen* such as Shahhat had to have one instead of the old back-breaking well sweeps and water wheels.

Hagg Abd el Mantaleb owned half-shares in a number of pumps, one of them with Salem, the *ghaffir*. After the two men fell out over some trivial matter and Hagg bought Salem out, Salem bought another one with Shahhat's friends, Abd er Rahman, and set it up at the same place along the canal. These two pumps, operating side by side, were an endless bone of contention. Hagg's son Ahmed, a surly, hot-blooded youth, or Abd er Rahman, equally hot-tempered, were forever dismantling each other's pumps and throwing the pipes into the canal. Soon both sides were recruiting allies and forming factions, saying, "We'll show those sons of dogs that we are real men." Salem and Hagg tried to preserve the peace. Salem's son, Jamal, who bore no grudge against Shahhat for holding him captive since he himself was on bad terms with his father, recruited Shahhat, who agreed to join his faction as long as no one told Ommohamed.

For days strategy and counter-strategy occupied the village youths; the feud might have become serious had not two strangers come to the village one Friday noon to attend the weekly prayers at Hagg Abd el Mantaleb's mosque.

This in itself was not remarkable. It was a custom to seek out other village mosques on Friday if a man could spare the time from his fields. But Hagg's mosque was so small, inconsequential, and so lacking in history or distinction, except for its miserly donor's failure to provide a minaret, that outsiders rarely came to pray there.

The two strangers, who first appeared in the village cafe just outside the temple gate, looked so sinister and menacing in their long, black wool tunics and black turbans, they at once became subjects of intense speculation. There are some men whose villainy can be ascertained by their face, voice, and laugh. These two happened to belong to that unfortunate class: judging by the brutishness of their faces, the harshness of their voices, and the stupidity of their jokes, everyone expected the worst of them. When the two men told Sha'atu, the cafe owner, that they came from the distant village of Gamoleh, a notorious lair for *harami* or professional bandits, that settled it. As soon as they paid their bill and left for the mosque, Shahhat and Sha'atu sent a small boy to follow them and eavesdrop on what they said. He soon returned to breathlessly report one had said to the other, "Let us go to Hagg Abd el Mantaleb's shop, buy some cigarettes, and see what is there."

"I'll tell Hagg not to sleep tonight," Shahhat exclaimed. "He has a rifle."

"No, quick, telephone the police!" advised old Yusef. No one else favored this course, it being felt that any involvement with the police was only asking for trouble. Once thieves had broken into Shahhat's house and told him to fetch his buffalo; instead he had leapt over the stable wall and hid, and the bandits, thinking he had gone to call the alarm, fled. Shahhat said that if he ever met these men on the road, he would pass them without a sign of recognition, for he feared the police as much as the thieves, as did most of the villagers.

The two strangers from Gamoleh left the village after the noon-day prayers. But the threat they might return some night united everyone. Feuds over diesel engines and the like were forgotten, and all the young men took turns standing guard at Hagg Abd el Mantaleb's house at night.

For days the village was in a state of seige. Cows, buffaloes, camels, goats, sheep, chickens, rabbits, and ducks were herded indoors early and locked in their stables. Families took refuge after dark behind heavy bolted doors. Sobhy handed out revolvers to all the servants at the inn. As the night fell, it seemed danger lurked behind every tree—the dogs had never barked so much—and once El Azap fired at nothing and was scolded by the older men. After a week went by and nothing happened, everyone began to feel sheepish; they stopped guarding Hagg's house and the two strangers were forgotten.

They came late one Thursday night, catching everyone by surprise. There was some speculation about the choice of a Thursday, since by Moslem tradition this is considered the most auspicious night for a man to sleep with his wife. Hagg Abd el Mantaleb himself later refused to say a word about the robbery, but rumor had it the thieves took away money, jewels, and gold worth five thousand pounds, a fabulous sum. This might have been exaggerated by civic pride, but no one disputed that Hagg's loss had been enormous since, like all villagers, he distrusted banks and kept his fortune in his house.

From what could be gleaned from Bahiya and the children, three men—stark naked, their bodies greased with oil, and with black hoods covering their heads—awoke Hagg at two o'clock in the morning by

81

prodding his head with the barrel of a pistol. One of the thieves was said to have demanded the key to the strongbox and another the key to a certain bedroom cupboard where Bahiya kept her jewels. Luckily, Hagg's two sons, Ahmed and Mahmood, and their little girl, Nadja, slept at the other end of the large house and did not awake. Hagg and Bahiya were bound and gagged. It turned out early reports that Bahiya had been raped were completely unfounded. Indeed it was Bahiya, according to most versions, who was able to struggle out of her bindings and free Hagg. A favorite detail, which Bahiya confirmed to Ommohamed, was that Hagg ordered her to scream and call the neighbors as she had the most carrying voice.

The police inspector came and interrogated everyone at Sha'atu's cafe. He asked questions in a mild, even tone, heard one villager after another, dismissed each with a muttered, "Get out," and then hurried off to the inn, coughing. There he could be seen with Sobhy at a table littered with beer bottles and ashtrays filled with cigarette butts discussing his own affairs as if he had forgotten about Hagg Abd el Mantaleb, the thieves, and the stolen money. Village speculation turned not to whether the thieves would be caught, but to who had informed them of where Hagg kept his money. "Who?" old Yusef would cry. "Hagg's enemies, that's who! Every man in the village is in debt to him. Who else?"

A Morning's Ride to the Suk

For months after his father's death, Shahhat slept badly. By August, a strong wind rose every night from the desert, crackling the palm trees and rattling the shutters. Shahhat would lay awake for hours, listening, and remembering that Abd el Baset was dead and would not be among them again. These days all the family slept badly, Ommohamed by the pain of her loss, Samah by anxiety, the boys by hunger and itch. Shahhat could hear them upstairs coughing, turning from side to side, mumbling in their sleep, getting up for a drink.

He slept below to guard the stable in the large front room with its bare earthen walls and ground, lit by a small oil lamp which smoked and burned dimly. If he moved in front of the lamp, a large shadow fell across the walls and bright moonlight could be seen. Toward morning, as the wind died and the lamp went out, the room's two small high windows were brightly illumined by moonlight.

Shahhat would try to sleep and forget, and for a while he would slumber, then suddenly it was as if he felt a familiar hand on his shoulder, a breath on his cheek, and he would awake suddenly expecting it was his father. But he was gone and it was impossible to bring him back. He thought of something El Azap had said. "Before you don't care about your life because your father looked after the family and fed them. Now the sadness of life has come over you and you must be a real man."

Shahhat turned onto his other side and his father was forgotten. But now came thoughts of money, of fodder for the buffalo and donkey, the rising cost of fertilizer, the mounting debt for flour and provisions at Hagg Abd el Mantaleb's shop. Shahhat groaned in his anxious thoughts. *"El hamdu li-llah,"* he muttered softly, "Praise be to God."

Sometimes he could hear muffled movement upstairs, but looking at the windows it was difficult to tell whether the moon was shining or it was already dawn. When Samah came down to wash and milk the buffalo, he knew it was after four o'clock. It would still be dark but already possible to discern objects. Sometimes he would hear Ommohamed's loud dejected sigh as she went about the kitchen, lighting the fire, evidently half-asleep and waking up as she moved about.

When a bluish light began to show through the cracks of the door, Shahhat would stir and go outside to splash some water on his face from an earthen jug, rinsing his teeth with a finger and spitting, then absently remembering to beg the pardon of any genii that might be there. His fine white teeth were badly stained with nicotine; unlike Ommohamed, who kept hers scrupulously clean with ashes, Shahhat did not care how he looked. Dogs would bark along the road, as if determined to wake everyone in the village. Then the voice of Hagg Abd el Mantaleb's cousin Amr could be heard from the mosque, beginning the call to prayer. *"Allahu Akbar! Allahu Akbar! God is most Great!"* he would cry, his

83

quavery tenor voice strained to its utmost pitch. "Come to security. Come to God." Old Yusef would come out of his house down the lane, coughing and wheezing, fuss about, spit several times, and go back to bed.

After washing Shahhat uttered a morning prayer, "Oh, Allah, protect me from Satan," and gathered from under his pillow his protective charms; a tiny copy of the Koran, a written magic charm, and a ring wrapped with white string. He had always carried them about with him since he had been troubled by genii.

Ommohamed would bring him his tea, her face looking pale and swarthy as people do in the early morning when the stars are fading and the first light is beginning to break. It worried Shahhat that he could not bring home the daily earnings from gambling as his father had to feed her extravagance. Instead they just got deeper into debt, and to speak with her about it at all was to quarrel.

Shahhat always felt a sense of release when he left the house each morning. This day, after harnessing his donkey, he headed for the *suk,* the village market held each Tuesday morning down by the ferry landing on the Nile.

Once out of the village and astride the donkey, where trees, houses, and the high temple walls no longer obscured the view, Shahhat could see the open sky, yellow cliffs, and flat green plain below for miles and miles. His spirits lightened in this spacious outdoor world and as he went he observed the crops of his neighbors. Shahhat's eyesight was remarkably penetrating—a gift perhaps inherited along with his hot temper from his Bedouin great-grandfather. What to others were empty landscapes were full of life to him. He had only to look at the distant cliffs to see a desert fox, rabbit, or hawk—seeing them, not running in flight as others could, but in their free daily life when they were not hiding or looking about in alarm. Thanks to his keen-sightedness, besides the world that everyone could see, Shahhat had another of his own, accessible to few others. When he gazed at something far away and grew interested it was difficult not to envy him.

The donkey passed the bean field of Lamei, the rich landowner, then followed a rough, well-worn path across the gritty stone ruins of some forgotten pharaonic palace. When he turned east onto the paved road leading to the Nile, Shahhat had to shade his eyes. A long way ahead across the Nile, where the sky was divided from the earth by the yellow cliffs of the Arabian Desert, a broad, bright yellow streak of sunlight was creeping across the treetops and houses of Luxor, two miles distant across the river. In a moment this light came nearer, and glancing around, he saw it had reached the Libyan Desert cliffs behind him. Then something warm touched Shahhat's shoulders. A streak of light came steadily up the road toward him, rose to meet the other streak and suddenly all the Nile Valley was flooded with dazzling sunshine.

The ripening maize, the reaped sesame lying in shocks to dry, the pale green shoots of newly-planted Egyptian clover, all half dead the evening before from the heat, now glittered with dew and revived. Two white egrets flew across a flooded field. A flock of pigeons, their white wings iridescent in the early sun, rose up, swooping gracefully in broad circles, and then flew away to the temple pylons, where they would roost all day in the shade. Far away, to the left somewhere, a dove cooed.

A crested brown and white *hoopoe* or *hodhod* bird with a flowing movement of his wings floated in the air beside Shahhat and his donkey, then suddenly stopped, as if remembering an important errand, and darted like an arrow across the fields. If a *hodhod* died and you hung it over the door, your house would become lucky; the Koran told how they carried messages from the Prophet Suleyman to the Queen of Sheba.

"*Atla! Atla!*" Shahhat urged his donkey forward, making a clicking sound with his tongue.

Ahead came a cart laden with sesame stalks. A young boy lay on top of the load. Sleepy and lulled by the ride, he just raised his head to look at Shahhat and called drowsily, "*Salaam aleikum.* Peace be on you."

"*Aleikum salaam wa-rahmatu-llahi wa-barakatuh,*" Shahhat replied, in the customary response. "On you be peace, and the mercy of God, and his blessings." Shahhat's tone changed and he called jokingly, "Are you married, Shaiyoma? *Inta majaues,* Shaiyoma?"

"Not yet. If God wills."

The boy lay down again and his cart passed on. His story was celebrated in the village. Although he was but twelve years old, he had tried to marry a girl of eighteen. The girl's father had been willing as Shaiyoma had inherited three acres of land. When Shaiyoma's mother, a widow, refused to permit the marriage, Shaiyoma poured kerosene over himself and was caught by neighbors just as he was about to strike a match. After the girl was married to a youth of her own age, Shaiyoma obtained a magic charm from Sheikha Daiyi so the girl would leave her new husband, which she did. Now Shaiyoma worked as hard as a man, drank wine and smoked cigarettes to convince his mother he was old enough to marry. And no one passed Shaiyoma on the road without smiling and calling, "Are you married, Shaiyoma?" "Not yet. If God wills," he invariably replied.

Shahhat had not gone far before the dew evaporated, the air became hot and dry, and the valley resumed its usual languishing appearance. The yellow cliffs, the green fields, the lilac distant along the river bank all seemed as dead and lifeless as a painting. The day promised to be suffocating. The district police station, a large white building, loomed up on the left and Shahhat rode by without glancing its direction. Among his friends he could boast, "Even if ten policemen surrounded me, I could fight them if I was innocent. I could do anything, hit them with a bottle, even beat my own head against a wall." In truth, like most *fellaheen,* although Shahhat was not lacking in courage in village quarrels, he was submissive toward authority; the villagers felt there was no protection against it but their own wit and cunning.

As Shahhat drew nearer the Nile, he passed large fields of government-owned cane on either side of the road; here jackals roamed at night—no one entered the tall cane after dark. Then came a bean field where six men in a line were swinging sickles, crouched low to the ground. Further on a black-shrouded woman gathering grass stood and held her aching back with both hands, following Shahhat with her eyes. He could not tell if she knew him or was simply resting. Anyhow she stood a long time looking at him without moving.

The road soon became peopled with villagers going to the *suk:* black-veiled women on foot or riding donkeys with enormous baskets of vegetables balanced on their heads; tall, striding men in clean white or pale blue tunics; rich *fellaheen,* proud in their dark wool robes despite the heat; poor men in rags coming to sell a sheep or a goat; girls coming to shop and gossip and young men coming to flirt with them. To Shahhat there were four kinds of people at the *suk:* those who sold sheep, goats, or vegetables for household expenses; those who bought them; traders who got livestock to resell at higher prices in town; and those who came just to be sociable.

The *suk* lasted from dawn to mid-morning, and if Shahhat wanted to sell something, he came at daybreak, chose a spot along the road to display his vegetables or tether his sheep, and squatted down to wait for customers. By eight o'clock the *suk* was a noisy, confused hubbub of men, women, children, cattle, and goods; though there was plenty of space along the road, they all crowded together in one small area for the *fellaheen* loved congested groups. When they crossed the Nile every-

86

one would throng onto the same small ferry so that it was a wonder accidents were rare. When they took the train, they would arrive two or three hours early, cluster on one end of the platform and then scramble all together into a single carriage, even if there was plenty of room in the next one. The road through the *suk,* with so many people hurrying by on donkey or foot—most of them laden with enormous bundles or sheep, goats, and rabbits under their arms, some stopping to loudly greet one another, others shouting to demand they move on—resembled an evacuation. Carts were heaped with produce, raising clouds of dust. Herds of sheep were driven forward by children with sticks. Antiquated taxis somehow pressed through, horns honking. Shahhat saw a small boy blowing a cheap paper horn as if to show he was there too. The boy was soon swallowed up in the crowd but still the toy trumpet could be heard.

Shahhat saw Bahiya and Su'ad, covered in black from head to toe, walking on the side of the road ahead. He pulled his donkey up beside them. They greeted him with the loud heartiness habitual to everyone at the *suk,* and Bahiya bombarded him with questions in her loud, assertive voice. "How are you, Shahhat? Are you busy? How is your sugar cane? How is your mother? Why do you not open your father's shop?"

The two women had passed through El Kom and were filled with gossip. "You know Fatna?" Bahiya demanded.

"Fatna who?"

"Fatna whose father Mohammed died last year. Tomorrow she is to be married."

"She's too young. How can she marry? She can't be more than twelve or thirteen."

"She is not so young," Bahiya told him. "You've not seen her lately. She looks tall as a palm tree. And she has no father now. There is a good man in El Kom who took her to the doctor in Luxor and got permission to marry her." Shahhat did not know the man.

"Why, Shahhat, until now have you not thought to marry?" Bahiya demanded in an accusing tone.

"How can he marry," Su'ad interrupted, "and Abd el Baset only three months dead?"

Bahiya shrugged. "If he marries, his father can rest in his grave in peace. Shahhat can restore the house, and his wife can help Ommo-hamed. They have a big house. There is much work to do."

"Shahhat is a man now and can easily marry after two or three years," Su'ad argued. "He can take any girl, Bahiya. But his sister Samah must marry first. She is already fourteen."

"You come to me, Shahhat," said Bahiya, who was impervious to other people's ideas. "I have a good girl in mind for you. *Helwa,* beautiful. A good housekeeper. And rich. She would not cost you much. She has many clothes. She also has some gold, rings, necklaces, jewelery."

Shahhat laughed, "First I must see her. I do not want the gold. I do not want the fine clothes. I want to see this girl. If she is good, I can live with her in the fields in a house of branches. Perhaps after the next crop is sown, I'll come to you." Shahhat stopped to dismount and tether his donkey beside a tea stall. As the women waited for him, El Azap came up, calling, "C'mon, Shahhat, tonight after dark we'll go to Abdullahi's and share a bottle." The women made clucking noises of disapproval. Shahhat laughed. "*Yulla!* Let's go!" El Azap went to light a cigarette but Shahhat snatched it out of his lips and the two youths began to wrestle for it. "Azap and Shahhat, stop!" Bahiya shrieked. "You both have hot blood. You want to take everything by force."

"Wah!" Su'ad exclaimed. "Shahhat always jokes. He never acts nicely."

"He's like his father," Bahiya laughed. "The son of a duck. He swims in the same direction."

Su'ad defended her late uncle. "His father was a good man. He drank much, gambled much, but you could always count on Abd el Baset if there was trouble. We demand from Allah that he becomes good in the afterlife."

The youths left the two women, Shahhat telling them, "May your day be black, ladies! Don't think of me!"

Someone hit Shahhat hard on the shoulder and he turned and saw it was Snake, another friend. "Take care, you buffalo!" he cursed him, then the two youths fell into an embrace, kissing each other several times on the right cheek and then on the left, for they had not met in some days.

"*Salaamet!*"

"*Teiyebeen!*"

"I congratulate you on your safety."

"I hope you are well."

"Peace be upon you."

"On you be peace, and the mercy of Allah, and his blessings."

"Welcome to you. Come to my house and drink tea."

"I have drunk, thank you."

Then Snake and El Azap embraced and went through the whole hearty social ritual again. Snake told them he had spent the night in jail after getting into a fight at the ferry landing. He laughed. "Forty men inside a small cell. I kept thinking the whole time, 'Oh, my God, how did I get here?'" Snake was from the neighboring village of Qurna just north of Berat. Qurna men, with their Horobat warrior blood, were forever getting into bloody fights.

Even in Berat a feud, once started over a diesel pump or some other trivial affair, could go on a long time. Antagonism might show itself over something so trifling as a trespassing sheep, missing fodder, or the shifting of a boundary marker, and before long it could seem as if human life counted for nothing. In Berat such feuds were quickly stopped by cooler heads among the older men.

But in Qurna life was lived in constant insecurity. As night fell, the dogs would start to roam and bark, and every man carried a heavy stave if he ventured out. Sometimes a fight could start for no good reason and before long men would come running to reinforce both sides, armed with rifles and staves and shouting, "Allah, Allah!" In no time both parties would vow to fight to the death and the police faced great difficulty in restoring order. In Berat such violence was rare as the *fellaheen* were too busy tilling the land. Though some Qurna men had become *fellaheen* and moved down to the plain, most of them remained with their families in the cliffhouses built among the ancient tombs, where they still made a lucrative, if illegal, living digging below their homes at night. Others sold fake antiques to tourists.

The people of Berat and Qurna shared the same road, *suk,* and ferry landing, and everyone had acquaintances in the other village. Yet intermarriage was scandalous, the Beratis regarding the Qurnis as a different lot altogether.

Each village was in fact a closed system, with its own headman, *ghaffirs* to maintain law and order, jail, mosques, Islamic schools, government schools, dispensaries, and doctors. Each had its own agricultural inspector. The Beratis preserved habits, customs, and taboos handed down from pharaonic times; the Qurnis had desert traditions.

Shahhat asked his friend if his father would beat him.

"Perhaps not. Perhaps yes. Nobody knows. Just him."

El Azap asked if the other side in Snake's fight would seek revenge. He laughed. "Oh, my God, nobody knows what will happen.

Just only Allah. Maybe some older men will mediate and it will be finished. Those dogs, the police, wanted money. Why should I give them and have nothing? I'll kill them first."

Snake also wanted to know why Shahhat did not reopen his father's shop. In truth Shahhat had no taste for gambling; he was a *fellah*. "Don't be angry about what happened, Shahhat," his friend advised him. "This is the way in life. I am going to die. You are going to die. Everybody's going to die. You must open your shop and get some money and be like your father. And day after day, you'll forget your bad memories. Because your friends and the friends of your father will come to drink and play dominoes again."

When Shahhat, looking grieved, did not reply, Snake seized his shoulder and told him, "Look, those who came before and gambled with your father, they don't even like to walk down that road any more. They hate the place now. Why is that? Because your father was so kind with the people." Then, seeking to cheer up Shahhat, Snake, grabbed his turban and dodged away, taunting him, *"Hung gesak! I steal your luck!"* Shahhat grinned at once and grappled with Snake until he got it back. Snake shook hands with them and joked, "Pray for me to be happy, men. Pray or hope."

"Go to the devil. *Wa-llah!*"

Their noise had aroused three mangy black dogs from sleep, and all at once they began to bark and sprang toward Snake as if in ambush. They looked vicious, with hairy pointed muzzles and wet eyes, and rushed at him, looking as if they were prepared to tear him to pieces. Snake, who loved fighting, rejoiced at the opportunity and seized some stones from the road to throw at them, a malevolent expression on his face. Two hit the mark—the dogs yelped in pain, and all of them retreated some distance to stand howling more furiously than before.

As they entered the *suk,* Shahhat looked about, interested in everything. He watched two old women, squatting in the dust, speaking in rapid sibilant whispers, their faces so close together their black cloaks seemed to make a tent. Fatih's voice could be heard, loudly bargaining for a sheep. "As true as Allah! I won't pay you more than twenty-five!" A young girl with a lovely face gazed around with a rapturous half-smile as if the dirty, crowded *suk* were something wondrous to behold. A squat, muscular youth clad in dusty sackcloth wandered about, a village halfwit from El Kom; women did not step aside but allowed him to brush against them for such lunatics were thought to be the favorites of Allah, their spirits being already in Paradise.

Old Yusef, squatting to one side with another elderly man, was making a great fuss over buying a goat. He would slowly unfold four old greasy pound notes with deliberation and ceremony, then hand them over to the other, who, with an expression of disdain, would slowly count them out and hand them back, snarling "Four fifty," between his toothless gums. Old Yusef gave a squawk of indignation. "Your goat is old! No one in his right mind would take it, even if you gave it to him!" Shahhat leaned over and whispered in his ear, "Pay the price. Perhaps it will give much meat. But that black one over there is better."

Su'ad's daughter, Batah, her eyes flirtatious beneath long drooping eyelashes, caught Shahhat's arm. She asked if two pounds had been a good price for her lamb. "If it's good with you, it's good," he told her, though in fact it was too little.

Salem's son, Jamal, greeted Shahhat. He was angry with his father for selling a ewe and lamb together for twenty pounds. "It's a bad price," the youth told Shahhat. "We wanted thirty, but my father is timid and wants to finish everything quickly without quarreling. By Allah, if I had had the twenty pounds I would have bought it myself and resold it for much more in Luxor. But, Shahhat, I can't speak. My father still considers Sayeed and me small boys. Both of us are getting to hate everything in the house."

"*Malesh*. Let it be forgiven," Shahhat advised him. "You haven't lost anything from your own pocket, Jamal. Patience is everything. Remember, in the end it will all come to you and Sayeed." Shahhat invited Jamal to join him and El Azap for breakfast since none of them had taken more than tea in the morning and it was now past nine. They stopped at a roadside stand for bread, hot spiced broadbeans, onions, and tea. As he always did, Shahhat ate quickly and moderately, afterward rinsing his mouth out with water and his finger and spitting on the earth.

Then they went to watch a quarrel; two men had become so excited bargaining over a sheep they had started whacking each other with their staves. Others were crying, "*Malesh! Ma-a-lesh!*" and trying to push them apart. On days when prices rose too high or the demand for sheep and goats exceeded supply, such fights were common at the *suk*. Often the buyer and seller were content merely to hurl insults at each other, but some had been known to become so enraged as to try to strangle an adversary, bite his nose, or even kill him. In such rare instances, the assailant would almost always instantly repent and weep over his victim's corpse. Hot tempers were the rule rather than the exception in Upper Egypt. Provided things did not get out of hand, such fights at

91

the *suk* were a welcome distraction for the onlookers and the subject of much gossip back home.

El Azap was diverted by Batah, who passed close by in a bevy of young, giggling girls. He leaned her direction and called softly, so no one else could hear, "Speak with me, *yah gameel*. Oh, beautiful one, come with me tonight." El Azap's overtures were so crude he never got anywhere, and when Batah flushed and threw him a disdainful stare, he said in a loud, resigned voice, "Well, she has good breasts but the legs are a little fat. The stomach is good. Thin ankles." As Batah hurried on, Shahhat called after her, "Her laughter is beautiful. The ear falls in love before the eyes." Batah flashed him such a coquettish smile, he forgot everything and wondered why he had not noticed how grown up she had become.

By the Fireside

AT HOME IN THE EVENINGS Shahhat always liked to wander over to pass some time in Sha'atu's cafe. It was always crowded between dusk and the supper hour; some men were usually playing dominoes, some of them singing softly under their breath or calling loudly for tea without getting it, for they had used up their credit. This evening Sha'atu had not yet taken the chairs and tables in from outside and Shahhat sat down for a cigarette, watching the evening fall over the dusty village plaza. From the inn Sobhy's voice could be heard, cursing one of his servants. "No, you work! Your father is a dog! Why do you want to go into town! Get back to work or I'll kill you!" In the open spaces between the trees and houses, he could see the newly planted fields of clover along the canal, bright green in the flat, late sun. Here and there men still moved about, gathering fodder and watering.

Down a rocky slope north of the houses a crowd of women and girls were returning from the well with water jugs on their heads. All wore their black veils, partly concealing their faces as they gossiped and laughed. Shahhat saw his sister, Samah, then Batah, who walked in front and called to someone in her high-pitched voice; she was looking about and up at the sky, turning this way and that, as if she had seen him and wanted to attract his attention. Then he saw Suniya was also among them; she fell behind and ran to catch up, looking as if she were out of breath. Her stomach bulged with pregnancy—she would soon have her first child.

Shahhat turned away and went inside. Old Yusef, something of the village bore, was holding forth as usual in one corner. Arms akimbo, he greeted Shahhat. "Yes, Shahhat, at the *suk* I agreed to buy that goat for four and a half pounds, of my own free will. . . . Yes . . ." Yusef, now that his sons cultivated his land, made a pretense of selling lemons and limes to tourists who visited the temple. If his wife had not nagged him continually, he would not have even done this, but spent all his days complaining and gossiping at Sha'atu's cafe. He would tell whoever would listen of certain enemies of his, complain of the insults he had to put up with from neighbors, how the authorities abused their power, and so on. He was tiresome to listen to.

The cafe was small, brightly-lit, and pleasant with clean, white-washed walls, and colored tablecloths; framed quotations from the Koran hung about, for Sha'atu was a religious man. He and his wife, Zeyneb, had once been very poor and had lived by peddling vegetables from door to door. Now, with the cafe, they had prospered a little, but Sobhy was forever intriguing with the police inspector to shut it down. Often Sha'atu was harassed by the police but they never went too far, as no respectable Moslem would set foot in the inn and the villagers had no other place to gather except in El Kom. When Shahhat found the cafe's door locked and the windows shuttered, he had only to call, "Sha'atu!" and the obliging owner would come downstairs, open up, and put on the teakettle to boil. Shahhat told everyone Sha'atu and Zeyneb, a pretty little woman, spent all their spare time upstairs making love.

Old Yusef took a long pull on the water pipe Sha'atu provided his customers. "Well, Shahhat, all right, so you see, I'm willing to buy that sheep of my own free will, *El hamdu li-llah,* not bothering anyone,

Shahhat, stirred by Arab music, dances at Sha'atu's cafe.

and in an evil hour up comes that Hoseyn from Qurna, you know, the uncle of Mahmood the donkey driver, and he. . . ." The old man rambled on and on and no one listened. His quavery unstoppable voice, like Sha'atu's geniality and Zeyneb's cheerful smile, was a familiar part of the atmosphere of the cafe, and would have been missed as much as the songs and curses of the domino players.

It was said that formerly, twenty or thirty years before, village gossip had been much more interesting. In those pre-revolutionary days, every man was said to look as if he were harboring some sort of secret, as if he knew something, expected something. Everyone spoke of the coming redistribution of the feudal estates like Sombat and of newly dis-covered pharaohs' tombs filled with treasure. Now the revolution had come and gone, all the tombs had been found, and the conflict with Israel had dragged on so long it no longer excited comment. It seemed as if the village people had no more secrets at all; their whole life was as though on the palm of the hand for all their neighbors to see, and they could talk of nothing but water, fodder, and prices.

"In the past it was better than now," said Shahhat, setting down beside old Yusef with a glass of tea. "There was much wheat and they fed loaves of bread to the dogs. Now who finds enough bread?"

"No, no, no!" old Yusef sputtered indignantly. He chuckled merrily and called to Sha'atu in his wheezy voice, "Shahhat is just a baby. He does not know the old days, eh?" He turned back to Shahhat and told him in a delighted manner, "In the past if we grew maize and wheat we ate all of it. Now we cultivate sugar cane and oh, so many crops and get much money to buy food."

The old man warmed up to his audience. "Now we are under the care of the government. We get everything. If a man is ill, he can go to the hospital." Yusef loved being treated by the doctor in the new dispensary near El Kom and often went there to get drops for himself and ointments for his wife. Sometimes he went to the Qurna dispensary instead or even to the hospital in Luxor. He knew all the doctors and medical assistants and not a one of them had escaped his complaints and opinions. He harumphed. "Now the government must treat us like human beings," he declared, thumped his fist on the table and glared about as if daring anyone to contradict him.

"But now there are so many people."

"Yes, yes, Shahhat, you are right. I too feel the number has doubled or tripled since I was a boy. But everything has doubled. Before, a hundred persons could not find anything. Now two hundred can find everything. Radio, television, taxis, we eat and drink much. In the old days we ate chaff, eh, Sha'atu? Do I not speak the truth, Sha'atu?"

Behind his counter, where he was preparing tea, Sha'atu chuckled; he was a tall, gentle man with a mild and even disposition.

"If I had an atom bomb, Yusef, I'd drop it on this village and start over," Sha'atu joked.

"Allah won't give it to you because he knows that," called Shahhat.

Old Yusef gave a hoarse groan. "Allah won't give me money because he knows I will do everything bad with it." He laughed at his own joke, then fell into a coughing fit.

"So tomorrow we die," Shahhat said, rising to go. "Everything is from Allah."

"*El hamdu li-llah!*" the old man exclaimed loudly, as if to say he was just faithful a believer as the next man.

It was chilly when Shahhat reached home, and he found his family huddled in a big circle around a brazier of hot coals in the front room. It cast a warm, red halo, and after quickly eating a supper of hot beef stew, onions, and bread, Shahhat lay down on his stomach on the wooden bench and rested his head in his hands, staring at the glowing coals. Samah went to fetch some wood and the two small boys and several of Ommohamed's grandchildren sprawled about like pups in a heap, drowsing off or watching the fire with wide, open eyes. After taking Shahhat's dishes, his mother went into the shadows away from the fire, saying, "*Allahu Akbar.* God is most Great," as she began her evening prayers.

Shahhat himself had not said his five daily prayers nor gone to the mosque for several years, but Ommohamed was very faithful.

In the Name of God, the Merciful, the Compassionate
Praise belongs to God, the Lord of all Being,
the All-merciful, the All-compassionate,
    the Master of the Day of Doom.
Thee only we serve; to Thee alone we pray for succor.
    Guide us in the straight path,
the path of those whom Thou hast blessed,
not of those against whom Thou are wrathful
nor those who are astray.

Her voice dropped as she went on. She stood, knelt, sat back on her heels, prostrated her head to the ground and stood again, all the while softly repeating Koranic verses. Some of the villagers rushed through their prayers, reducing them to an unintelligible litany. Ommohamed pronounced every word clearly and distinctly. When at last she turned her head each direction, saying in a soft voice, "Peace be onto you, and the mercy of Allah," Shahhat knew she was finished. He watched as she sat quietly for some time, just moving her lips, as her fingers went down a string of prayer beads. Each time he heard the name of the Prophet, Shahhat would whisper in response, "May Allah bless him and save him!"

Just as these whispered invocations on behalf of Abd el Baset's soul came to an end, there was a rude knocking on the door. Shahhat's friend, Abd er Rahman, burst in, breathless and excited. "What's the matter?" Shahhat asked. "Your face seems handsome tonight. Have you found a treasure in the earth?"

The tall, raw-boned youth burst into laughter and heartily seized Shahhat's outstretched hand. "I come directly to you," he exclaimed in his deep bass voice. "I know you love me and I wanted you to know first."

"That's the truth," Shahhat replied. "Not only in front of you do I say I love you, but behind your back also."

As they sat down, Abd er Rahman told them his father had announced at supper that he would buy him a taxi. "He says it is a good investment," the youth went on in his excitement. "He said, 'I am in good health, praise Allah, but I am old, my son. You now have a wife, children, and a house. But I want to die satisfied that I have done my best for you. You have been an obedient son and labored hard in the fields.' " Which was true; when it came to harvesting no one could match Abd er Rahman's strength. He gave a loud hoot and slapped Shahhat on the back—they both burst into laughter and started cuffing each other.

Ommohamed took no part in this merriment. An anxious look passed over her handsome face. "Oh, Abd er Rahman," she protested. "It is not your work! Better your father buys you an acre of land. Taxis are forever in need of repair, you have to spend much on spare parts and sometimes must take from your pocket. In the end, you'll want to be rid of it." In truth, her objections were otherwise; the taxi drivers had much time to idle at the ferry landing where they drank much and smoked hashish.

Seeing their chagrin, she threw her hands up and exclaimed, "Well, I give to you my opinion and you are free to do what you will!"

Shahhat objected at once. "How many times do I have to tell you not to talk so much, my mother? Here the poor man is coming and he is happy and hopes to buy a car, and your words make him feel hopeless and lazy."

Soon they were quarreling. "You are *fagri*, miserable, Shahhat!" his mother flared up. "You put yourself in matters of which you know nothing. What do you know about taxis? Your work is with the buffalo, the donkey, and the fields!"

Abd er Rahman burst into hoarse laughter. "By my God, Allah!"

he exclaimed, slapping his thigh. "I come here for help and find it is you two who need the help!"

He and Shahhat went into convulsions of laughter until tears came into their eyes, and they rose to their feet. Ommohamed, for decorum's sake, also laughed, though her eyes were anxious. "By God," Shahhat exclaimed, still laughing, "I will sell the buffalo and the donkey and the fields and buy a new Mercedes with Abd er Rahman!" Ommohamed gave a little shriek of dismay, which made them laugh all the more. She indignantly pressed Abd er Rahman to stay for tea, but the big youth winked at Shahhat as a sign he wanted to go. Shahhat knew Abd er Rahman was secretly meeting a widow in El Kom and was anxious to be on his way.

After his friend had gone, Shahhat began to entertain the children with a story about a man from El Kom who had once been set upon by thieves. Ommohamed's good humor was restored; on the cold winter nights when everyone was gathered around the fire, Shahhat often told such tales and she was most contented at such times, her children all gathered around her. Nubi was sent to the roof to gather more dry sesame stalks. Shahhat joined the circle crouched on his haunches and, putting his hands just above the flames, watched them devour the stalks. Samah came with water and Ommohamed filled the teapot and fixed it over the fire. Her shadow danced over Shahhat and at times hid and at times revealed his handsome face. Everyone stared at the sticks over which danced a fiery light.

"It was about five years ago," Shahhat began and he told them about two thieves, both of them from Gamoleh village, who waited one night behind the Colossi of Memnon on the road to the Nile. It was winter. Darkness had fallen early and a rich woman came by on a donkey. They seized her, muffled her screams, dragged her into some acacia trees, raped her, took her gold necklaces, and cut off her head.

No one around the fire took a breath. Ommohamed, trying not to make a noise, shoved some sticks into the fire. After waiting for them to stop hissing and crackling, Shahhat went on.

"A man from El Kom was passing by on his donkey, carrying two baskets of vegetables home. He was a cousin of Faruk and his name was Mohammed Abu Madj. When he saw what had happened, he tried to escape but the thieves ran after him, caught his donkey, and pulled him off." Shahhat's voice rose to a strangled cry of terror. "Let me go!" he cried, as if his own life was at stake there by the fire. "I have many children who will starve! I will give you my potatoes, my onions, my tomatoes, my baskets, and my donkey, but in the name of Allah, the merciful, spare my life!" Shahhat's contorted face in the firelight no longer looked like his own, but rather like some evil spirit one might dream about.

The water was boiling and Ommohamed poured some into a glass with some tea and sugar to taste it. "Is it ready?" Samah whispered. "Wait a bit. Soon," her mother whispered back. Nubi and Ahmed sat side by side listening in silence, enthralled. Ommohamed filled the tea glasses and passed them around. No one drank but sat staring wide-eyed at Shahhat as if they were hearing the footsteps of the thieves approaching the door.

"But the thieves would not listen to the man, and cut off his head also. Then they cut his body into pieces and stuffed them into the baskets, putting the vegetables back on top. They slapped the donkey and told it to go home, 'Get going! *Yulla!*'"

Seeing the children's terrified faces, Shahhat burst into laughter and exclaimed, "Drink your tea!" No one moved a muscle so he paused, took a brand from the fire, blew on it and lit up his own face. "Then a boy came along from the Nile," he went on, "and he found the donkey without its master and took it to his own home. It was soon recognized by Mohammed Abu Madj's family, who called the police. The police inspector came and questioned the boy but he became so frightened he could not speak. Everyone thought he was guilty of killing Mohammed Abu Madj. The inspector told him, 'You will be hanged for murder.'"

"Just then the head of the dead man, still buried under vegetables in the basket, called out in a loud voice. 'It was not this boy! It was two thieves who killed me and one rich woman also. You can find her body buried in the ground under the acacia trees by the Colossi of Memnon!'"

Shahhat paused, resuming his normal voice. "Today that man is buried in El Kom and his grave is a holy place because he had such strange power." Feeling a sense of anti-climax now that his story had come to an end, Shahhat added, "There are many such thieves about."

"Many," affirmed Ommohamed, who drew nearer the fire. "Many," she repeated in fierce whisper. "The devil take them!"

Shahhat liked to spin such yarns around the fire on the long winter nights. In all of them thieves or evil genii played their role, and all had the same note of terror and unreality. Some tales he had heard from others and some he himself had invented in the past and later, forgetting, had mixed with his experience and ceased to be able to distinguish one from the other.

Life in Upper Egypt was so fearful and wonderful that, however frightening a story Shahhat might tell, it always evoked in his listeners' minds that which had been. Had not naked thieves, their heads masked with black hoods, actually come to Hagg Abd el Mantaleb's house in the night and had not Shahhat himself been tormented by genii in the guise of horned devils, a beautiful girl, and the dreaded *marid* taking the shape of a desert whirlwind? An educated outsider might be expected to grow bored and skeptical, noting the impossibilities and contradictions. But the villagers had spent all their lives surrounded by desert that stretched for thousands of miles, lifeless and empty, and by granite pharaonic temples which had stood unaltered for thousands of years. To anyone so isolated in space and time as they were, it was not surprising that the most fantastic unreality easily paled and mingled with the real.

Shahhat broke the spell by relating humorous things which had happened to him during the day; again, as was second nature to him, acting out all the characters. One moment he was a scowling, abusive Sobhy, cursing his servants, and the next, speaking in a high falsetto and clasping his hands and clutching his head, he was unmistakably Bahiya. Samah, Nubi, and Ahmed, even while they feared his hot temper, adored their oldest brother and nothing could tear them away once he got going on a story. Even when they already knew what happened or had even been present at the time, it seemed to them so much more dramatic and exciting in Shahhat's version and often more interesting than the event itself. Although veracity was not a common virtue among the villagers— no more with Shahhat than anyone else—there was such sincerity and earnestness in the torrent of his words, in his flashing eyes, and the movement of his long thin hands, it was hard not to believe what he said.

This night, as soon as Nubi and Ahmed had drowsed off, Shahhat carried them one by one up to bed while Ommohamed and Samah brought the smaller visiting grandchildren. As the fire died, Shahhat wrapped himself in a heavy, wool blanket and for a long time he gazed into the red halo round the glowing embers. As a pleasant drowsiness crept over him, he regreted opposing Ommohamed's advice about the taxi; she had been right that Abd er Rahman should buy land instead. He wanted to tell her but she would be asleep and if he woke her she would not understand. *"Malesh,* let it be forgiven," he told himself, rolling over to face the wall and pulling the blanket over his head, feeling sleepy, warm, and comfortable. "There's always tomorrow, *in sha Allah.* May Allah in his mercy look after her." And feeling strangely contented by the quiet evening at home, he slept.

Of Course, a Woman!

NOTHER TUESDAY MORNING at the *suk.* Shahhat went to see Faruk, who always on *suk* days sat down by the ferry landing buying grain from *fellaheen* who wanted to spare themselves the trip into the town grain market. Shahhat found Faruk bullying an old man on a donkey, whom he recognized as Mitri, a rich landowner from Basili, Berat's only Christian hamlet.

Mitri was widely believed to be a hundred and five years old and looked it; he was so tiny, frail, and wrinkled he resembled an old gnome out of Arabian Nights; his rheumy blue eyes were almost blind with cataracts; he was almost deaf and was said to be so miserly he put even Hagg Abd el Mantaleb to shame. His wife, a bent, toothless old crone almost as old as Mitri himself, stood beside her husband's donkey, wailing loudly, her spidery arms all akimbo.

The old man was screeching furiously at Faruk. "No, I don't want to sell my beans! Go away from me!" Faruk was laughing and the old lady was shouting into her husband's ear that he had already agreed to sell Faruk two sacks of beans for three pounds. She waved the money in front of his face and demanded they return home.

Mitri, who had already forgotten what he had done a few

101

moments before, kept making a fuss. "If you don't go far from me, Faruk, I shall shout, '*Ya wahid,* help!' and call the police!"

"No, no," protested Faruk. "I gave you a good price."

"How much did he pay?" Mitri demanded of his wife.

"Three."

"No, I want four! I told you earlier, woman, that we must get four. *Ya wahid!* Help! Help! Police!" A constable standing by the ferry gate, seeing it was senile old Mitri, paid no attention. When Mitri refused to budge, his old wife began to cry. "Please give me one more pound," she begged Faruk, "or my husband will beat me when we get home."

Faruk was amused. He shouted into the old man's ear, "What a cold-blooded man you are, Mitri! For one pound you would take a stick to your wife? You have much money!"

"Give me one more pound, you robber!" Faruk gave the old woman another pound note, telling her, "Here, Mother, take this. He has his pound so you won't be beaten." Then Faruk lifted the old man off the donkey with one arm and held him in the air for a moment while he put Mitri's empty sack on the saddle. Mitri, all skin and bones and so fragile he looked like he might crackle into bits like a dried leaf, stayed suspended in a bent sitting position until Faruk set him back upright on the saddle. "Now he cannot go to the police and say that Faruk has stolen his sack," he told Shahhat. Faruk turned the donkey around, pointed it toward the Nile road, and slapped it hard to make it go. He shouted after Mitri's retreating figure, as the old woman hurried to keep up, "Take your pound, Mitri! I hope it burns you! Go to the devil! Your father is an infidel!"

Shahhat laughed. "All rich men are the same. They bury their money in the ground."

Faruk grinned. "As the Christians say, 'Keep the white piastre for the black day, your stacks small, and your enemies happy.'" Then he turned serious. "Where's my twelve pounds, Shahhat? Your mother owes me for *Nitrokima.*"

Shahhat was embarrassed. Ommohamed had given him the money but before he had time to give it to Faruk, something had happened and he had spent it himself. Now he confessed to Faruk what he had done and begged him not to tell his mother; he promised to find the money to pay him from somewhere.

Faruk burst into laughter and slapped Shahhat on the back. "*Inta jagri,* Shahhat! You are a worthless bastard! You spent it all on a

Batah, Shahhat's willful, flirtatious fourteen-year-old cousin, recklessly flaunts stern village and social conventions.

woman, eh?" Faruk understood such folly; had he not himself often done the same? Shahhat stayed sheepishly secretive but he was visibly relieved when Faruk agreed to wait and keep the matter between the two of them. Faruk told him, "You know many people gossip to Ommohamed about me. They say I do bad things and neglect the land. Well, I shall give you and your mother a good part of the maize harvest and say nothing to her. But you must pay me the twelve pounds, Shahhat."

In a moment of infatuation, Shahhat had given the money to his cousin, Batah. It happened this way:

Until the day he saw her at the *suk*, Batah had never particularly aroused Shahhat's interest. Batah was the daughter of Su'ad, who lived just next door, and the grandchild of Abd el Baset's sister Fatnah. Because Fatnah was old, frail, and almost blind, with an ailing husband who kept to his bed, Batah lived with her grandparents and looked after them. They lived in the old large family house where Abd el Baset was born up on the slopes near the Tomb of Marai. Shahhat had seen Batah coming and going on her daily visits to Su'ad for years, but until she had flirted with him at the *suk*, he had not noticed how grown up she had suddenly become.

Since then Batah's visits to her mother had grown more frequent and Shahhat was somehow often standing by the upstairs window when she passed through the lane. At first they merely smiled and greeted one another as always, but soon Batah took to giving him long glances under her drooping eyelashes and then, turning quickly into Su'ad's door, would burst into shrill giggles.

Batah was fourteen, of marriageable age, a handsome, svelte girl with a pair of bright, if calculating, black eyes in a lively face. She was vain and by nature passionate and willful. She was hardly very intelligent and hardly good tempered or kind, but she was extremely pretty.

Soon Shahhat began to dream of her at night and like the genie earlier, she became the object of his fantasies. In confusion Shahhat began to suspect Batah had bewitched him. Why had he never noticed her before? He had heard tell of how Sheikha Daiyi, by wrapping sulphur from a match or an acacia thorn inside a magic written charm, could cast a spell for a girl so that any man she chose would feel an intense burning and pricking and desire her. He suspected Batah had so bewitched him.

One day, seeing her come down the slopes, he went to meet her on a lonely stretch of road outside the village as if by chance. After the customary salutations, he walked beside her and said in an urgent low voice, "I cannot wait for you by the window any more because Su'ad will guess that I love you and you love me. When you come to see her and look up each time, I'm afraid. If your grandmother hears anything she will not let you come here any more. We must be careful. I want to see you but must come to your house."

"When?" Both of them spoke in low voices and avoided looking at each other in case they were being observed.

"Tomorrow night after supper. I'll come after dark."

"Are you not afraid? There are many dogs in *Gurnet Marai*. They will bark and maybe attack you."

"Afraid of a few dogs? Never! I'll bring some bread in my pockets to throw at them."

"Are you sure no one will see you and gossip?"

"Yes. Your grandmother will be saying her prayers then. But wear your red dress. It is very beautiful." Batah flashed him a self-absorbed glance and smiled prettily. Encouraged, Shahhat went on in the conspiratorial tone they both were enjoying, "Tomorrow when you visit Su'ad I'll be sitting with some men along the road and will not greet you, so no one will have suspicions about us. But I'll come tomorrow night."

Batah agreed but added petulantly, "Keep away those two little boys, your brothers. I'm afraid they will spy on us and spoil everything."

Shahhat turned to go a separate direction as they were nearing the village houses. "I will be as if on fire, Batah," he whispered. "So, after. If God wills, tomorrow. *Bukra, in sha Allah.*"

Batah let her fingers brush against his sleeve and whispered softly, "Oh, Shahhat, I want to stay with you now. But I must go." And she hastened away, saucily swinging her hips.

Soon Shahhat was secretly slipping away to see Batah almost every evening. Fatnah, the grandmother, was fond of Shahhat and noticed nothing. Once she had greeted him and chatted for a time, she would pay them little more attention but go to say her prayers or sit the rest of the evening by her husband's bedside, crosslegged on the floor, eating nuts. Sometimes she made such a noise cracking them with her teeth, Shahhat would be startled, just as if it were a pistol shot. His strategy of scattering bread to the dogs did not always succeed; he was bitten several times and bore the scars on his ankles.

But by then he had fallen under Batah's spell. Though he had known her all his life, she now seemed to have acquired fresh beauty and vitality. When they sat talking on the open rooftop terrace of Fatnah's house and Batah would sigh deeply, toss about, and complain about her life, or suddenly quiver and laugh coquettishly, her white teeth flashing and her eyebrows lifted in an amused fashion, he would think what a proud, lovely creature she was. As she did with other young men in the village, Batah played with Shahhat like a cat with a mouse. Sometimes she would flirt with him until he was almost overcome with desire, then she would burst into mocking laughter, stamp her feet with rage at some pretended slight, or push him away, pout, and not speak to him. She began to demand presents, and Shahhat took small amounts of grain from his mother's storeroom and sold them to El Got.

Yet Shahhat realized he did not care for Batah in the way he had cared for Suniya. The feeling Suniya had aroused in him, that intense, deep, tender feeling, was not repeated. Batah's intuition told her this and her vanity suffered from it. One evening, seized by jealousy, she disclosed to Shahhat that she was also secretly meeting his friend Snake.

"Why not?" she asked and gave her mocking laugh. "I get plenty of money from him. All these Qurna men have money." Then, seeing Shahhat's face darken, she hastened to tell him in a soft, caressing voice, "But I want nothing from you, Shahhat. Only your smile." She dropped her long eyelashes. "Somebody told Snake about us and he was angry. I told him, 'I'm only speaking with Shahhat. After all, he's my cousin. Besides Shahhat never gives money to girls. They must always give money to him.' I told Snake you were too jealous and dangerous and asked him, 'Why would I want to go with Shahhat?' "

Ashamed of his poverty, Shahhat took the twelve pounds Ommo-hamed had given him for Faruk, and in a dramatic gesture, threw it all in Batah's lap one evening. She shrieked with delight, clapped her hands, and embraced him. "Now you must love me more and more," she whispered. "Because you make me too happy. Don't worry about Snake. I won't see him again."

But Batah was not satisfied, and soon, wanting to buy this dress

106

or that necklace, began meeting Snake again. She flaunted his presents before Shahhat.

Shahhat could have told her how Snake came by so much money, but he proudly kept his silence. Snake had often told him that if the foreign tourists who came to visit the tombs of Qurna were more interested in himself than the fake antiques he peddled, he took them out into the desert where he would provide any service, as long as he was paid handsomely. It was not an uncommon way of earning money among the young men of Qurna.

Shahhat himself had little to do with tourists. Some days, idling away an hour in Sha'atu's cafe, he would watch them get in and out of their buses and taxis at the temple gate; thin, fat, short, tall, male or female, they would swarm about in bright uniformity, looking rich and carefree in their red, yellow, white, blue, and green hats, dark glasses, shorts or trousers, shoulders festooned with cameras, purses stuffed with pound notes, and bags of every description.

One moment the sun-baked plaza would be empty of life. The next it would spring into noise and activity to a honking of horns and clouds of dust. Children came running to hawk cloth dolls or beg for *baksheesh*. A servant would come from Sobhy's inn, peddling agate necklaces, crudely painted fake antiques, or authentic mummy beads, which were found by the hundreds in the fields. Old Yusef would rouse himself from a nap in the shade of the temple walls and drowsily run about, holding up his basket of lemons and limes. Sha'atu would hurry to put tables and chairs in the shade outside his cafe, and his wife Zeyneb, who habitually seemed to be far gone in pregnancy, shyly advanced toward the tourists calling, "Lemon, coffee, tea, madam, Coca Cola!" the only English she possessed.

While the tourists disappeared inside the temple, the hawkers and children hung about the gate like predatory birds. Once they came out again, the hawkers would make their long, sobbing cries, the children wail for *baksheesh* and the guides shout directions as they herded their charges back to their buses and taxis. A policeman would run about with a switch, thrashing whichever begging child did not dodge him fast enough, so that their screams and sobs added to the din and confusion.

"Madam, you lika this. It's uh-lovely. It's uh-bootifool Alabaster. Not too much. Five pounds."

"My friend, lady, how much you wanna pay?"

"Missoo, a cigarette! For the papa! For the papa!"

"Two pounds, lady. No money more. Nice price from my God, Allah. Okay, you buy?"

After the buses and taxis roared off and the children, evading the policeman, gleefully caught rides on the bumpers as far as the edge of the village, old Yusef would go back to his nap, the servant return to the inn, Sha'atu would whisk his chairs and tables inside, and the children vanish as quickly as they had appeared.

Shahhat spoke a little English, picked up from listening to foreigners in the cafe, but he never talked with them. If his friends asked why, he would say, "God gives me my work. I have land. Why should I speak with these foreigners, sell antiques to them, beg for *baksheesh?* Let the Qurnis go with them. My work is to cultivate the land."

Late afternoon. Shahhat was climbing the cliff face above the valley on his way to the desert. There was no wind, hawks circled lazily overhead, and the rocks were a blinding white in the strong light. Shahhat was lost in his own thoughts when he heard a girl's voice cry out. Somewhere high above him on the ridge she was screaming for help.

Without another thought, Shahhat left the trail and began scrambling up the rock face. Some moments later, breathless and his heart beating fast, he advanced up a narrow corridor of rock not far below the highest ridge. As he emerged he found himself face to face with a blonde foreign girl who was about to smash a rock down on his head. "Oh," she gasped in astonishment. "Oh!" She dropped the rock and stared at him speechless for a moment, then cried, "Please help me!"

The girl burst into a torrent of excited speech. Shahhat could not understand much of it, but he caught enough words and gestures to grasp what had happened; just as he had remarkably keen eyesight, he was also unusually quick of comprehension. Little escaped him.

The girl had wandered up the narrow path from the Valley of the Kings directly below, where she had left her bicycle. The cliffs descended from the ridge where they stood in an almost sheer drop to the narrow gorge where the pharaohs had their tombs. But a trail, cut into the rock long ago, traversed back and forth so that it was possible for someone with no fear of heights to ascend the precipitous cliff. She had almost reached the summit when she met three boys. She guessed their ages as around fourteen to sixteen. They had exchanged greetings and tried to sell her mummy beads. One produced a shriveled mummy's hand from his pocket and another was carrying a live scorpion in a box.

After she refused to buy anything and continued her climb, she saw that they were following behind and speaking in rapid Arabic. They caught up with her and one of them seized her arms while another ran his hand inside her blouse. Angry, she broke away, and, pushing them aside and telling them to go away and leave her alone, started up the trail. She had not gone far when she heard them whistling and calling—when she turned around she saw the biggest boy had pulled up his tunic to expose an erect penis and that the other two had pressed their bodies together and were hunching back and forth in an obscene, rhythmic way. They gestured for her to join them and when she turned and ran up the trail, they started up after her. Frightened, she scrambled over the rocks as fast as she could, frantically seeking a place to hide. When the boys tried to enter the narrow rock corridor, she forced them back by throwing stones. They seemed to go away. She had been screaming for help when she mistook Shahhat for one of them.

Shahhat listened, eyed her with amazement, and tried to form words in English, all the while thinking she was the most beautiful creature he had ever seen. Her eyes were naive and clear and blue as the sky, her every movement was charming and graceful, and her hair long and yellow as ripe maize. Even her panic did not spoil her good looks, but intensified them. She was breathing rapidly and trembling all over, and his anger mounting, he groped for words.

"They . . . they want to make bad things with you?" he managed to say. When the girl nodded he opened his mouth to say something more, but uttered no sound. Instead his face grew dark, his eyes watered, and he clenched his teeth. "I know boys in the mountains," he finally said. "They want to make bad things with the tourists. If they find you alone in the mountains, they can make anything they want."

He took her arm and silently they climbed up to the ridge's summit, just fifty yards or so above them. Deeply relieved, but apprehensive, the girl kept stealing glances at him. Shahhat was dressed in black, with his face half-hidden by his old grey scarf which was wrapped about his chin and throat in the Bedouin manner. A fringe of moist, black hair hung down from his skullcap and beads of sweat stood out on his forehead. He was agitated and angry, but also entranced. The girl's

109

eyes were so blue, her hair so yellow, and she moved with such inexpressible grace. He could scarcely keep his eyes off her. Without a word, they sat down upon a jutting rock and watched the path below. He lit a cigarette. They both felt a sense of communion and neither wanted to speak, as if it would break the spell.

Some minutes passed and then, far down the mountain, a lone figure could be seen coming up the trail toward them. The girl watched for a time and then stiffened; she recognized the white turban and tunic.

"That's him!" she cried out involuntarily. Then, seeing the fury in Shahhat's face, she covered her mouth.

"The same boy?"

"No. No. I can't be sure." But she was sure. "He was also wearing white, that's all. Why would he come back now that you are here with me?" Shahhat stood up, scowling; seeing how angry he looked, the girl began to worry about what he might do. The boy kept advancing until he was less than fifty yards away. He stopped and squatted down in the path, facing them.

The girl jumped to her feet and shouted, waving her arm, "Go away! Go away!"

"Don't speak!" Shahhat whispered harshly. "Let him come here!"

Shahhat and the boy began to shout back and forth in angry, gutteral Arabic and the girl could not understand. Shahhat demanded, "Did you try to rape this foreigner? She is our guest!"

"No, I made nothing," the boy at first protested. "There were some others up here. Maybe it was them."

"Go away!" the girl called.

The boy sneered. "If she was alone, Shahhat, I could do with her what I liked, even throw her off the mountain."

In an instant Shahhat swept down the slope, his black robe flying and his face terrifying in its sudden explosion of temper. He seized the boy by the shoulder, ripping his tunic, and knocking off his turban. The girl came running down the slope behind him, tripping, almost falling, and crying out, "No, no! Stop! This is the wrong boy! Let him go!" She seized Shahhat's shoulders but he shook her off and she fell.

Shahhat flung himself at the boy, with bloodshot eyes and upraised fists. "I know you!" he thundered. "I know all the people here! You are bad! Your family is bad! *Yah erajeh!* Your mother is a whore!"

110

He began to shake the boy so furiously his teeth rattled. "You sons of dogs think that if someone comes here in the mountains alone, you can do anything with them!"

Terrified, the boy sobbed and whined, begging Shahhat to let him go. "No, no, I don't do anything, Shahhat. I came back to see the girl and ask her. Maybe she wants to fuck. You can go first. Okay?"

Shahhat began beating the boy with his fists. In panic, the boy tried to fight back, waving his fists and trying to ward the blows away from his head. The girl, seeing they were perilously close to the cliff edge, which dropped more than a thousand feet into the Valley of the Kings, seized one of Shahhat's arms and pulled on it with all her strength. The boy was able to wrench himself free, and he rolled down the rocks, crawled to his feet, and ran down the trail. Shahhat made no attempt to go after him and when the boy was some distance he turned around and shrieked, "*Malesh,* Shahhat, let it be forgiven! I know you! You want this girl for yourself! Do with her as you like!"

"I know all the people like you!" Shahhat shouted back at him. "The men and the women, the boys and the girls!" He spat at the boy in contempt. "You are all dogs!"

For a long time Shahhat was too enraged to speak. He roughly seized the girl's hand and pulled her down the trail. She saw he was trembling; to the girl's eyes Shahhat, in his black robes against the blindingly white rocks with the open blue sky all about, seemed very much of a wrathful Old Testament figure. They descended in silence to a low lying ridge just above the Valley of the Kings where the trail divided, one path going down into the plains. There were tourists about, and the girl prepared to thank him and say goodbye. Shahhat was still scowling and he told her, his first words since the fight, "I want to beat his head in with a rock!" He had intended to use a normal voice but instead it came out in a hoarse, strangulated shout.

Impulsively the girl put her arms around Shahhat's neck, put her cheek against his, and gave him a resounding kiss. Then she turned and ran down the path and was gone. Shahhat nearly shouted but stood frozen, staring after her retreating figure, an expression of adoration gradually appearing on his face. As he turned toward home, his heart beat violently and his hands trembled so much he stuffed them into his pockets. His neck, warm from the embrace, seemed touched by a lingering scent; near his moustache, where the kiss had come, a nerve trembled. From head to foot he was soaked in a warm, new sensation.

111

At lunch he ate and drank mechanically what Ommohamed put before him and heard not a word of what she said. He abruptly left the table before he had finished and hurried back to the place where the girl had left him. He went to the Valley of the Kings, the cliffside temple of Hatchepsut, and the slopes of the nobles' tombs, spending the rest of the day searching in vain for a distant yellow-haired figure. He imagined meeting her once more, falling in love, perhaps accompanying her to the distant land where she lived, even becoming her husband. He returned home after dark, hope dead, exhausted, realizing it would be a miracle if he ever did see her again.

For several days Shahhat was in torment. He was so ill-tempered and quarrelsome, Ommohamed suspected some malevolent person had worked a spell over him. When not quarreling with whoever spoke to him, Shahhat did nothing but walk about the house whistling, then— remembering the scene on the mountain—he would stand quite still, absorbed in thought, fixing his eyes on the ground. He was absent-minded and in such temper that at supper one night he exploded in fury over some small annoyance and flung the table over, spilling food and dishes onto the ground.

When he heard Batah was being seen with Snake, he was indifferent, muttering absently, "Batah's like a buffalo." When Batah herself saw him at the *suk,* she stopped him and demanded, "Why don't you speak to me, Shahhat? Why do you not come to my house?"

"I have no time," he said, anxious to get away. "I'm busy in the fields."

"Come tonight. We can talk."

"No. I have no time."

Ommohamed went to Sheikha Daiyi who decided Shahhat had been bewitched. She told Ommohamed to return home and look between the third and fourth bricks from the ground to the left of her doorstep. There Ommohamed found a loose brick and, removing it, discovered a small piece of paper folded into a tiny triangle and covered with illegible writing in red ink. Sheikha Daiyi identified it as a *hegab* or magic charm prepared by a certain Coptic priest, who was notorious for his mastery of the powers of darkness and evil. The two women recited prayers from the Koran, the sorceress burned incense and chanted an exorcism to drive the evil demon from the paper. Then she instructed Ommohamed to have Shahhat burn it just at sunset at the time of Magreb prayers in the village mosque.

Shahhat became good-natured again. Yet he did not forget the girl with the yellow hair whom he had saved and who had once caressed him. For a long time, remembering those moments on the cliffs, it seemed to Shahhat as if his whole life in the village was unnaturally thin and wretched.

World Enough

VILLAGE LIFE was governed by the seasons. As the maize ripened for harvest, Shahhat rode his donkey to Sombat every day to rip off a load of green maize leaves and tassles to feed his buffalo. Like all *fellaheen*, Shahhat never entered cultivated fields other than barefoot; shoes and sandals were always left on the dikes. As it was stifling hot in the tall, airless maize, he also stripped off his headscarf and tunic and worked in his underwear. Since the *fellaheen* had abandoned the old breechclout, this underwear comprised a sleeveless white undershirt, a pale blue many-buttoned cotton vest, and loose white cotton underdrawers which reached to his knees.

Faruk was right; the maize was almost ready to be cut. Shahhat considered when to seek the agricultural inspector's permission to harvest. He would have to rent two or three camels to carry it to Faruk's house in El Kom. As was the custom, Ommohamed and other women would gather to shuck it. Unlike in the northern Delta, this was the only field work Upper Egyptian, or Saidi, women did.

Shahhat worked with remarkable speed, as he habitually did in the fields, throwing armload after armload of the green fodder into a growing heap on the grassy dike. After he had gathered all the donkey could carry, he went about carefully selecting a handful of small green ears for Ommohamed to roast; he chuckled, thinking how his small brothers, Nubi and Ahmed, would probably fight to see who got the most. Shahhat had many things to think about. He must also arrange to hire two cows to plow the field once it was harvested to sow the next crop. The inspector had told him to plant lentils this year instead of the traditional winter crop of wheat that most his neighbors would grow. He was also troubled about the twelve pounds he owed Faruk; he realized how foolish it had been to give it all to Batah when he had no way of earning such an amount.

With so much to think about, Shahhat felt a radio was buzzing inside his head. Irritated and perplexed by his entangled affairs, he sat down on an irrigation canal's grassy bank, lit a cheap Cleopatra cigarette, and stared into the water. He was suddenly aware that tiny fishes were frisking about, some no bigger than his fingernail, but others two inches long and more. The next time the canal was drained, he thought, he would get Nubi and Ahmed to help him build a mud levee to trap some of the bigger fish in an irrigation culvert. Then he was diverted by the sight of a snake, swimming from one bank to the other. He threw a small stone at it and it disappeared.

Suddenly hungry, he took a piece of bread and two leeks from his pocket and began eating them. Oppressed by the heat of the midday sun, which always seemed worse after eating something, Shahhat stretched out on the grass, enjoying the stillness. It did not last long, for in a few minutes a helicopter appeared overhead, coming from the Libyan Desert. He listened to its drone and shaded his eyes to watch it whirr away in the direction of the Nile. Then he heard the putt-putt of a diesel engine as someone started a pump down the canal and the soft, very soothing splash of water rushing out of a pipe. He leaned over the grassy bank to see who was watering and felt something cool on his face like some other kind of air. The water from the pump looked so clear as it gushed into its channel from an iron pipe and glistened so brightly in the sun, it made Shahhat feel intensely thirsty. He feared the bilharzia parasite carried by the water snails that flourished in the canals, especially since the Aswan Dam had brought year-round irrigation. Both Nubi and Ahmed were weakened by it as they sometimes had blood in their urine.

Somewhere far away a donkey brayed, and Shahhat looked to see if his own donkey was paying attention, for to him it sounded like a female in heat. Like all *fellaheen,* Shahhat believed animals conversed with each other in languages of their own, as did birds; what to a man might sound like mere aimless twittering might really be a hymn of praise to Allah.

The softly splashing water and the engine's steady putt-putt did not break the stillness nor stir the stagnant air within the tall maize; rather they seemed to lull it to sleep and made Shahhat drowsier than ever. He dozed off, then awoke and stood up to shake off his lethargy before putting the load on the donkey and starting home. Shaking his head and rubbing his eyes, Shahhat turned to gaze westward to El Kom, whose houses rose along the ridge of a *tell* or artificial mound created by ancient debris so that it was plainly visible. On the eastern boundary of the old Sombat estate, hidden behind a thick row of acacias, were the new square, whitewashed buildings of the government primary school, dispensary, and agricultural office. But El Kom was the real heart of Berat village. Here were the headman's house and the jail, the Moslem school where Shahhat had learned the Koran as a boy, here the cemetery where Abd el Baset was buried, the houses of Faruk, Sheikha Daiyi, Fatih, and Lamei, and Abdullahi's dimlit den. Now in the hot sun there was no life to be seen, just as if El Kom had been overcome by the heat. To the right of El Kom, the granite ramparts of the Ramses III temple with the cliffs behind were just visible in the dusty lilac distance and below them the acacia trees along the canal path which concealed Shahhat's own mudbrick house.

It is sometimes said by city men that one Egyptian village is like any other; Berat was Shahhat's whole universe. The vast open expanse of fields around him, the old Sombat estate, together with El Kom, were Berat's center. Around them, like spokes on a wheel, spread the ten other hamlets with their ancestral landholdings that made up the whole village. Five were named after common ancestors of their present inhabitants: Lohlah, Azooz, Azbah, Tot, and the only Christian hamlet, Basili. The others were known for some feature of the terrain and were called the places of the railway, market, island, reeds, and Tomb of Sheikh Marai, or, in Arabic, El Gutter, El Rozbah, El Gezira, El Helfayah, and Gurnet Marai.

The village population had fallen during World War II and the malaria and cholera epidemics that followed it so that Berat, with less than seven thousand people in all its eleven hamlets, did not suffer the acute overpopulation of Cairo or Lower Egypt, where density was the highest on earth. In ancient times, the Theban Plain was much more

115

crowded, the pharaonic temples alone possessing eight hundred thousand slaves, taken as prisoners of war.

Half of Berat's people owned no land at all. Those who did had average holdings of two acres; the distinct exception, Lamei, whose father had been given two hundred acres by an aunt of King Faruk just before the 1952 revolution. Lamei kept more than fifty laborers but worked as hard in the fields himself as any of them. He kept within a legal fifty-acre land ceiling by jointly cultivating with his brothers.

To Shahhat's eyes, everything he saw had its special flavor, a unique value and meaning. Here was a white minaret, there a clump of date palms; each field could be located by familiar canals, dikes, wells, and trees. All these things Shahhat unconsciously perceived; he knew their feel, their sound and smell. To him Berat was more; its eleven huddled hamlets formed a community, seven thousand human souls who thought in terms of relationships, families, kinship, ties, rights, obligations, factions, feuds, and friends. He took all this for granted, and yet gazing about these familiar surroundings felt a warm sense of satisfaction.

A yellow butterfly fluttered close by, then lit on a henna bush. Shahhat looked at the bush, forgot his reverie, and becoming very serious and alert, dropped to one knee. He fixed his eyes on the spot, slowly raised a henna branch with one hand, and arching the other, suddenly lunged forward, clapping his hand over something in the bush.

"*Yah ragil!*" he exclaimed aloud with the excitement of a small boy as he opened his hand upon a large scarab bug. Imagining the scarab liked it, Shahhat stroked its wide yellow and black back and touched its feelers. As a boy Shahhat had made small water wheels from maize stalks, attaching a scarab to them by piercing its outer shell with an acacia thorn. The insect, struggling to get free, would spread its wings and fly furiously around in a circle, turning the wheel round and round just as two cows did a real one. Sometimes the beetles would keep this up an hour or more; the village children never tired of making these wheels. Now Shahhat let the scarab go and it flew away with a whirring sound; like the ancient Egyptians, who reproduced them in stone temple images, Shahhat believed them sacred.

Preparing to load his fodder, thirsty, Shahhat glanced at the flow of water from the pump. "My God," he said aloud, "If I get bilharzia, I get bilharzia! I'll go to the hospital and sleep for a month in bed!" He put his mouth to the water mechanically and swallowed just enough to quench his thirst, then, having gone this far, he drank im-

116

moderately, until the punget cold in his mouth overran his body, and his vest and singlet were soaked.

Just then he heard a low singing. Somewhere, quite far away, a girl was singing against the faint groan and creak of a water wheel. "*Yah loblee, yah loblee. . . .*"

Shahhat held his breath and listened, recognizing the voice. In the tall maize the song sounded now to the right, now to the left, now in the air, now on the ground, as if some unseen genie were floating about him and singing. In her song, plaintively and simply, the singer was trying to persuade someone that she was in no way to blame, that she passionately desired to live, that she was young and loved him still and would be pretty if it were not for the heat, the dry desert wind, and the incessant labor. It was no one's fault, but she begged someone's forgiveness, singing it was unbearably painful, and a pity for her.

"Hello, you across the Nile, take my hand, my love, take my hand. . . . "

It was Suniya. He listened a long time to her song, then suddenly the airless field seemed hotter, stuffier, and stiller. He hummed loudly as if to drown her out, cursed his donkey, put his clothes back on, and loaded the fodder. Once he had the heavy load balanced, he leapt astride it and commanded the donkey to go, "*Atla! Atla!*"

When he reached the high cart road by the main canal through Sombat, he could look across the maize tassels to where Suniya, in a black dress, was seated on a water wheel beneath some palm trees at the field's edge. The wheel was being slowly drawn round by two brown cows, and it was evident it had been Suniya who was singing. As he rode along he watched her unyoke the cows and water them. He could not be sure, at this distance, whether she noticed him or not. Then some trees came in the way and she was no longer in sight.

He remembered how each August, when the Nile flooded its banks, they caught small fish called *garmot* and put them into the well at Abd el Baset's old water wheel. In the spring, when the water level fell, and the long chain of earthen pots that were engaged in rough cogs to the big horizontal wooden wheel had to be dipped deep into the well, the jugs filled not only with water but also fish, which had grown bigger with the passage of time. Suniya would clean them, build a fire, and cook them, without salt, right there by the canal path, and the two of them would enjoy a secret feast. There were ruins of a pharaonic water wheel in the temple grounds and once they had been excited to find some

117

garmot fish portrayed on an ancient stone freize. "We took everything from them," Suniya had said, but Shahhat had teased her and called her *pharaoni*. He remembered how Suniya one morning, seeing the sun rise over the eastern cliffs, had said it was like the land expressing thanks.

Now only a few villagers still used their water wheels and Suniya would soon bear another man's child. Shahhat began to sing the same melancholy song as Suniya had but with words he had once made up to serenade her as he worked all night on his father's water wheel.

> Oh, girl, you who have much money
> And now sleep, I am poor.
> I work not for riches, it is my choice.
> Oh, beautiful, beautiful girl,
> Come out to see the night,
> Come out to see the stars,
> Come out to see my eyes,
> Deep as the deepest well.
>
> Now I forget my two friends, my cows who
>   labor all the night,
> Asking nothing but grass from me.
> I am not rich, oh, beautiful sleeping girl.
> But I am free.
> You idly sleep, you feel nothing.
> Come out to me in the night.

The Christian hamlet of Basili was situated in the southwest corner of the village on the edge of the desert, where, away from the Nile, the soil was poor. Except for old Mitri and a few priests, its land-holdings were tiny, small fractions of an acre. Basili had been a Christian settlement, it was said, almost since the Apostle Mark had brought the gospel of Jesus to Egypt; its church, a whitewashed, multi-domed building which stood some distance out in the desert sand, had been in continuous use since Roman rule. The Coptic families of Basili, isolated and inbred for centuries, were among the most illiterate and impoverished of Berat's people.

Shahhat was passing along the canal path by Basili one day when he heard angry shouting and saw Zacharias, a poor Christian share-cropper, running toward him, a hoe raised over his head. He was pursued by an old woman and a boy who shouted after him, "No, no! You cannot stop the water coming to our land!"

Zacharias called back, "I paid the same as you! My land is closer to the canal. I shall water first!"

"You cannot!" cried the boy, catching up to Zacharias and raising his hoe as if to strike him.

"I can! Because my maize is thirsty!"

"You cannot! If you don't wait until we finish, we'll have our water by peace or by force!" Shahhat recognized the old woman as the wife of Zaki, another Christian now in Cairo with tuberculosis.

Zacharias waved his hoe at the boy. "I'll hit you! Get away or I shall go to prison for what I shall do to you!"

"I'll cut off your head, Zacharias!" the boy shrieked and his mother began screaming too.

Zacharias turned his back, ran in long strides to the canal, and began hacking through an earthen dike with his hoe. Zaki's wife ran after him, panting, sobbing, her veil falling to her shoulders. "I won't let you take our water, you devil!" she shrieked.

"Get some sense into your head, woman!"

Seeing real trouble threatened, Shahhat ran toward them as did some other men tilling nearby fields. Soon everyone was shouting excitedly. Fathers and mothers were cursed on both sides and there were cries of "son of a dog," "pig," "donkey," and "you stupids," as Shahhat and the other men cried, "Malesh! Let it be forgiven!" Just when it seemed blows would be struck, Zaki's wife, Zacharias, and the boy sat down on a dike side by side and began talking as calmly as if they were the bystanders. "The next time Hagg Abd el Mantaleb gives water, one must first get his full time and then the other," the old woman said. "Not like this, all this confusion and quarreling. It is not good, Zacharias."

He agreed and said in the same sociable tone, "I have been waiting here three days for my water. Hagg told me I could come. His worker said, 'Come and take water.'"

"For three days there has not been enough water," one of the neighbors explained to Shahhat. "We told Hagg Abd el Mantaleb, who owns the pump, that everyone is fighting over water and he is the cause.

119

He doesn't turn the flow on high enough, he's such a skinflint. So the water comes so slowly, nobody gets his fair share and there are many quarrels. That Hagg Abd el Mantaleb's heart is black."

"He is rich and so he must love money much," said Shahhat, who sat down on the bank and companionably passed about cigarettes. "Only yesterday his little girl, Nadja, came to Sharhomi's shop to take a quarter kilo of tomatoes. She paid four piastres. But when she took them home to her mother, Hagg complained they were too dear and made her bring them back again."

"He keeps his money in the ground," sighed Zacharias.

"He's afraid to put it in the bank for fear the government will see how rich he is and tax him," said Zaki's wife.

"El Azap came to the shop afterward," Shahhat went on. "You know how poor he is and must sometimes work in the fields of Hagg Abd el Mantaleb. El Azap took potatoes, tomatoes, and onions worth forty-five piastres and gave Sharhomi fifty. Five as *baksheesh*."

"His nature is that way, that Hagg Abd el Mantaleb," the old woman said.

Zacharias sighed. "Better I use my old water wheel. I am a poor man. Nineteen pounds rent I must pay the priest for my two acres. I planted maize, but now it has dried up and I will get nothing. And with eight children to feed and another on the way." Zacharias, a small, thick-set man with a lined, weathered face put his gray stubbled chin in his hands and groaned in mock despair.

"You still use your water wheel?" Shahhat asked.

"Every day, every day. In my opinion, the water wheel is much better than these new pumps, Shahhat. The water is warm; if you want to take a bath in early morning, you can. I know the water wheel from my father and grandfather. I run mine all day, from dawn to sunset."

"In the summer we used to work them at night," Shahhat said.

"It is best you do it at night."

"How we used to sing at the water wheel!"

"I still do it, Shahhat. Until this moment. Well, God give us patience! In my sandy soil, only tomatoes, watermelons, and beans do well. Oh, my God. Eight children and the ninth on the way!"

Shahhat laughed. "Women take tablets today to not get babies. People are getting intelligent about the life. How can you feed nine?"

"Our land is good. But we are lazy. We do not serve the land as we should. The government should help us more, Shahhat. If you go for

120

Shahhat and his younger brother, Ahmed, wash their buffalo in the Ramses Canal, ignoring the bilharzia-infected snails that float by the hundreds near its banks.

your *Nitrokima,* if you need it right away this minute, you go there and none is available. The inspector says to come back next week, and if you haven't money to buy on the black market, you are finished. When the flood came each year before the High Dam, the land did not need *Nitrokima.*"

"The speaking of Zacharias is good," said Zaki's wife, their quarrel forgotten.

"Yes, the soil becomes weak," Shahhat agreed. "In five more years maybe the land is dead. Everything will stop growing." He grinned. "*In sha Allah,* God willing. *In sha Allah kolo duniya mot.* God willing, all the world is dead."

"I see Hagg Abd el Mantaleb got a very poor maize crop," said Zacharias in a pleased voice.

"He would spend nothing," Shahhat joked. "He wanted the plants to grow up by themselves. That's why he is rich. I hear tell, Zacharias, that you are so poor that when you go to the church you fill up your pockets with bread from the altar to feed your children."

Shahhat left the Christians in good humor and headed homeward along the canal path. The canal water reflected the blue of the sky, and with the air so stagnant and suffocating, it looked maddeningly inviting. Seeing no one about, Shahhat scrambled out of his clothes, slid down the bank, and flung himself into the water.

It was wonderfully cool. He dove under the surface, splashed about a good deal, then swam on his back and blissfully closed his eyes. Some small boys, playing on the canal bridge near Hagg Abd el Mantaleb's mosque, saw him and came running. They too quickly threw off their clothes, and one after the other, with loud shrieks of anticipation, they leaped into the water. Soon the quiet canal resounded with splashing and snuffling and shouts. Shahhat chased two small boys, the sons of Amr, the village *mueddin,* who gave the call to prayer five times a day from the mosque. The boys laughed and screamed and choked as if they were drowning. Then they chased Shahhat, trying to catch him by the foot to duck him.

"Hey, hey!" they screamed. "Catch Shahhat! Get him!"

Shahhat dodged away, laughing and enjoying himself. He plunged into the muddy water, touched the slimy canal bottom, and kicked himself back to the surface. He sputtered and snuffled, blew bubbles, and opened his eyes, and found the sun was shining on the water almost exactly in his face. At first there were blinding sparks, then spots danced before his eyes. He squeezed them shut and breathed so deeply he felt refreshed down to his stomach. Then, so as to make the most of the cool water, he lay and floated on his back, splashed himself, turned somersaults, swam on one side, on his stomach, and just as he felt inclined. The maize on the further bank glistened gold from the slanting sun; the dust shone golden in its wide rays; the mud of the bank was thickly overgrown with hyacinth weed; hundreds of greenish-brown snails bobbled up and down at the water's edge.

There was the sound of an angry voice and Shahhat saw Amr— a small skinny man with his tunic tucked up at the waist so that his long, loose drawers dropped down over bony legs—standing on the bridge. He

122

waved his arms about and cursed his two sons. The boys, horrified to be caught in the canal, emerged from the water, and without drying, hurried to put their clothes on.

"Why do you go into the canal?" their father demanded, in the same strained pitch in which he called the faithful to prayer. "I told you not to go into the canal or you'll get bilharzia. Mahmood, you can read books? Ishmail, you can recite from the holy Koran? If you don't want to read books or learn the Koran, then finish! *Khalass!* From now on you can help me in the fields!"

The two boys stared down at the water without saying a word. As if this made him angrier, Amr strode up to them, seized one by the neck, and began thrashing him. Then he turned to beat the other. With stifled cries, the boys pleaded with him, saying they would never go into the canal again. Their mother, hearing the commotion, came running up the path. "Now what?" she demanded. "Allah give me patience!" Then seeing Amr so angry and the boys in tears, she at once changed her tone and begged her husband to forgive them. "They won't go again. You can let them go this time, my husband. For my sake."

Amr looked sternly at the boys. "Because your mother has spoken, I will let you go this time. Now go to the house and study your books." He gave each of them a sharp slap on the cheek. Sobbing again, their faces as wet as when they had just come out of the water, the boys ran off. Amr, as poor and illiterate as anyone, possessed less than two acres of land but he had great respect for learning. At great sacrifice he had managed to send his eldest son, Shamsuddin, to a commercial institute in Aswan to study accounting. Amr was also a very pious man.

Shahhat, who meanwhile had come out of the water and dressed, went to shake Amr's hand in the customary village greeting. Amr complained to Shahhat, whom he considered quite worldly, that Shamsuddin had come home that day angry that his father had not sent him enough money. Amr said he had posted five pounds but his son had not received it; the mail was too slow. "Shamsuddin is far too free with money," Amr complained. "Perhaps he goes to the cinema every night."

Shahhat laughed. "Perhaps Shamsuddin loves a girl in Aswan." When he was home, Shamsuddin could usually be seen seated with his books under the shade of his father's date palms. Here Shahhat found him, a pale and sorrowful-looking youth who wore a sanctimonious expression on his handsome face. As they shook hands, Shamsuddin gave Shahhat his usual disapproving look as if to say that while Shahhat might

Shamsuddin (left), a pious student, reads the Koran while Shahhat irreverently tunes in to popular Arab love songs on Shamsuddin's transistor radio.

find pleasure in jumping in canals, making jokes, and idling his hours away, he himself spent his time reading the Koran or edifying books.

Shamsuddin rarely came home, only on the biggest feasts or when his father failed to send him enough money, though Aswan was but a three hour journey south by train. However, he regularly sent letters to his family. These were written in careful, magnificent handwriting and on stiff white paper such as only found in towns. The letters were full of expressions which Shamsuddin never used in conversation: "My dear father and mother, I am in dire need of sufficient funds to enable me to undertake further studies in the duties and skills required of an executive secretary." At the end of each letter, in the most excellent handwriting, appeared his signature and below, "Aswan Commercial

Preparatory College." These letters were read aloud several times, even to the neighbors, and Amr, touched with pride, would say, "There now, my wife, we sacrificed to send Shamsuddin to school, well, quite right! He is making something of himself!"

Shamsuddin was one of five college students from Berat, unthinkable in their fathers' days. Yet he was no longer at home with the village youths like Shahhat, and unable to enjoy their company and jokes, took refuge in Islam. He was very pious. Every day he read the Koran aloud like a *maulana*. Much of it he did not understand, but the sacred words moved him deeply and such words as "verily" and "blessed," he pronounced slowly and reverently. In contrast to Shahhat's faded and torn black tunic, dirty bare feet, and stubble chin, Shamsuddin dressed immaculately, always wore sandals, and shaved each morning.

He made much of following Koranic strictures to the letter. He never drank inebriating liquor, gambled, or used the name of Allah lightly, as Shahhat and his friends did. He spoke of war against the enemies of Islam as his sacred duty, though as a student he had applied for a deferment from the army. He was fond of quoting verses from the Koran; when he did, his pale face became tender and reverent. Shahhat had great respect for his childhood friend, but felt ill at ease in his company—he found himself lapsing into the crudest obscenities and vulgar oaths as if to show Shamsuddin what a low and uncouth person he had become. Shahhat was always relieved to leave, yet deep in his heart he longed to be educated.

Healing Laughter

BAHIYA'S BROTHER FATIH is going to marry my cousin, Namat."

"When?"

"He says next month."

"Next year, more than likely. Has he bought the furniture yet?"

"No."

"Then what will the bride sleep on?"

The women laughed while their fingers quickly and deftly ripped open the maize with a twig, then tore off the husks and threw the yellow ears into baskets. As they shucked and absently gossiped, they sat half-buried in the large heaps of maize. Ommohamed was there, and Faruk's wife, nursing a baby in her lap, and two older women, widows who received a basket of ears as payment each day.

Ommohamed was out and about for the first time since Abd el Baset's death. The day before, Shahhat had harvested his maize, and she had gone to the field to help, making tea, sending Nubi and Ahmed to fetch and carry, and keeping a sharp eye on a crowd of women and children who came to glean. Wave after wave, the harvesters, gleaners, animals, and birds moved down the field as the maize was harvested. First came Shahhat and three hired men from El Kom who chopped the stalks off at the roots with hoes; from time to time they stopped to stack and load it onto camels to carry everything to Faruk's yard in El Kom. The gleaners followed, black-shrouded women and children with baskets tucked under one arm. Herds of sheep and goats came after them, driven by little girls who carried switches and ran about with shrill cries, tossing stones at laggards and strays. Last came a flock of white egrets to feed on the newly exposed insects. Finally, in late afternoon, El Azap arrived with a plough and a pair of cows to begin turning the soil so that Shahhat could at once sow his lentil crop. Nothing could be wasted, not even time.

Toward sunset Faruk appeared, paid each of the harvesters a generous fifty piastres, and let each load his donkey with fodder. So many gleaners came at the end, Shahhat grew angry and sent them away with shouts and curses. The last camel was loaded just as darkness fell—Shahhat tied a large bundle of fodder on the donkey and the family followed it home on foot. Ommohamed often stopped to greet women along the way and had to keep running to catch up; she was weary, flushed, and breathless, but satisfied now that the first harvest without Abd el Baset had been safely gathered in.

Shahhat's maize crop was poor, less than a ton on his single acre. But then Hagg Abd el Mantaleb himself did little better, and while Lamei had harvested four tons per acre, who else could afford to use so much *Nitrokima?*

Hagg for one, but he was to stingy. He hired four women to help Bahiya shuck his maize, but paid them so little Shahhat could hear them loudly complaining back at Sha'atu's cafe. They first tried flattering

126

him, crying in loud voices. "Every year may you have good health, Hagg Abd el Mantaleb! May you return to Mecca! May you be generous, and Allah will give you more!" This got them nowhere, and soon they passed the cafe on their way home grumbling and cursing Hagg, "May he burn in the fire! These baskets are too small!" After that none of the women would return, and Bahiya had to shuck alone, working late into each night.

Ommohamed, in contrast, was so generous and improvident, not only to the women who helped her but also to El Kom's water man, barber, and other poor souls who happened by, that she ended up taking less than half a ton home to her storeroom. When Shahhat grew angry, she replied, as she habitually did, that Allah would reward such generosity with more.

Faruk's wife, a broad-shouldered, homely woman with kind, gentle ways, was also hospitable and each day brought tasty meals to the women of spiced broadbeans, leeks, cheese, and spicy omelettes which they ate gathered around a small wooden table, scooping up the common dishes with small pieces of bread. Despite the dust that rose from the dry maize stalks, Faruk's wife kept a baby in her lap. It was wrapped in a blanket, but when its face peeped out, it seemed such a small, wizened, piteous baby that it was strange that it should even cry, look, and be reckoned a human being. The baby would kick his pink little legs out of the blanket and laugh and cry, and then at the same moment, cough so dryly and fitfully he sounded like a sick old man.

All the small children in the village went about filthy and shabbily clad and appeared just as neglected. Their eyes were dirty and dozens of flies seemed to buzz and perch, without being waved away, around every eye. In fact, the village women deliberately left children dirty and unwashed for fear of the Evil Eye; it was considered injurious to wash, or even touch, the eyes of a child when they were discharging the matter that attracted the flies. In truth the villagers cherished their children and lavished them with affection. But they had such a horror of illness and loss of sight, infant mortality and blindness being so common, that they failed to take the very steps needed to prevent them.

The shucking lasted five days, and on the last morning Ommohamed looked up to see Nubi and Ahmed sheepishly approaching. "Why aren't you in school?" she demanded, since they were supposed to be at the *kuttab* memorizing the Koran now that the harvest was in. Nubi's eyes were red-rimmed from crying, and he rubbed them with a dirty sleeve. When his mother asked what was wrong, he burst into tears and sobbed, "The teacher struck me in the face with a stick!"

"He what? Oh, my God, what next!" Ommohamed was at once all indignation. "Don't go back. Never go back. Now you stay here and work with us, Nubi. Here, fetch some more stalks." She told the other women, "Nubi is such a good boy. I love my Nubi too much. He has already memorized all but fifteen chapters of the holy Koran. If he learns the rest he can win a hundred pounds from the government." Her pride turned to anger. "I want to strike that teacher in the face with a stick!"

She noticed one of the women tearing the husks off with her hands. "Use a stick to tear it or your fingers will get sore, my sister."

The old woman laughed. "Oh, daughter, I never use one. Nothing can harm old hands like mine." Soon she was diverting Ommohamed with a new piece of gossip; the old woman leaned forward and told in a hushed voice how Batah's grandfather had caught her walking with Snake. He had thrown a fit and dragged her home.

"Everyone knows Batah's reputation," Ommohamed said. "She will destroy her grandparents' house."

Around noon the Moslem school teacher or *fikkee* came, a tall man whose small and hollow eyes had dark rings around them for he was almost blind. He was a distant cousin of Ommohamed's and she was fond of him. But now she ignored his salutation and called angrily, "I will not send my sons to your school if you are going to beat them! I won't send them unless you are kind to them."

The teacher opened his wide mouth in surprise. "I'm your near relation," he protested. "I want to teach your sons as if they were my own."

"I'm paying three pounds a month for them," Ommohamed went on in the same haughty tone. "Better I save my three pounds and not send them to be tortured. If you're going to beat them I'll save my money. Better they help Shahhat in the fields."

"I'm sorry," the teacher replied. "But Nubi has not spoken the truth. He can be very naughty. He is always hitting some other boy." The teacher explained that he had intended to punish Nubi for hitting Ahmed twice during the lesson. As was the customary punishment at the school, Nubi was ordered to take off his sandals, lie down on his back, and put his bare feet in the air, so the teacher could hit his soles with his switch. But when he went to strike the first blow, Nubi pulled his feet away and the switch came down on his face.

128

"What the teacher says is true," volunteered Ahmed, the younger boy. Nubi glared at him angry at such treachery.

"Is it true?" Ommohamed demanded. Nubi, his eyes to the ground, muttered it was. Ommohamed threw up her hands. "*Yah rab!* How you have lied to your mother!" She turned apologetically to the teacher, "If he is naughty like this again, you can tie his hands and feet and beat him all you want." Hearing this, the corners of Nubi's mouth went down, he rubbed his eyes with his fists, and seemed about to give a loud sob. Just then Shahhat came, leading a camel loaded with maize. "Bring that other camel," he told the boys. "We'll put a saddle on him. This one has a bad leg." Relieved to be so rescued, Nubi scrambled to help. "It was late to be sowing lentils," Shahhat told his mother. "We've got the crop in but I hope they do as well as the maize." A pigeon fluttered past their heads. When one of the old women cursed it, Shahhat laughed. "No, the pigeon is my brother," he told her. "Its singing is too good."

Shahhat was amused to hear about the trouble in school. He himself had spent six years in the *kuttab* and was all too familiar with the *fikkee*'s switch. All the boys sat around the edge of an open courtyard reciting the Koran aloud and making a frightful din. One by one they would have to go before the *fikkee* who squatted in the center of the yard, his switch in his hand. One mistake in the recitation of the day's verse and you get a painful stroke on your open palm.

The teacher promised Ommohamed he would come by that evening to hear Nubi and Ahmed recite the lesson they had missed. He arrived by donkey just at sunset and crouched near the doorway to catch the last shaft of warm sunlight. Nubi and Ahmed sat down cross-legged in front of him and began reciting in sing-song voices, their bodies rocking from side to side as this was believed to help the memory.

Ommohamed sat on the doorstep, and even Shahhat and Samah came to stand behind her to watch. The boys knew the lesson by heart and hearing them, Ommohamed exclaimed proudly, "*Yah salaam! Yah salaam!*" The *fikkee* had to stop and correct them only once, and when they had finished, he told Ommohamed, "Your boys are doing well."

She laughed happily and told the boys with mock indignation, "Why can't you recite in front of me like you do before the teacher? In front of the sheikh you know it all! Oh, I could throw dirt in your eyes!" The boys grinned, seeing her pride.

Just at that moment Ommohamed's brother, Ahmed, turned into

129

the lane. He stopped, froze, a look of consternation on his face, and rushed toward them, crying, "Oh, my God!" Without another word, he swept past them and burst into the house. Then he stopped and stood speechless, a foolish expression on his face.

"You come so suddenly!" Ommohamed exclaimed.

Ahmed opened his mouth to say something, but uttered not a word as if his power of speech was gone. Then he stammered, "I saw all of you sitting here with the sheikh and thought someone had died. You know my poor sick wife. I thought it was her."

Ommohamed burst into laughter, got tears in her eyes, and rose. Ahmed's wife was as healthy as an ox except that she suffered deafness in one ear where Ahmed, in a fit of rage some years before, had slapped her. Ever since he had been tormented by guilt and was forever worrying about her health. "I hope she has died," Ommohamed said, still laughing, "and gone to her well-deserved rest after a lifetime with you!" Her voice rose several notes higher, and she laughed so much she could hardly stand on her feet.

"No, please! Don't joke about it!" Then Ahmed, his mistake at last dawning on him, looked painfully chagrined, making the family laugh even more, until Shahhat began to choke. Ahmed, feeling foolish, also laughed, sputtering and waving his hand. The house echoed with hilarious laughter.

Hearing it from her house next door, Su'ad raised her eyebrows, sniffed, and said to Batah, "Well! By my God Allah! They have forgotten poor Abd el Baset already!"

PART THREE

The love of the son for his mother, even when he is grown up and married, is the most noticeable attachment in the *fellah* family. If he has been lacking in respect for her, the whole village is shocked. . . . She is the mistress of his household until her dying day.

Father Henry Ayrout in
The Egyptian Peasant

Buffalo and Evil Eye

$\mathcal{A}$ PERFECT BLUE SKY, a cool and breezy morning, very mild for the second week of May. Shahhat was resting from his field work, smoking a cigarette on the canal bridge near Hagg Abd el Mantaleb's house, and talking with Hagg's youngest son, Mahmood.

They watched as Abd el Baset's friend, Fatih, rode rapidly on his donkey toward them on the canal path. He looked red-faced and agitated, and Shahhat was curious about what Fatih would have to say; he had just scandalized the village by sending his new bride back to her parents' house after less than a week of marriage. Since Fatih was Bahiya's younger brother and his bride, Namat, a cousin of Ommohamed, Shahhat had heard the two women discuss the episode in great detail. As the shrewdest cattle dealer about and a handsome, hot-tempered man who was forever getting into quarrels, Fatih was a favorite subject of gossip.

Mahmood hailed him, "Good morning, my uncle!"

Fatih met this pleasantry with a burst of insults. As he rode up, he shouted, "May your father's house be destroyed! May all the houses in his sight be destroyed! I demand to see your father, Mahmood. I want to kill him! He's a dishonest, crafty son of a dog! I know his bad character! The miserly pig! And you, you little donkey, you're a damned catamite!"

The boy, stunned, looked down at the road, muttering, "What have I done? I know nothing, my uncle."

Greeting Shahhat, Fatih dismounted and came to shake hands. He complained that he had paid Hagg Abd el Mantaleb to water his sugar cane, but this morning he had found the diesel pump had been taken away. Hagg had left word it was broken and that he would get it repaired. But how was Fatih to water his cane in the meantime?

"*Salaam aleikum.*" Shahhat greeted him in the solemn bass voice

133

he habitually used when saluting someone. Then he grinned and invited Fatih to come to the house to drink tea.

Fatih said he had heard the buffalo Sobhy had given them the previous summer had calved; he wanted to see the calf, he told Shahhat, but he feared to meet Ommohamed. "You know I sent Namat home after only four days of marriage. I fear your mother will blame me. What happened was that some enemies of mine got a sorcerer to cast a spell so we would quarrel. They put some secret dust in my tea. After that every time I looked at Namat I saw a buffalo instead. I sent her away." Fatih seemed beside himself. "Oh, Shahhat," he went on, "I demand from Allah that those persons who have cursed me shall die and their houses be destroyed! I love Namat and want her back."

Shahhat persuaded him to come to the house. Mahmood took the donkey, and as they walked down the canal path, Fatih pressed Shahhat not to sell the calf to anyone else. "I'll give you one pound more than any other man offers," he promised. "If they'll pay seven, I'll pay eight. And please don't take any milk from the buffalo until the calf is fattened up."

Shahhat laughed. "If you want it without money, you shall have it." Shahhat was also apprehensive his mother might be angry. Namat was seventeen and very beautiful. She had been married before to a rich, elderly landlord, but Fatih had fallen in love with her, left his own wife, and broken up Namat's marriage. Yet Ommohamed greeted Fatih warmly, calling from the door, "A great weclome to you! *Hababak, fuddel,* Fatih! Come in and sit down." They had not counted on Ommohamed's hospitable manners, to say nothing of her curiosity.

"Thank you, Ommohamed, but I have no time. I just wanted to take a look at your new calf." Fatih's uneasiness was evident.

"No, no," Ommohamed protested with a little laugh. "First you must drink tea. The Arab custom. For are you not an Arab? No, you are a sheikh among the Arabs."

"And you, dear lady, are a sheikha among the Arabs. If you have a guest, you must lavish them with food and hospitality even if you have to run and borrow from the neighbors." The two of them bantered compliments back and forth, reminding both of the old days when Abd el Baset had been alive. Fatih, realizing he had not seen Ommohamed since Abd el Baset's death ten months before, felt ashamed and declared emphatically, "No, Ommohamed, I cannot take tea."

"Why?" she exclaimed, reading his thoughts. "Are you sitting at a funeral? You must."

Moisture filled Fatih's eyes. "Oh, Ommohamed, how I remember the good times we used to have when I came to this house with Shahhat's father. The talk and the jokes and the drinking." Fearing they both might start to cry, Shahhat hurried Fatih and his mother out to the stable. At once Fatih's composure returned and he became the cunning trader of the marketplace. He briskly examined the calf, opening its jaws and counting the teeth, pinching its muscles, and lifting it off the ground to judge its weight, all the time commenting what a poor specimen it was. "It's too skinny," he said in a disapproving tone. "I advise you not to sell it now. Perhaps you don't give it enough milk."

"Who said to you I wanted to sell it?" Shahhat asked, also slipping into the bargaining manner of the *suk*.

"I thought you wanted to. When I heard about this calf, I told myself, 'You must be the one to buy it.' Even if I took it without money. I knew you wouldn't say no to me, Shahhat."

"You put me in a difficult position," Shahhat said in mock perplexity, for he was enjoying the contest. "We expect to get fifteen pounds." He threw up his hands in a gesture of sacrifice. "But if you want the calf, yes, then go ahead and take it."

"Fifteen? Later. Let it fatten up a bit. Then we'll see."

Ommohamed saw Fatih out, calling from the door after another long and gracious exchange of compliments, "Our house has been honored by your visit." As soon as Fatih was out of earshot, Shahhat said, "Fifteen is good, my mother. I suspect Fatih is trying to get a cheap price."

"Fifteen?" she snorted. "Seventeen. The calf takes much milk." Then, thinking of Fatih's evident grief, she softened. "I will sell it to him at any price. He loved your father much."

"No!" Shahhat knew too well Ommohamed's love of the grand gesture. "I would kill the calf before I sold it at just any price!"

"As you like," she sighed. Fatih must have been interested, as he returned that evening, this time bringing Faruk with him. Ommohamed had latched the door against the night chill and Faruk, who sensed her disapproval of his drunken ways, teased her, "It is the first time I see the door of this house closed. Well, may Allah make Abd el Baset good in the afterlife!"

While Ommohamed prepared tea, Fatih boasted about his bean harvest but complained that Hagg Abd el Mantaleb had cursed it. "Hagg praised my yield as the highest he had ever seen. The very next day the market price dropped. *El hamdu li-llah!* What Allah gave, Hagg with his

Evil Eye took away. It there a man who can leave his neighbors in peace and not curse them with compliments?"

As she served tea, Ommohamed joked to Faruk, "Fatih has not entered our house except to visit the new calf."

Faruk laughed. "He's always busy but in his heart he loves you and Shahhat. Because you are a true lady. You are generous to everyone who enters your house." In his coarse, good-natured way, Faruk knew how to ingratiate himself with the women.

After some discussion it was decided Fatih should go to the inn to ask Sobhy's permission to buy the calf; as the buffalo's half-owner, custom decreed he had the right to dispose of the first calf. Fatih went but soon returned. He said he had found Sobhy sitting with Hagg Ali. "The two cousins spoke with one mouth," he told Ommohamed. "Sobhy wants to sell both buffalo and calf. He said he would take a hundred and twenty-five pounds for the lot. He promised to buy you a better buffalo."

Ommohamed was indignant. "No! He's lying. They want to take the money, that is all. I know Sobhy and Hagg Ali all too well. There would be no new buffalo." She was stunned. Then her handsome, anxious face took on a set expression. "No," she declared, "I refuse to sell the buffalo. How can we get milk, butter, and cheese? How? If all the city came to buy it, I would never sell. I will kill anybody who comes near my buffalo. This is all the talk of Sobhy and Hagg Ali. They speak with the mouth of the devil. They can say anything."

Seeing her so upset, Fatih declared, "That son of a dog, Sobhy. I heard Hagg Ali telling him, 'How can you give that family a buffalo? Are you crazy?' Never mind. On market day, I'll come here, Ommohamed, and take the calf to the *suk* to see its price. If Sobhy gets in my way, I'll kill him! You need to feed your children. I'm not afraid. I'll stand by you. We'll make a gathering in front of the headman. That son of a dog is not in need of money. And you are, my sister."

"Let us have nothing more to do with this buffalo and her calf," Shahhat interrupted, his temper rising. "We'll buy another. Let them pay us for the fodder we provided and they can take the buffalo and calf."

"No, wait!" Ommohamed silenced them both. "*Bas, bas!* Stop, stop! Fatih, it is forbidden to me by the Koran to take anything that belongs to another. The buffalo is Sobhy's by law. Anyone can take back his possessions if he chooses. I cannot claim what does not fully belong to me. Perhaps if I tried to take the buffalo, my house would fall under a cloud. The little finger of any one of my sons is worth a hundred buffaloes. But

136

I shall demand from Sobhy the price of the fodder Shahhat has given it these past ten months."

Shahhat quickly estimated the cost as coming to seventy-eight pounds; with that they could buy a new buffalo.

"You could sell some land," Faruk suggested, always keeping an eye out for cheap property. Shahhat cut him off. "No! Anyone who sells land is not a man."

"God will not forget us," Ommohamed cried. "Allah will provide." What she feared most was the social disgrace. "Now I will not be able to take the buffalo outside the house. I am so ashamed. I'm afraid of these gossips. They will say, 'Oh, Shahhat must sell his buffalo. He walks proudly but has nothing in his pockets.'"

The next day Ommohamed collapsed into helpless, petrified gloom, refusing to set foot outside the house. She could not bear the sight of her neighbors' eyes. She could only guess too accurately what Su'ad and the rest were saying, and she was tortured by each turn of her imagination. She knew they felt she was vain and haughty, and that she put on airs. Now they had her at their mercy.

She forgot her brother Ahmed's pride was as fierce as her own. As soon as Ahmed heard the story, he gathered together the necessary money and set out for Sobhy's inn.

Handsome, vain, and cold, Ahmed took an intense pride in appearing well before the world. His pale *gallabiyas* were tailored from the most expensive cloth, his turban was always immaculate, his watchband real gold, he scorned the usual sandals for shoes and stockings, and did not smoke the cheap Cleopatra cigarettes the other villagers did but a special brand only townspeople could afford. He was frugal at home, forced his wife to run an austere household, and rarely invited anyone in. The extreme hardship of his childhood and youth and the years as chief watchman in a large hotel had left him with a contempt for human nature. But he also possessed a desire to cut an impressive figure wherever he went. With his lean, good looks, his carefully trimmed moustache, his broad shoulders and staid, important manner, he succeeded. Ahmed was not one to let his family be humiliated by the disreputable likes of Sobhy.

As he entered the village he met Kamil, a gaunt, workworn man who was married to Shahhat's second-oldest sister. Kamil—who went about in old, dirty tunics, his hands encrusted with the soil of the fields— looked older than his forty years and worked for little pay as Sobhy's sharecropper. Now Kamil was anxious. He told Ahmed that if he stood

137

beside Ommohamed as his mother-in-law, Sobhy might turn him out, and then how would he feed his wife and five children? Ahmed listened impatiently, knowing that it was really Ommohamed who mostly fed and clothed Kamil's children as he feared to ask Sobhy for money and was a poor provider. To Ahmed such weak, craven souls mattered little in a hard world.

"I will stand against anyone who fights my sister and nephew," Ahmed declared, cutting off Kamil's mournful complaints impatiently. "I have no relationship with Sobhy or his family. Return with me."

"Can you pay Sobhy?" Kamil asked, trying to keep up with Ahmed's long strides. "So the family can walk respected in the village again?"

Ahmed stopped and scowled so fiercely at him Kamil stumbled backwards. "I can beat the very earth to get the money if I haven't got it!" Ahmed thundered. Then he added haughtily, "But I have the money."

When they reached the inn, Ahmed glared at it in disapproval. From the outside its peeling walls, rows of crudely-painted red-shuttered windows, and the domes of its arched open upstairs terrace gave the place a medieval Arabian Nights air. Yet the hotel had been built only ten years before. They entered the dim-lit hall that served as a dining room and salon, a long corridor to one side was lined with empty rooms where cobwebs and drifts of desert sand forlornly awaited nonexistent guests. Ahmed sent Kamil to fetch Sobhy and took a chair. His eyes swept contemptuously over the discolored oilcloth on the tables, divans in one corner of some grimy blue material, and walls of the same depressing color. It seemed to Ahmed that if one hung a dozen lamps about, the room could not be otherwise than dingy. Pillars supported a high ceiling, and Sobhy had once hired a local artisan to decorate these with murals of pharaonic gods; but these grotesque portrayals, which included a leering god of the penis, merely added to the shabby, degraded air of the place.

Soon Sobhy appeared, his enormous pendant stomach protruding from a loose, white tunic. Seeing Ahmed, he pulled at his long, drooping black moustache, looked about with red-rimmed eyes as if searching for some servant to bully and curse, and with a muttered grunt beckoned Ahmed to come to his private apartment upstairs.

"No, I can speak here." Ahmed spoke with such harshness, even Sobhy flinched. "Without further speaking," he went on, "I want to enter into the main question. How much do you want for the buffalo and calf?"

Sobhy settled his heavy body into a chair. "One hundred and twenty-five," he muttered in a surly tone.

"And that's it?"

"I want what's mine."

Ahmed rose, took a wad of pound notes from his pocket and threw it into Sobhy's lap. He ordered Kamil, "Count it for him." Then he said in a solemn voice to Sobhy, *"Salaam aleikum,"* and strode out the door without another word.

Stunned, Sobhy followed him to the door, clutching the money and calling, "Come, come! I want to say to you one word! Come, Ahmed. For the sake of Abd el Baset's memory!"

Ahmed hesitated at the gate. Turning about he demanded, "Well, what do you want now? From the first I said we would go into the main problem without speaking."

"You are so angry. Why?"

"On the contrary, Sobhy, I am happy. My sister has paid for her buffalo and is now independent of you and your relations. If you were a man, Sobhy, you would not take back what you have given. Now she can go out of her house and be seen by all the world." Then, gesturing angrily to dismiss the need for further words, he declared emphatically, "Enough! We stop speaking, everything! *Salaam aleikum!*"

Sobhy was left sputtering at Ahmed's retreating figure, a spectacle much enjoyed by all who witnessed it. Soon the story, exaggerated and dramatized, spread through the village to everyone's entertainment.

Ommohamed's relief at being rescued was short-lived. Ahmed came at once to her house and vented his wrath upon her and Shahhat.

"I am happy and not happy we have solved this problem, my sister," he told her. "Now you can keep your buffalo and walk proudly before all the world. But I am unhappy because Shahhat is not a man. He is a boy and like all boys of his age, he spends money easily and does not take responsibility. And he tires you, making you weep."

Shahhat, hearing his name, came into the front room; Ahmed sternly ordered him to sit down.

"Your father died ten months ago," he told Shahhat in his cold, relentless way. "Yet you do not change anything in this house or on the land. This family does not go up, it goes down." He turned to Ommohamed. "Shahhat does not do anything. I am tired, I am sad for him. And I will not stay with him. What about you and the small boys? This household costs much. What does Shahhat do to bring in money?"

Ommohamed started to speak but he cut her off. "And you—you entertain everyone who comes along. You spend much. But times are changing, my sister. It is not like the old days when you were a girl. In

In the past if you hadn't a loaf of bread in your house, you could demand one from your neighbors without shame. You could enter any house to eat. But in the past there were fewer people. We have doubled in number in Egypt, my sister. And now every person has to see to his own problems, and cannot always look after you and your family. For all these things, I am very, very sad."

"Allah will provide," Ommohamed protested.

"Yes, of course, everything is from Allah. But a person must also look to the future himself. We do not know what will happen in another five years, another ten years. There will be many people then. Is my speaking wrong, Shahhat? By your dead father's soul, speak the truth."

Shahhat's head was bowed, and his eyes were watering. Ahmed's words made him feel more of a failure in trying to fill Abd el Baset's place than ever.

"I have much experience in life, Shahhat," Ahmed pressed on harshly, annoyed by his nephew's show of emotion. "You must love the person who makes you weep, not those who make you laugh." He turned back to Ommohamed. "I want Shahhat to be a better man than those sons of dogs like Sobhy. I do not want him to stand in front of them and shout, 'I can beat you! I can kill you!' but with empty pockets."

Shahhat rose and went about the room, aimlessly swatting flies with a cloth. Ahmed raised his voice.

"Shahhat has been given the name 'beggar.' He is like a beggar truly. The beggar takes from you a loan and then acts as if he's your master. But what cock can crow on an empty belly?"

Shahhat went out to the yard, pressed his face against the earthen wall, and could not control his grief. "I'm not my father," he told himself, "and I never will be. I am myself. Shahhat." Did they not see that Abd el Baset was gone and would not come again?

When Shahhat recovered himself and went back inside, Ahmed was describing the scene at the inn. "If Sobhy had uttered one bad word, by God, I would have killed him! I would have taken from him twenty-five years in prison!"

He criticized Ommohamed for not giving Sobhy the calf at once. "By custom the first calf was his anyway. After that you could sell the second in the market and split the price. You know the custom."

Ahmed rose to go. Ommohamed protested he had not yet taken tea. He refused and spoke even more harshly. "My sister, this house if full of faults and falsehoods. A person should face the truth. But you and

140

Shahhat live on dreams. You spend much more than you can afford, and then when it catches up with you, you don't know what to do." Then, seeing Ommohamed was starting to cry, he softened his tone. "Well, you are my sister. I must stand by you."

Ommohamed had to be brought down to earth now and then, and despite her tears, she knew Ahmed spoke the truth. Yet within minutes of his departure, she was forming wonderful pictures in her mind of how their lives might be changed. It did not occur to either Ommohamed or Ahmed that people rarely do change nor should they expect too much of Shahhat. He was built to a larger scale than any other youth in the village. Built to a larger scale for all his faults and frailties. And they had to accept him as he was or lose him.

The very next day the buffalo stopped giving milk. It remained dry for three days. "We must find some way to feed the calf," Ommohamed told Shahhat. "Nothing has come except a little spurt once in a while, and it is sour."

Ommohamed sought everyone's advice. Her son-in-law Kamil merely lamented in his apathetic, shiftless way, "What can we do? I am tired and you are tired. We demand of Allah but he gives us nothing. Allah has the freedom to give and take. We are his creatures."

El Azap told her it had probably eaten too much green clover and would be all right in a day or two.

Bahiya was convinced that Fatih had given the buffalo the Evil Eye. "Even if he is my brother, you know what a shrewd cattle trader he is," she told Ommohamed. "You always say you are clever. But you understand nothing. I dare say you haven't even your wisdom teeth. Why did you ever allow Fatih in the stable? No stranger must ever see a new baby, human or animal."

"Oh, Bahiya," Ommohamed lamented. "These days I have so many troubles, I don't know my head from my leg."

"Yes, your face is yellow. You must send for Fatih at once. Engage him in speaking and then have Shahhat or one of your boys sit near his feet. When he is not looking they must cut a small piece from

141

When Shahhat's *gamoossa,* or buffalo, stopped giving milk, suspicion arose that Fatih had cursed her with the Evil Eye.

the hem of his *gallabiya*. Then you must let him know so that he becomes angry. And burn that piece of cloth at the time of Magreb prayers."

"No, no, I could not!"

"Then you must catch Fatih. Whether he wants to or not. Pull up his *gallabiya* and demand that he urinate on the buffalo. It is the only way, Ommohamed.

Ommohamed was deeply mortified. "No, no, Bahiya, we must consider Fatih's feelings. I shall go to Sheikha Daiyi in El Kom."

"Why spend money? And you must not let Fatih see the calf again. If you won't do it, I'll fetch him and attend to it myself. You need the milk, don't you? Are you rich? Do you have ten acres?"

"If Fatih saw Shahhat cut his clothing he would be angry. I have such a hot-blooded son. They might quarrel. No, Bahiya, I shall go to the *sheikha*."

"Do as you like. Allah knows you are in need of money. I said from the first you were a foolish woman and understood nothing."

Ommohamed laughed. "Allah stays in heaven. He will give more than it costs perhaps."

Fatih, too, heard the buffalo was not giving milk and came to the house. Ommohamed rushed to block the doorway and, flushed and breathless, told him, "Yes, the buffalo is good. The milk is sweet."

"I want to see it," Fatih demanded. "I heard it has stopped giving milk. Let me take a look, and perhaps I can tell you what is the matter."

"Oh . . . uh . . . uh . . . yes, Fatih. Next time. Just now I must go to my neighbor's house. There is no one else here."

Sheikha Daiyi told Ommohamed to bring her some hairs from the buffalo's tail. She wrapped these inside a written paper charm and said it must be buried in the stable underneath the buffalo. Henceforward, the sorceress said, the buffalo must be milked by none but a virgin. Ommohamed had Samah keep trying, but for two more days the buffalo remained dry. "Wah," Ommohamed told Shahhat. "I lose two pounds and get nothing." Just after dawn the third day, Samah woke her with excited cries; there was again a flow of sweet milk.

At Fatih's urging Ommohamed went to see her cousin, Namat, who fell into her arms and wept. "Please, aunt, I need your help," the girl

143

appealed to her. "I love Fatih. Tell him he must come to my father. My father is wild with anger. He says if I go back to Fatih he will kill me. What shall I do?"

"Oh, Namat, Namat," Ommohamed tried to console her. "Don't break my heart with such words. I'll try to help you. Perhaps your father will listen to reason. Don't cry, my dear."

She was furious at Fatih, and the next time he came to the house, told him angrily, "What do you want from me? Namat is my cousin. You sent her home after only four days. You know these gossip mongers. You are not a good man, Fatih. Now I suspect you didn't come here about the calf at all. What a snake you are!"

"Those bastards bewitched me!" Fatih protested. "Every time I looked at Namat, I saw a buffalo. I was mad. Now I want her back as my wife. By God, I'll take her back by force!"

"No, no, not by force. Everything must be done peacefully, Fatih. I'll think of something." Finally Ommohamed arrived at a plan. She and Fatih would take Namat's father, Hagg Ahmed, by surprise, suddenly entering his house in early afternoon when he had returned from the fields. Fatih would at once kiss his turban and beg his forgiveness. Ommohamed's imagination pictured a happy reconciliation and she predicted confidently to Fatih, "After that Hagg Ahmed will be ashamed and will let you take your wife. This is good advice."

It did not go so smoothly. When they entered Namat's house and Fatih tried to kiss her father's turban, Hagg Ahmed leaped up, pushed Fatih away, and bellowed at him, "You son of a dog! You are the reason I can look no one in the face! I must change my turban's color from white to black! You have shamed me before everyone!" Before Ommohamed could speak, Fatih was shouting insults at Hagg Ahmed, Namat was shrieking and tearing her hair, and neighbors came to seize Fatih and throw him out into the road. Then the old man turned on Ommohamed and shouted, "I'll never trust my daughter to that man! He's the son of a dog, sending Namat home after four days. I won't allow women to speak. If I don't run my own household, I'm not a man. I hear Fatih is often at your house these days, Ommohamed. Well, you tell him for me that Hagg Ahmed will humble him if it's the last thing I ever do! I'm going to take his eyes in the divorce court, everything I can get! When I get through with Fatih, he'll be lucky to walk through the village like some poor, mindless lunatic!"

Shahhat noticed Ommohamed abruptly dropped all mention of Fatih. He was agreeably surprised when she favored selling the calf to the poor Christian Zacharias, saying that, after all, he had nine small children to feed.

Ommohamed and Faruk

STUNG BY AHMED'S CRITICISM, Ommohamed resolved to take a firmer hand. When they had almost lost the buffalo, Shahhat had taken it for granted that she was the stronger character; it had been her brother who had saved them. As the days passed, Shahhat made less of a pretense of stepping into his father's shoes. This made Ommohamed all the more anxious; as the spring harvest approached, her fears grew that Shahhat was lazy and neglected the land, and that Faruk might try to cheat them.

Sometimes her suspicions irritated Shahhat and he would explode, "I've told you a thousand times not to talk so much! A woman should be still like the blanket on the bed!" Ommohamed would retreat in pained silence for awhile, yet once their lentil harvest was cut and stacked to dry at Faruk's threshing ground, she kept after Shahhat to keep a close eye on it. Was their stack of lentils getting any smaller?

Shahhat himself did not entirely trust Faruk. One afternoon he arrived on his donkey at the threshing ground to find two cows munching on his stack of lentils. No one was in sight except a single laborer riding a *norag,* or threshing sledge—a heavy machine with a seat and eleven iron disks which was drawn about in circles by two cows to crush the grain.

Shahhat found Faruk lying on a bench in his shed beside a young man from El Kom; the voice of Egypt's famed late singer, Um Kalthum,

145

was loudly amplified from a blaring transistor radio and the air smelled of hashish fumes. The youth scrambled off the bench as Shahhat entered.

"Why do you let your men tether cows by my lentils?" Shahhat demanded. "Why? They are eating my harvest! You have no blood, Faruk!" As Shahhat went back to his donkey, mounted, and started to ride away, the man from the *norag* called, "It wasn't Faruk. I brought the cows. I let them wander free, and if they went to anybody's stack of grain, they ate from it. Not yours alone."

"No! You lie! One of you tied those two cows by my stack. You or Faruk! You meant for them to eat it!"

"Come, come, Shahhat!" Faruk called from the shed, but Shahhat kept going. At home he told Ommohamed, "I fear you are right and Faruk is a thief. If I had gone back to speak to him again, God knows what I would have done. By God, I won't cultivate with anybody else in the future. I'll do everything myself. Not with Faruk or anyone!"

"No, my son," Ommohamed said. "If you cultivated the Sombat land by yourself you would have to stay right in the field and sleep there like Faruk does. We would not have a man in the house. It is better we find someone else for the next crop."

"When I saw those cows, I felt they were eating my stomach. It is my fault, my mother. I have been lazy."

Faruk was not happy either. He came to the house and told Ommohamed, "Every day I send a boy to fetch Shahhat, but he does not come. What to do? Well, I shall give a good part of the harvest to you. I know many people gossip to you about me, those sons of dogs!"

Shahhat went to the threshing ground every day after that; he stayed for hours, helping on the *norag*. Faruk cultivated with seven other *fellaheen* besides Shahhat, and their harvests of lentils, wheat, and beans were stacked about, waiting to be threshed. Faruk seldom went home; despite his new prosperity he lived in the same lowly house he always had. Cattle were tethered right in the front room and his family kept the habits and discomforts of the very poor.

"Tell me, Shahhat," Faruk would ask, seeing Shahhat so silent and sullen, "why don't you speak more these days? Are there demons in your head?"

"There are no demons," Shahhat would reply. "I think all the people these days act like demons. Where is the man who serves another in his heart? When two men work together, they should be honest and trust each other."

146

"Let us always be like that," Faruk answered. "But no two men are alike. Each thinks differently. If the world was not like that, it would be dull."

Faruk did not press Shahhat for the twelve pounds he still owed him, the money he had squandered in his infatuation with Batah. Yet Faruk himself was deeply in debt. Shahhat discovered this when Faruk's father, an old, shrunken little man who did little but sit about smoking cigarettes, one day complained that the inspector had come to demand Faruk repay three hundred pounds he owed to the government. In response Faruk bullied his father half-jokingly, "If you will not increase the money we spend on fertilizer, my father, so our sugar will fetch a better price, I shall bring soldiers to put you in irons."

Shahhat by nature would have liked to trust Faruk but something always came in the way. One day two men who drank with Faruk at Abdullahi's, Hasan and Suleyman, came to the threshing shed with three bottles of cognac. Shahhat knew them well as drunken scoundrels who were said to bully everyone, abuse women, and steal from their neighbors. It was rumored they had once set fire to the field of a man against whom they bore a grudge. Nor was either above bearing false witness to the police if there were a bottle in it for them. Shahhat had long suspected these were the two who had beaten Faruk so badly in the fields that night, though he kept this suspicion to himself. Hasan, a tall, long-legged man with such a short, thick neck he looked hunch-backed, was the worst of the two. Shahhat only paid him respect because he was a distant relative, an uncle of Batah's. His evil reputation and the dark color of his skin had earned him the name of El Abd, or the Black One. Now Hasan teased him, "Why don't you shave, Shahhat? You look like an old man. Come, come, *Sheikh,* you must be smart. You are young and handsome. You are a man now and your muscles become full for your sleeves."

The cognac did not last long and Faruk, his face becoming flushed, proposed going to Abdullahi's for more. "C'mon, Shahhat," he insisted in a thick voice, "what do we have to do here until the lentils are dry enough to thresh?"

"Come, Shahhat," Hasan joined in, throwing one of his long arms around Shahhat's shoulders. "We must be happy."

Suleyman, grinning to expose a mouthful of rotting teeth, demanded, "Why have you changed, Shahhat? In the past you drank much." He took a small packet of greasy paper from his tunic, glanced slyly about, and unwrapped some opium. As the others crowded

147

closer, he made a small pellet and offered it to Shahhat. "Here, take this and you'll forget your troubles." When Shahhat refused, Hasan and Suleyman tried to force it on him, but he broke away from them and left the shed, followed by their harsh laughter. He angrily suspected Faruk had put them up to it. Everyone knew Hasan and Suleyman were the two worst drunkards and bullies in the village; whoever went with them came to grief, and he wanted nothing to do with them with the lentils still to be threshed and safely carried home.

Batah's father, a ne'er-do-well who spent much of his time in Cairo gambling, was a half-brother of Hasan, and it was rumored about that he had agreed to her betrothal to one of Hasan's sons, a young soldier named Ali. But Fatnah, Abd el Baset's elderly sister and Batah's grandmother, had objected, declaring such a marriage would take place only over her dead body. It was said the matter had ended there. Hasan and Batah's father had village tradition on their side; it was an old custom to marry one's first cousin. As family law was everything and vendetta law still applied, it was the honorable thing to do.

Nor was Hasan poor; he owned three acres. But his son, Ali, was a dull, slack-jawed youth who showed every sign of becoming just as dishonest, drunken, and coarse as his father. The family was disreputable in every way; one of Hasan's younger brothers, discovering his wife had committed adultery, sexually abused her all night, slit her throat at dawn, hid her jewels, and then claimed thieves had come and raped, robbed, and killed her. Neighbors, who heard her screams, knew the truth, but since the adultery was proven, the police had chosen to take his word.

Ommohamed was contemptuous of Hasan and had dismissed the rumors, saying that Fatnah, as strong-willed a woman as herself, could not possibly let Batah marry into such a dissolute family. Yet if it came down to it, neither Fatnah nor Batah's mother, Su'ad, had any say once Hasan and Batah's father had agreed to it. The Prophet Mohammed had decreed a girl must give her consent in marriage. But this, like other Moslem strictures that went against the village creed of male dominance, was often ignored.

Shahhat's uncle, Ahmed, hearing how sober Shabbat had become, was approving when they met one day at the ferry landing. He told Shahhat, "Ah, take care of yourself and be a man." Ahmed was angry when Shahhat told him his mother had sold the calf. "I told her never to sell it," he said. "You should have kept it in your house and we could have sold it profitably in the future. The way prices are rising, we might have

148

bought a cow. Now you are the man of the house, Shahhat, and everything depends upon you. You must decide things, not your mother."

"She is your sister."

"We haven't any woman who can speak. A woman's advice is not good. Only one should make the decisions about the livestock and cultivation. If Ommohamed speaks against the things we want to do, I shall leave her. I told her about the calf, not to sell it. When I say no, I mean no."

Yet it was Ahmed's criticism that made Ommohamed determined to replace Faruk with Taiyar, who, despite his divorce from her eldest daughter, had remained on good terms with Ommohamed. Taiyar, like Hagg Abd el Mantaleb, was rising in the world; he not only owned land, ran a shop in El Kom, and held shares in several diesel pumps, but had also been appointed to help the agricultural inspector with the many small landowners at Sombat. Ommohamed cursed the day Abd el Baset came home drunk to tell her, "If my daughter is finished with Taiyar, I want to finish with him too! From now on I shall cultivate with Faruk!"

Ommohamed decided to go to the field the day the lentils were threshed and sacked and have it out with Faruk once and for all. Buoyed up by the thought of action, she waited until the day came, and that afternoon, almost with exhilaration, she put on her best black wool gown with its long sleeves of some diaphanous black material. She adorned her ears with long golden earrings set with green stones, put on a new sequined head veil, and wrapped about her best black wool cloak. Soon, riding through the village astride Shahhat's white donkey, her face flushed, the long cloak flowing almost to the ground, and with the upright carriage that was second nature to her in moments of extreme dignity, she looked a very grand lady.

Ommohamed had asked Taiyar and her eldest daughter's new husband, Hassan, to await her at the threshing ground, and when she arrived they were already there. Faruk, Shahhat, and half a dozen of Faruk's laborer's were working near the *norag*. Ommohamed greeted the men with the customary salutations, dismounted, went past the piles of sacked grain, and sat down on the ground in the shade of the shed. For some time she rested, modestly pulling her veil across her face.

This humility fooled no one; Ommohamed had such presence, the men instinctively gathered at the shed, taking seats on the grain sacks and a bench, waiting for her to speak. Faruk, warned of the confrontation, stood about with a hangdog expression. Women almost never came to the fields in this manner, especially one as haughty and proud as Ommohamed.

149

Ommohamed dresses in her best on one of her rare visits to the fields.

"Faruk," she began in a low voice, hardly audible through the veil, "this is the last season we shall cultivate with you. You can take anything you want." She gestured contemptuously toward Shahhat's stack of lentils. "This harvest is not good enough. All our neighbors have double the yields. You did not fulfill your part of the bargain."

Not a sound was heard. Shahhat, seated on the bench with some other men, kept his eyes on the ground, his face expressionless. Faruk coughed and cleared his throat. "All right. Finish. I wanted that. Thank God the words came from you, not from me. It's up to you. I help you much, Ommohamed. If I was not here in Sombat looking after your crops every day, you would get nothing."

Ommohamed flared out with anxious authority, pulling back her veil. "My uncle, Hagg Ahmed, harvested nine sacks from his one acre. Shahhat says you will be lucky to give five or six. Why is that? You look like the village headman, Faruk. You want to take something from everybody without earning it. But it is not all your fault. It is also the fault of my son. If he were a real man, I would not have to leave my house to come here now. These are the feelings I have in my heart. You are a bad influence on my son."

Shahhat kept his eyes down and moved not a muscle.

"I want from you money," Faruk stammered. "Because I plowed the land, watered it, and protected the crops."

"It is good. Call your father and Taiyar will be with me. We shall discuss it. To decide who gives money to whom." She spoke with such angry authority Faruk avoided meeting her eyes.

"Not my father and not Taiyar," he told her. "The issue is clear." In an awkward attempt to ease the atmosphere Faruk threw a bean at Ommohamed, chuckled nervously, and asked her in a bantering manner, "Why did you not greet me when you came?"

"When you are a man, Faruk, I shall greet you," she responded grimly. "I am the same as your mother, and I know much about your affairs." Faruk flushed but said nothing. "You have destroyed more than you have built for our family," she went on. "When we shared with Taiyar, he brought the harvest to our house. I have not had to come to the field before." Now that she faced Faruk and gained the upper hand, Ommohamed was keyed up by the ordeal.

"Why do we speak in front of all these people?" Faruk demanded.

She flashed him her haughtiest, most sarcastic smile. "This is a suitable time for me to speak. Why hide such things? Everyone knows them. You are a devious man, Faruk."

"We should speak between ourselves only," he grumbled.

Taiyar, a big, plump man with an air of authority, interrupted to say he had discussed Ommohamed's harvest with the inspector. Since the crop was so poor, he said, glancing in Faruk's direction, the inspector had agreed to reduce the quota to be sold to the government to one-and-a-half sacks. Taiyar helped Ommohamed to her feet and they went behind the shed for a whispered conference.

151

"Don't be angry," he counseled Ommohamed. "And don't speak so much with Faruk. I'll stand beside you and we'll solve everything."

"How can you cultivate with us, Taiyar?" Ommohamed asked him. "You have so many jobs. You are busy."

"Yes, I am busy, but I promise you, I shall find the time to do it if you wish." With a third of each harvest in return for little time and investment, Taiyar jumped at the opportunity to cultivate more government land.

When they returned to the others Taiyar told Faruk. "This is real speaking. Because it is the truth. The words of the mother should anger no one if she speaks so frankly. Everyone must get his fair share. If you want to cultivate with her, you must agree to her conditions. If you do not wish, she can even plant branches in her fields if she likes."

Faruk's laborers, who had left their threshing to watch the spectacle, loudly applauded Taiyar's words. All speaking at once, they exclaimed, "This woman speaks like a man!" "You are in the wrong, Faruk!" "If you had done right, she would not have to come to the fields!"

Encouraged, Ommohamed demanded, "Why did you not harvest nine sacks like everybody else? No wonder we are suspicious. You are bad, Faruk. You are lazy. You want everything for nothing. In the past, when you were not with us, I never saw these fields." Ommohamed's eyes were bright—she had great dignity when she was most upset. "My husband is dead. Does this mean we neglect the land? Every day you try to bleed me of money. I understand. I have lost half my lentils. You have stolen them."

She had gone too far and Faruk, his face reddening to a purple color, had difficulty controlling himself. "Only Allah stands between you and me!" he warned.

"I want to insult you even worse," she went on; nothing could stop her now. "But because Taiyar is here, I shall hold my tongue. Taiyar is here and he knows the story now. I shall follow his advice." She turned to Taiyar. "I shall come tomorrow and take all my lentils, and if anyone tries to stand against me, I shall do what I must!"

"No, no, leave these things to me," Taiyar interrupted. "Your place is not here, but in the house."

Ommohamed heaved a deep sigh and Taiyar helped her to her feet. "I shall return home," she said, then casting about for a final insult, she told Faruk scornfully, "You are a man of many houses," which, worse than anything she had said, implied he was an adulterer. Shahhat mut-

152

tered a scarcely audible, *"Salaam aleikum,"* mounted the donkey, and headed for home, Ommohamed following behind on foot as was the custom. But it was plain who was the master; from now on, the men guessed, nothing would be done without Ommohamed's consent.

Shahhat did not let a word fall until they got home, and then he did so calmly. "Taiyar and my father did not care well for the land," he told her. "They planted seeds and put on water and *Nitrokima* and left it. If they got a good harvest, they did. If not, they didn't. Father would say, 'It all depends on Allah.' Now the Nile no longer floods, the soil is weaker and the yields are less. The Nile no longer enriches the soil. You were too hard on Faruk, my mother."

"No, I want Taiyar again," Ommohamed said. She was exhausted now. "He is *baraka,* saintly. He can bring workers easily. He is well connected with the inspector, everyone respects him and is afraid of him. Faruk gives our house a bad name." She admitted to Shahhat, "I made a fuss because I don't want Faruk any more. Perhaps the amount of lentils he has taken is small. But he is a big shame to me. I want to have done with him."

The scene had given Shahhat new respect for Faruk. Despite all the insults Ommohamed had flung at him, he had chosen to keep silent about the twelve pounds Shahhat owed him—he had not humiliated his mother before all the men. Faruk, for all his drunkenness, had his own code of honor.

Early the next morning, as he worked at his well sweep watering his clover, Shahhat saw Faruk coming up the cartroad from El Kom. When Faruk reached him, Shahhat called, "So, what's the matter? Good or not?"

Faruk grinned. "Good," he called back cheerfully. "I've come to make an accounting, Shahhat. I want from your mother twelve pounds."

"Look, Faruk, that money is between you and me," Shahhat protested. "I told you I would repay it some way. Why speak to my mother about it?"

"When shall you repay me? Eight months have gone by. Your mother said yesterday she wanted a settlement. Well, by God, she will get one right now."

Shahhat's temper exploded. "Why bother my mother? Burn your religion, Faruk! You are a boy, not a man! That money was between us alone!"

"Come, come, Shahhat, don't be angry," Faruk interrupted, but

Shahhat turned back to his work and began to furiously splash water about. Faruk stepped back to avoid getting wet. "Be calm, Shahhat. Come, smoke a cigarette." When Shahhat kept working and refused to speak, Faruk shrugged and continued on to the house.

Ommohamed greeted him proudly. "Well, why did you not bring my lentils?" She at once became wary as Faruk greeted her politely and said, "You must ask why I have come to see you, not why I don't bring your lentils. We will not get enough sacks until tomorrow. Now I shall tell you all the things I have done. I spoke with my father last night. I mean to give you a full accounting."

He produced a notebook. Ommohamed, like all the village women, was illiterate, but she understood figures. She saw Faruk had kept a detailed account for each of the eight separate landholdings at Sombat he helped to cultivate. He was soon able to convince her that Shahhat had withheld money due him.

"Now," Faruk concluded. "I want from you twelve pounds."

Ommohamed was bewildered. "Since the death of my husband I thought I paid for everything. I gave Shahhat the money to give you each time, for the plowing, the *Nitrokima,* everything."

"And, as you can see, he pocketed twelve pounds of it himself. I just told Shahhat I would tell you, and he made a big quarrel with me. But it has been eight months."

Ommohamed said nothing. She was lost in thought, the deep private thought of someone whose many calculations have suddenly been proved wrong. After a moment she excused herself and went upstairs to her strongbox, returning in some minutes with twelve pounds. She gave it to Faruk.

"All right," she said firmly. "But don't speak of this to Shahhat again. Now what about the lentils?"

Faruk was amazed. Ommohamed seemed to have taken her son's dishonesty to her in her stride. Faruk did not understand that when it came down to it, she forgave Shahhat everything, that her love for him was unqualified. Indeed, she was even now blaming herself for not seeing he had been given more pocket money. She knew Shahhat was too proud to ask for it.

Seeing Faruk waiting open-mouthed, Ommohamed asked him if he would sell half her share of the lentils in the *suk.* She would need the cash now. He agreed.

"In the future," she went on, "I shall pay you myself for the needs

154

of the land. I shall not send the money through Shahhat. A person must see his head from his feet. I shall come to you or you can come to me."

"As you wish." Faruk felt a little ashamed. "You see, Ommohamed, Abd el Baset was a very dear friend to me. You may take all the lentils if you wish."

She smiled. "No, Faruk, Allah will give to you all that benefits you." They spoke like two old friends.

Faruk hesitated. He was moved by her strength of character. "The fault is Abd el Baset's," he began awkwardly. "He did not accustom your son to take on responsibility. When Shahhat ran away to Cairo after you forbade his marriage to Suniya, Abd el Baset quickly forgave him. Shahhat is not lazy. He works as hard as two men in the fields. But he is not accustomed to disciplining himself. Also, he's young. I wonder, if I were not here, who would look after this family. I hope, in my mind, Shahhat will become a good *fellah*."

Four young girls from El Kom came to Faruk's threshing ground the next day to glean for bits of fallen grain. In late afternoon when Shahhat again saw his mother approaching across the fields, he expected another angry scene. Ommohamed had said nothing to him, and now he was surprised to see she seemed in good humor, greeting Faruk sarcastically, but with a smile, "What, Faruk! What are all these young girls doing here? In the future, you will destroy everything!"

"What is the matter, aunt?" one of the girls saucily asked. "Why does your Samah not come and help us glean? There is much grain left from the winnowing."

Ommohamed gave an indignant snort. "If any daughter of mine came here, I'd kill her! I'd no longer have a daughter. Why do you girls come here? I know who your fathers are, and they are not poor."

The girls burst into giggles. Ommohamed gave a deep reproving sigh. "Oh, I'm afraid Faruk will try to marry the lot of you!" Faruk gruffly told the girls to stop making such a noise and prepare Ommohamed tea. They stopped their work to gather some brush and squatted around, starting a fire and listening to Ommohamed and Faruk.

"Without these four beauties," Faruk said sheepishly, "my threshing ground would be destroyed. None of my men is willing to fetch

155

drinking water. These girls save our lives." He and Shahhat took off their tunics and spread them out on the ground. Then, wearing only their loose, long white underwear, they carried over five sacks and dumped the lentils in a large heap.

When the tea was ready one of the girls offered Ommohamed the first glass. Faruk snatched it away, gave it to Shahhat, and hit the girl hard on the shoulder with his fist, cursing her, "May your house be destroyed! Never serve a woman before the men!" The girl rubbed her shoulder and stamped her feet in anger, telling him, "You burn the religion of your father!" Then she burst into shrill laughter and all the girls giggled. In the bright sunlight Faruk's pitted, swarthy face looked so ravaged by dissipation it was a wonder to Ommohamed that the girls seemed attracted by him.

Soon Faruk was measuring out the lentils in a straw basket as Ommohamed stood over him, watching like a hawk. "Why do you shake your baskets and not mine," she complained. "Oh, the weight and measure men! May they all burn in the fire!"

"No, Ommohamed, I mean to be fair."

"Why?" joked Shahhat as he straightened the sacks. "So you can go to Mecca?"

"Never, never shall Faruk go to Mecca! How?" Ommohamed burst into mocking laughter. Faruk, too, laughed and shook his fist in her face. "Go away!" Ommohamed shrieked, pushing his arm aside. "Taiyar never cheated me like this. He never shook his own baskets and not mine."

"I am the cleanest one here," Faruk retorted. "I mean it. This harvest was better than the fields on this side or on that side. When the government weighs their share and says it is too little, Ommohamed, go and tell them that Faruk has stolen your lentils."

"Wait, Faruk! Did you fill that basket completely?" She intended to miss nothing. "Be still, Ommohamed. You already have your share. This basket is for me," Faruk said.

Shahhat laughed. "When my mother comes to the field she confuses everything."

"I'll take five baskets home and leave seven with you, Faruk, to sell for us," Ommohamed calculated out loud.

"Do you need money?" Faruk grinned. I can give you five pounds right now from my pocket."

"No, no. If I need money I can take from my brother, Ahmed."

"Why do you admit in front of these girls that you take money from your brother?" Faruk teased her.

Embarrassed, she hastened to change the subject. "The sugar this year is not good, Faruk. You know that."

"Yes, those nine days I went away, you and Shahhat didn't give it enough water." He got to his feet in a gesture of settling things. "By God, Ommohamed, now in front of everyone, I'll call one of my men and you ask him if by Allah Faruk gave the sugar cane enough water or not!" Faruk called loudly to a man winnowing some distance away. "Now, Mahmud, speak the truth. If you don't speak the truth I hope Allah takes all your children and destroys your house. Did I give the sugar enough water or not?"

"Yes," called the man, hardly looking up from his work.

"Yes and he rides about on his donkey like the village headman and gives his orders," Ommohamed called to the worker. "Maybe the men give water and maybe they don't. Is that not true?" The man grinned and went on winnowing.

"Don't be angry, Faruk," said Shahhat, who could not understand this cordial banter between his mother and Faruk.

Faruk laughed. "I am never angry. How could I be angry with the widow of Abd el Baset? Your father was a great friend to me. Every day he came here, all his pockets full of cognac and brandy. He never asked about money or the crops. I just brought the harvest to your house."

No sooner had Shahhat taken their sack of lentils home on his donkey than Ommohamed spread out a cloth on the front room floor. She poured out the lentils and enthusiastically began measuring out baskets to give her family and friends. There was some for Ahmed and his wife and her two married daughters. And the mothers of El Azap and Abd er Rahman. And poor Sha'atu and Zeyneb at the cafe had so little, she would give to them too. And when Su'ad stuck her head in the doorway and exclaimed in a shrill, sarcastic voice, "You'll eat your lentils all alone, Ommohamed?" even she could not be slighted. Then there was Bahiya, and she could not leave off Sheikha Daiyi, and so it went.

The next morning when Shahhat went to get some grain for the livestock he discovered that, far from having enough lentils to last the family six months, half of them were gone. He went upstairs, roughly shook his mother awake, and shouted at her, "Where are the lentils?"

Dazed and still half asleep, Ommohamed asked, "Lentils? What has happened, my son?"

Shahhat was enraged. "Now who is the bad one?" he shouted at her. "Me or you? Always you say that I'm lazy, that I don't work the land properly, that I don't care about anything! I want to know, what have you

157

done with our lentils? Are you a rich *princessa?* Who are you? You are hungry, poor, and without clothes!"

Frightened, Ommohamed flared out in anxious anger. *"Yah, fatees!* You have no manners!" she cried out in a high-pitched voice. "How dare you shout at me? This is my house and I am free to do what I want. Go! I hope the dogs eat you! What have you done for our house? Now you have a fit over a few lentils?"

"You must go, not me! I hope the dogs eat you and all your family!"

Ommohamed was shocked. Shahhat had never spoken to her this way. "I shall go to Ahmed," she threatened. "He'll teach you to respect your mother!" In truth, she feared Ahmed's tongue even more.

"If he comes, I'll tear him to pieces! You are at fault, not I!"

Downstairs Ommohamed tried to seek reassurance from Samah, but her daughter sided with Shahhat and quietly asked, "Why did you give away half our lentils, my mother?" Samah started naming off everyone who had received lentils; Ommohamed was aghast. She had forgotten there were so many. "How do you know them all? Oh, Samah, everybody asked about our new harvest. I was ashamed not to give them some."

When Shahhat carried fodder into the stable, Ommohamed anxiously called to him, "It is nothing to give lentils to our friends, my son. When one is generous, Allah will give again. Come, dear, and take tea."

"No! I don't want that slop!"

Ommohamed raised her hands to heaven and pleaded, "Oh, dear God, please change my son to make him calm and quiet."

Pieces of the Game

LIFE IN A VILLAGE is governed by the seasons, and Shahhat, although he had grown lentils on the inspector's orders, was soon helping El Azap, Abd er Rahman, the Salem brothers, and Hagg Abd el Mantaleb harvest wheat, the main winter crop. The scorching heat of the Upper

Egyptian summer was drawing closer and the mowing lasted each day from dawn until noon, but Shahhat was content and at peace with himself, as he always was when he worked hard in the fields.

As the days became hotter, the sky seemed to pale; the once-green fields turned burnt yellow and the village was dustier than ever. Dust settled like pollen on the sweating backs of the harvesters. By noon, when work stopped for the day, a gray haze of dust spread over the sky, and the sun would turn a livid white. Each morning the bent figures of Shahhat and his friends could be seen in one field or another, slashing their sickles at the ripe stems, grasping a handful at a time and trying to avoid thorny weeds, advancing slowly, rocking from side to side, standing or squatting on their haunches to rest. Steadily and rhythmically they would move from one end of a field to another, spread out in a wide line, their sickles flashing in the sun and all together making the same sound: *grrch, grrch, grrrrch.* From the glint of their sickles, from their wet backs, and the way they gathered up the swaths after cutting, you could see how suffocating and oppressive the heat had become. Abd er Rahman and Shahhat went the fastest, El Azap was slow and steady, and the Salem brothers quickly tired. As muscles began to ache, the youths joked more and gossiped; often they sang in the wailing *fellaheen* way that sounded more like weeping. *"Yah loblee, yah loblee. . . ."*

Only in the fields of Hagg Abd el Mantaleb did the mowers seem to make no progress. A dozen of the oldest, laziest, and most foolish men in the village, they cut so little that Hagg's overripe wheat soon began to dry and shatter. "Why should we tire ourselves?" his lazy mowers asked themselves. "Hagg is such a stingy bastard he gives us only thirty-five piastres when most men are paying fifty." Hagg Abd el Mantaleb himself sometimes came to the field carrying a white parasol against the sun, and would stand about complaining how busy he was, what poor workers the men were, the high cost of labor, the low price of wheat, and how much money he was losing. Bahiya, who brought the men tea, would scold them, "You are no good! You leave stray stalks all about. And what little you have cut this morning! What am I to do? I cannot do everything myself, inside the house and outside the house. I give you so much tea you think we will get much money for this wheat. Little do you know the costs! The seeds and the water, the labor and the *Nitrokima!*"

Bahiya begged Shahhat to come and help. He told her, "Hagg is too stingy. He won't pay high enough wages to get good men and is letting his wheat shatter for nothing." Shahhat went to cut Hagg's wheat for a day and told the mowers, "Look, men, Bahiya brings us tea but

159

returns to her house sad. Please work harder because Hagg will lose much of his harvest. We must help him whether Hagg is good or bad. Because his wife is good."

The mowers jeered. "Bah! Why should we tire ourselves? If Hagg loses his harvest it is because Allah knows him for the miser he is."

Coming home at noon one day, his face and tunic wet and grimy with sweat and dust, Shahhat saw his friend, El Got, hurrying down the canal path in front of him. Shahhat hurried to catch up, but El Got, seeing him coming, quickened his pace. Despite the mid-day heat, El Got was wearing his best black wool *gallabiya;* his pockets were bulging, and Shahhat shrewdly guessed he must be wooing a new bride and taking her presents.

"Why the long face, El Got?" Shahhat called teasingly, catching up, but staying a few paces behind. "Are you running to a funeral, El Got? You look like an orphan who ate his parents. Ah, but you would not move so fast to a mere funeral. No, you run more like a dog chasing a bitch in heat." Shahhat laughed at his own joke.

"Go away, Shahhat! Leave me alone!" El Got called out without slowing his pace or looking around. "If all the village died, I would not go to the funeral. I go only to important things."

"Why do your pockets hang out so, El Got?"

"It is a black hour that I have met you, Shahhat. I carry with me chocolates, sugar, tea, and perfume. And a comb and a bracelet."

"Where did you get such things, El Got?"

"I stole them."

Just then Bahiya came out of a field and seeing El Got she exclaimed, "Where are you going now in your black *gallabiya* in the heat of the day, El Got?"

"To my sweetheart."

"Ah," Bahiya burst into laughter. "It is up to you."

El Got hurried past her, calling, "If anything bad happens to a man, you can be sure a woman is behind it. When a woman is under your body she is good. Anywhere else she is trouble."

Bahiya gave a loud, indignant squawk. "Wait for me here, Bahiya!" El Got called back. "Perhaps you are the fifth wife for me!"

"May your house be destroyed!" Bahiya cursed him.

"Ah," he retorted, "you say you will come to me even if my house is destroyed." Fearing to hear even worse, Bahiya hurried the other way.

Shahhat and El Azap were cutting wheat one morning a few days later when El Got returned along the canal path, his new bride riding

160

a donkey beside him. Men came running from the fields, gathering at the canal bridge to welcome them. Since there was no time to fetch drums or a band of musicians, everyone grabbed sticks and started beating tin pails. "Why has the weather turned so hot these three days?" Shahhat shouted above the din. "Because El Got has secretly been on his honeymoon!" There were more shouts and cheers, and Bahiya and Ommohamed came running from Hagg Abd el Mantaleb's house.

"*Mabruk!* Congratulations!" the women called. "Welcome to our village!" They hurried to shake the hand of the bride, a widow from the distant village of El Maurice, whose inhabitants were said to be descended from the French troops of Napoleon and were famous for their looks. The widow was not young but still handsome; she was very plump, with a glistening pale skin that gave her the look of a ripe melon. She offered Ommohamed and Bahiya some cookies. Ommohamed laughed and exclaimed, "I hope from Allah, El Got, that she becomes the mother of your many sons!"

"Why do you laugh in front of the new husband?" El Got blustered, indignant at this boisterous reception.

"I'm laughing because you are so brave," Ommohamed told him. "All the people said El Got cannot win this new wife. And here you are!"

For days whenever Shahhat and El Azap would pass El Got's house after dark they would shout, "El Got! El Got!" If he made the mistake of opening the shutters and looking out, sleepy and disheveled, they would call, "Why such a long face, El Got? Are you not good with your wife?"

The villagers were so preoccupied with their own and each other's affairs they took little notice of the outside world. Many listened to the president's radio speeches at Sha'atu's cafe and, since the 1952 revolution, even the poorest felt some of the half-tamed impulses of a newly-liberated people. But until Nasser, rulers had always meant tyrants, coming to tax, compel, and conscript, and by custom the villagers were not politically minded.

One morning on the canal path Shahhat met a large group of Christians from Basili; they were all dressed in black, stared vacantly ahead of them, and their eyes were red-rimmed from weeping. At first Shahhat thought it was a funeral party, but they explained they were taking a young man named Romanni to the railway station in Luxor. He had been drafted into the army.

Old Mitri, Romanni's great-grandfather, led the mourning group; he could scarcely control his sobs when he greeted Shahhat and tears

161

welled up in his rheumy, nearly blind eyes. Even Romanni himself, a sturdy, hot-blooded youth who showed no lack of courage when it came to quarreling with his family, now sniffled like a man whose death sentence has been pronounced.

"What is the news of the army, Shahhat?" old Mitri demanded in his loud, quavering voice. "Is there war? Will Romanni die in the army? What is the news? Speak to me the truth, Shahhat."

"How can I know?" Shahhat replied. "I cannot read well. Leave it for God to decide."

"How can he return?" the old man went on. "If he does not lose his eyes, if he does not lose his arms, if he does not lose his legs. If he goes to the army, Romanni is as good as dead."

Shahhat had heard how in past times young men in the village had been known to cut off their fingers or put out an eye to be rejected, or try to hide in the desert and escape. If there was no way out and they could not avoid going into the army, their families received condolences and abandoned themselves to formal mourning as if their sons were already dead. In the old days, to leave the village was to die.

But times had changed. Now Shahhat's friends came back from the army literate and aware of the world outside. Shahhat had twice tried to enlist but been rejected as underage, and now, as the only adult son of a widowed mother, the army would not take him.

"Don't be afraid," he advised Romanni. "The first time it only takes two or three hours, and then they send you home again. They strip you naked and look you over. If you are good, the next time you go you are a soldier. The life will agree with you, no doubt. They give you a uniform and all." Thinking to cheer the forlorn youth up, he added, "Take some packets of cigarettes. That's all the soldiers want. They'll put you in before the others and you can come home early."

To Romanni he might have been describing a coming execution. "Speak to God, Shahhat, don't speak to me," he sniffled, and the mourning party went its way.

"Shahhat! Shahhat!" Ommohamed called anxiously from the edge of the field. She said Hagg Ali had telephoned from Cairo to Sobhy asking him to bring Abd el Baset's death certificate to Cairo so she could claim her widow's pension. Shahhat left his work and Ahmed was summoned for a hasty family conference. It came out Hagg Ali had specified to Sobhy that he bring the paper himself and not send Ommohamed or Shahhat. Sobhy was prepared to go, but Ommohamed and Ahmed, neither of whom had ever been to Cairo, decided no one but Shahhat could be trusted with the certificate.

Ahmed provided a few pounds for railway fare and gave Shahhat his shoes and stockings to wear. Shahhat caught the third class night train; it was crowded with soldiers, and he had to stand the entire ten-hour journey, arriving at dawn in Cairo's main downtown station grimy and exhausted.

As most arriving *fellaheen* do, Shahhat headed at once across the great open square of Midan Ramses, dodging the unfamiliar heavy traffic, and scarcely glancing at the colossal granite statue of the ancient pharaoh. Once inside the twisted lanes of Bab el Sharia, the city's most congested quarter, there were more men in turbans and long tunics, and he felt more at home. If the village had a timeless quality, with its pharaonic temples and empty desert all about, Bab el Sharia was medieval. A gigantic wall built by Saladin against the invading Crusaders loomed up to one side, and there was the great mosque of the insane caliph Al-Hakim, who massacred Christians in the Middle Ages.

Shahhat hurried past the crumbling tenements, mosques, and Mameluke palaces seeing cadavers of buffalo meat, stained violet and hanging from hooks, chopped-off camel's feet awaiting buyers, a domed bathhouse, and cafes with tattered awnings offering Turkish coffee or milk sweetened with cinnamon. He dodged out of the way of a donkey-drawn draycart, which splashed muddy water on his *gallabiya*. "Oh, cart-driver, your mother is dirty!" someone near him cursed. A tall Nubian, with a glistening black face, came close and whispered, "Opium?" A voice cried, "N'na!" as if in alarm, and Shahhat quickly turned and saw it came from a man selling mint.

Everywhere there were people hurrying, pushing, shoving, indifferent, shouting with raucous voices, angry and hot-tempered, humorous, noisy. Shahhat felt vulnerable and defenseless, and he was relieved to reach a large, dingy cafe with a faded sign, "The Qurna Friendship Club." A bare, cavernous, ill-lit place, it was crowded with men in village dress who sat about playing cards, dominoes, backgammon, or were just gossiping. Some smoked water pipes, and waiters ran back and forth with trays of coffee and tea. All the men in Cairo from Qurna or Berat gathered in this haven, and Shahhat, who had never strolled along the Nile where the

163

great luxury hotels and government buildings rose, or visited the museum or the pyramids, seldom left the cafe when in the city.

A waiter recognized him and said Hagg Ali was staying at the Merina Palace Hotel, which despite its grand-sounding name was a cheap, rundown tenement where everyone from the village went. Shahhat found a corner table, ordered tea, and fell asleep at once, awaking only when Hagg Ali appeared and shook his shoulder.

"Why have you not come until now?" Hagg Ali sputtered. "I sent a telegram. And spoke with Sobhy on the telephone."

"Why did you tell Sobhy to come and not me?" Shahhat asked, gathering his wits about him.

"No, no, I never said that. Who said so? I knew you would be busy tending your fields. I thought if you just sent the death certificate along with Sobhy it would be less fuss for everybody. Now just give me the paper."

But Shahhat refused to let it out of his hands and the next day was at Hagg Ali's side when they visited a government office. The clerk seemed to be on familiar terms with Hagg Ali, and there was a good deal of passing cigarettes back and forth and lighting them for each other. Finally Shahhat was told to return in a month's time, having certain papers Hagg Ali was to bring certified by a judge in Luxor. There would be a lump sum payment to Ommohamed of three hundred pounds, and Samah, Nubi, and Ahmed would receive two pounds each month apiece as long as they were under twenty-one.

This business dispatched, Hagg Ali was in high spirits. He took Shahhat to a good restaurant for beer and *kabob,* and after several bottles Hagg Ali became loquacious.

"Now let's close this subject of the pension, my dear nephew," he told Shahhat. "I become tired talking about it all the time and all the coming and going. Now don't go back to the village and speak too much. You know that Sobhy is a bad one. All my troubles with your mother are the fault of that nephew of mine. He demands that I don't help you and Ommohamed. He has money, but still he is envious of everyone. He says, 'Shahhat and his mother walk proudly as if they were better than us.' Well, let us forget him. You can rely on me to look after your interests."

As soon as Ommohamed heard about the pension, she began planning how she would at last make her pilgrimage to Mecca. Neither she nor Shahhat gave a moment's thought to using the money to pay back their debts.

Ahmed was furious to hear they were accepting Hagg Ali's help. As soon as he met Shahhat, he demanded, "Why do you speak with Hagg Ali? He's crafty as a snake. Don't have anything to do with the man. Have you and your mother learned no lessons from life?"

Shahhat tried to reason with his uncle. "I cannot treat Hagg Ali badly, Ahmed. He was my father's cousin. In front of the people, no. After we finish and take the pension money, everyone will go his way. Don't be nervous. If you want to get things done, you must be wise and patient."

Infuriated Shahhat should be lecturing him, Ahmed refused to shake his hand. "All right, go do as you like."

Angry in turn, Shahhat swore, "I'll never set foot in your house again!"

"If you do anything to your mother, I'll cut you to pieces!" Ahmed warned him. "And no one shall know!"

The reconciliation with Hagg Ali proved shortlived. Abd el Baset's sister, Fatnah, now elderly and almost blind, sent word to Shahhat that Hagg Ali had tried to persuade her to file a rival claim to Abd el Baset's pension, but that she had refused. She and Ommohamed had been estranged for thirty years, but once, hearing Fatnah was being treated for her failing eyesight by a Luxor doctor, Ommohamed had impulsively sold a sheep and paid the medical bill.

Fatnah was not poor. Her husband was a feeble, ailing old man who kept to his bed, but they still owned three acres near the canal bridge which El Azap cultivated for them. Embarrassed by Hagg Ali's proposition and seeking to make peace with Ommohamed before she died, Fatnah invited Shahhat to supper one night. He had not visited since the days he had been courting Batah. Since Hagg Ali lived next door to Fatnah's house on the rocky desert slopes near the Tomb of Marai, Shahhat stopped off there on the way.

Hagg Ali greeted Shahhat with his customary effusiveness, and was interested to hear he would spend the evening at Fatnah's house. He said he himself would have joined them, but he was spending the evening with his friend, the police inspector. Even as he spoke, there was an impatient honking of a horn from the road below. Anxious to be off, Hagg Ali gathered the papers he had promised to bring from Cairo with considerable irritation. "Here," he said, giving them to Shahhat, "tell your mother to fill them in and sign them and take them to the judge to certify. I will take them back to Cairo with me when I go."

"I shall take them," Shahhat told him firmly.

"Yes, you take them," Hagg Ali retorted sarcastically. "You know how to do everything."

Shahhat enjoyed Fatnah's company. Batah had set out a meal of roasted chicken and rice in a room upstairs. As was the custom with male guests, Fatnah did not eat with him, but sat and reminisced about the old days when his grandfather had been alive and the big house was always filled with people. Now, except for Batah and her bedridden husband, the many rooms were empty, gloomy, and still.

"You are like your grandfather, Shahhat," Fatnah said. "You know how to speak with everybody and are always joking." Then since she had paid him a compliment, she hastened to add, "God protect you from the Evil Eye."

There was a commotion downstairs. Someone was talking in a low, gruff voice, and Fatnah went to see who it was. Then Shahhat could hear her speaking loudly, too, and also Batah's shrill soprano. Hearing the voices rise in anger and excitement, Shahhat opened the door to listen.

"You are Fatnah!" someone was shouting. "You are the cause of everything! You have encouraged her in her sluttish ways!"

Shahhat crept out on the landing and looked down the stairs to see who was abusing his aunt. The hall below was dimly lit and he could just make out the speaker, a tall, flatchested, bony man with sunken temples, long arms, and a hunched-over look. It was Hasan, the *El Abt* or Black One, from El Kom. He was very drunk, and shouted into Fatnah's face, "Every time she wears tight dresses to excite the boys! The slut! I must take her to my house tonight before anybody gets killed! Batah is to marry my son!" So the rumors were true after all, Shahhat thought. Hasan raised one of his long arms as if to strike Fatnah. "It is you, old woman, who have put my head in the mud! I know what you speak to people about me! By your doing, you shall kill many!"

"You cannot take Batah, you drunkard!" Fatnah shrieked, in a voice as furious as his. "Why should you take her? Your son chases whores, and your daughters beat Batah every time they catch her at the well. They insult her with filthy words. You cannot take her!"

Batah too was screaming hysterically. "Your girls beat me! I do not even speak to them! I'll never go to your house! Never!"

It was a terrible scene. Shahhat stepped back into the upstairs room, seized the first thing at hand—a glass water pitcher—and went back to the landing. He saw Hasan had taken Batah's arms and was trying to

166

drag her toward the door. Fatnah frantically held her back. "Keep silent!" Hasan roared at the screaming girl. "By God I shall slit your throat and cut you into small pieces! Not even the maggots will find your body when I'm through with you! I shall take you to my house! Now! Tonight! We do not allow women to say yes or no!"

Fatnah kept shrieking and refused to let go. Another man came from the shadows; Shahhat saw it was Batah's father. "Yes, you speak the truth, my brother," he shouted above the women's cries. "We cannot leave things for women to decide. You can take her. Be still, my mother-in-law! Do not speak! We want to close this subject!"

Fatnah screamed all the louder. "Hasan, you and your family go far from us!" she cried. "There will be no marriage with your son. Batah is mine. If you find her false, that is no business of a drunkard like you. If anyone tries to take her, I shall fight you until I die! Men like you are not real men! Women are better than you!"

Shahhat could hear shouts outside. From a window he saw that a crowd was gathering. Some carried flaming torches. There were men armed with wooden staves, hoes, and pickaxes. There were women, too, who started to scream and cry. Everyone was excitedly shouting in hysteria and confusion.

Another man entered the house. It was Suleyman, who followed Hasan everywhere. He too started abusing Fatnah. "Your father is a dog, old woman!" he roared. "Why has God not taken you! The good ones die and the bad stay alive!" Batah broke away from Hasan's grasp and cowered behind her grandmother, sobbing. From somewhere Fatnah produced a butcher knife which she raised as if to strike, forcing the men back.

Fatnah's voice rose above the rest, a piercing, blood-curdling shriek. "I am an old woman and blind! But if you do not leave my house this instant I will kill you and stay screaming all the night!" The men retreated, and Shahhat started down the stairs, pitcher in hand. Batah's father blocked his way. "No, no, Shahhat!" he cried, seizing his arm. "It is finished!"

"I do not do anything!" Shahhat roared, pushing him aside. Batah, her hair falling over her face, weeping and giving little screams in hysterical gasps, started to rush for the door. Shahhat slapped her face hard and said "Get back inside!" He shoved her violently back, and she collapsed in a heap in the corner, whimpering and holding her face. Her father seized Shahhat's arm again. "No, no, Shahhat, leave it! Let it be!"

167

"Your father is a dog!" Shahhat cursed him. "You understand nothing. I know Hasan and Suleyman. If they come near me, I'll break this pitcher over their heads."

He paused in the open doorway, and saw that Hasan and Suleyman, followed by several men, were going down the slope toward El Kom, shouting and cursing in their coarse drunken voices. The rest of the crowd was still there, and from the men's voices and movements he saw they were still in a state of violent agitation. Exactly as if they were bent upon killing someone, they could hardly restrain their hurried breathing—they held their staves and hoes poised in the air ready to strike blows, and shouted loudly at each other in trembling voices. Someone called out, "Do you know yourself, Shahhat?" Another cried, "If he makes trouble, we'll throw him into an old tomb!"

"All of you are dogs!" Shahhat roared at them, but he was frightened too, and he let Batah's father pull him away.

Once out of the torchlight of the crowd, it was very dark, and Shahhat could barely see his way down the rocky slope. Batah's father turned back to the house, crying to the crowd *"Malesh! Malesh!* Let it be forgiven!" Then Shahhat saw someone approaching who could be distinguished only by his middle height, white turban, and dark face, so dark it seemed part of the night itself. For a moment Shahhat thought it was Hasan coming back, but then a familiar voice called *"Salaam aleikum"* and a hand stretched out. It was Hagg Ali and, with a startled cry at seeing Shahhat, he squeezed his hand hard in his own. He was evidently out of breath for he gasped as he demanded, "Who insults Shahhat? What is this I hear? What happened at Fatnah's?" Shahhat said nothing and went on. As soon as he saw Hagg Ali had climbed some distance toward the house, he dropped back into the shadows and waited. Soon he could hear Hagg Ali angrily calling, "All of you are cowards! You are dogs! Why did you let Shahhat get away? You are nearly twenty men! Why did you let him leave without blood? You know you can do anything and I'll stand beside you!"

As Shahhat went home the thought came to him that Hagg Ali, perhaps coming across Hasan and Suleyman while he was out drinking with the inspector, could have been behind it all. How else explain the coincidence that Hasan had picked the very moment when he was upstairs taking supper with Fatnah to come and try to drag Batah away? He realized now that Hagg Ali was capable of anything.

Batah came to see Su'ad the next morning. From the upstairs

168

window Shahhat watched her come up the lane. She wore her sequined red dress and the flimsiest of veils. As she drew near, her hips swung saucily, and her face looked flushed and pretty. There was a pleased and excited expression on her face. Shahhat withdrew into the shadows so that she might not look up and see him.

He did not go back to Fatnah's house or seek any further help from Hagg Ali with his mother's pension. That day Hasan went about El Kom cursing Batah in the foulest language and vowing, "That girl shall never enter my house!" The marriage contract was broken. In time it came out that Batah had been secretly in love all the time with a youth named Abdul Satar, a cousin of Suniya from the despised water carrier tribe. It was said the young Jamasah, hearing of Hasan's words, had gone to Fatnah and declared, "I'm prepared to marry Batah. I love her and she loves me. I'll save the money, prepare the papers, and see to everything." Fatnah had given her consent.

Hasan, when he heard this news, exploded, "*Wallahi Azeeb,* by the Great God, that girl should be driven from the village!" His son, Ali, was away in the army, but there were fears of a blood feud between the Jamasahs and Hasan's family when he returned. Sympathies in the village, first favorable to Batah, turned against her once it became known she wanted to marry a Jamasah. "Batah is a bad girl," said Ommohamed. "She will disgrace all her family."

Ahmed, when he heard that Shahhat had fallen out with Hagg Ali once more, was pleased. He had heard rumors that Shahhat and the cousin had exchanged blows. He was disappointed when Shahhat told him the true story and complained, "These gossips. How quickly they change everything."

Late at night. A pounding on the door. Ommohamed roused herself and flung open the upstairs shutters. "What a strange coming!" she gasped. It was after midnight and there below were Hagg Abd el Mantaleb's two sons, Ahmed and Mahmood. She thought at once the robbers had come back. "What's happened?" she cried. "Are Hagg and Bahiya all right?"

The boys looked sheepish and the eldest shoved his brother forward and hissed, "Speak!" Little Mahmood, scarcely more than ten, called up in a high, shrill voice, "We want to take our sheep. Tomorrow we'll take them to the *suk* to sell."

"Wah!" Ommohamed exclaimed with indignation. She and Bahiya jointly owned two sheep which she kept in her stable. "What do you mean by coming at this hour? Who told you to come? Is your mother so hungry she wants to eat her share right away? If Bahiya wants to sell we can go together to the *suk*. Now run along, boys. I could beat you. You have no religion, waking up people in the dead of the night!" She slammed the shutters and went back to bed.

Bahiya came early the next morning, flustered and embarrassed. "My boys were naughty. When Hagg found out, he beat them with his shoes and would not rest until I came to you. I hope by our holy Prophet whom you want to worship in Mecca that you are not angry with me."

"No, no, my sister. But when your sons came at midnight, I was afraid something had happened to you. Why should they come at such a late hour?"

Bahiya laughed heartily. "No, my sister, believe me. I hope if I have not punished them for being so naughty, I will be struck blind and cannot see the way back to my house."

Ommohamed sent Samah to fetch some tea; as they seated themselves on a floor mat, she sighed deeply. "I am so tired, Bahiya," Ommohamed said in a weary voice. "Since my husband's death, every day there have been problems, problems. You stay in your house and do not know the troubles I have. Every day those cousins of my husband, Hagg Ali and Sobhy, speak in loud voices at the inn. They mean to insult me and my Shahhat. And Faruk does not look after the land well. And my brother, Ahmed Abu Sayeed, is always angry with me. When your sons came last night it was as if they came to complete the wreckage over my head."

Tears brimmed up in Ommohamed's eyes and she began to sniffle. "What am I to do, my sister?" she sobbed. "I am only made of flesh and blood. I am not made of iron." She was crying now, the tears streaming down her face. Bahiya also began to cry—she took Ommohamed in her arms and they wept heartily. They wept not so much from sadness as from long years of shared experience and an unquenchable hunger for something they could call happiness.

"Is it Shahhat who troubles you?" Bahiya asked accusingly, drying her eyes and loudly blowing her nose.

170

"No, no," Ommohamed protested. She dabbed her wet, swollen face with a handkerchief. "He is so young. He cannot take the place of his father." She gave a wan smile. "I know he is hot-blooded, but he would never make a big quarrel with his mother." Shahhat's anger over the lentils flashed through her mind, but she dismissed the memory. "I don't worry about his temper because most of the people in the village love Shahhat and pay no attention to it. He is like his father, quick to anger but easily good again."

Bahiya held her tongue. In her opinion Ommohamed, like Abd el Baset, was prepared to forgive Shahhat too easily. Yet she had to admit everyone was fond of him; without him the village would have been a much duller place.

"I fear one thing only," Ommohamed went on, her voice hoarse from crying. "If Shahhat suddenly married just any girl, a Jamasah like Suniya or a flirt like Batah, and she was not good for him, then I might lose everything."

"You'd still have Nubi and Ahmed."

"I know."

"And Shahhat inherits but a fifth of his father's land." Under Moslem law, Bahiya meant, each of the boys had equal shares, the three girls half-shares, and Ommohamed one-eighth of the total.

This was not what Ommohamed meant. She spoke quietly now in a thin, broken voice. In her honesty, she wanted Bahiya to know that now that Abd el Baset was gone, her whole life turned about Shahhat. She loved all her children, but there was something that set him apart. Gradually, and not very coherently, she told Bahiya that her deepest fear was that Shahhat would find the pressures upon him too great and would leave her. Did he not have the blood of Khalifa, his Bedouin great-grandfather? She told Bahiya, groping for the words, that her need for Shahhat was more than economic: his presence was vital for her being. Without him, she would be lost—her house, her family, her life, drab, dull, and without meaning. She wanted to see him married—indeed, felt some urgency about it. She said she planned to build one or two new rooms for Shahhat and his bride to keep him by her side as long as she lived. Was it not the custom for a man's eldest son to live on in the family home, perpetuating the household for another generation?

Impulsively, Bahiya kissed the top of Ommohamed's veil. "When I hear you speaking from your heart this way," she said with evident

171

emotion, "I know it is all right between us." Then, resuming her usual flat, loud tone of voice she went on, "Well, we both know how difficult boys can be. We've had our share."

"Yes, they don't always respect their mothers as they should." Suddenly Ommohamed smiled radiantly. One had to see the full force of her brilliant happy smile to see how beautiful she was. She burst into laughter; it made her seem easy and simple.

If All Sombat Flows with Blood

S HAHHAT had come to dread the yearly sugar cane harvest since it had to be loaded on freight wagons, and there were never enough to go around. Since a man's cane could be left to dry in the sun for some days, losing half its value, there could be violent fights or even killing.

Sugar had only been introduced since the end of the Nile's annual flooding and the redistribution of the Sombat feudal estate. Each *fellah* given land was to set aside one of his two new acres to grow sugar. This new cash crop, which took a full year to ripen, and was harvested from February to May, had tripled the incomes of all those alloted government land on the old Sombat estate. Her ability to use future sugar harvests as collateral had enabled Ommohamed to borrow such a large sum from the government as the three hundred pounds she spent on Abd el Baset's death rites.

The government had opened a new sugar refinery in the river town of Armand, ten miles south, and laid out railway tracks to the cane fields. Two of these tracks crossed Sombat, and during the harvest each *fellah* was alloted two freight wagons. The agricultural inspector told each

172

Ommohamed watches Shahhat cultivate what is left of the family's ancestral land; the walled garden of date palms and grape vines is in the background.

man what date to cut his cane, when to bring it by camel to the nearest railway track, and when to load it. Since the factory was not efficient and the engine hauling wagons back and forth was invariably late, and since the inspector and his men such as Taiyar were not always above favoritism, bribes, or even spite, there could be trouble.

Shahhat was happiest working the half-acre of land between his house and the canal that was all that remained of his father's inheritance; here were his fields of clover and onions and the walled garden with its grove of date palms and grape vines. These he watered with his ancient well sweep and cultivated in methods that went back to pharaonic times. At Sombat, with modern methods, all was frustration, delays, and complications.

173

This year the cane harvest was going badly. By early April great heaps of cane could be seen beside the railway tracks waiting to be loaded. Sometimes they stayed there for days. "Right from the start it has not been good," Faruk complained to Shahhat. "The cane gets all dried out in the sun. Some men will get a low price, maybe only half as much as they should. Those sons of dogs at the factory in Armand do not send the freight wagons at the promised time."

Shahhat was notified that his acre of cane would be among the last to be cut and shipped. The Armand refinery would shut its gates May tenth. Shahhat and those with fields in a row to the north and south of his were told not to begin cutting their cane until the second of May. When the day came, Taiyar assured him, "I must serve you in the matter of freight wagons, Shahhat. It is my duty. Three or four days from now, I'll send a wagon to you. Now don't be lazy. Work hard and don't worry. Depend on me." Taiyar touched his chest, a gesture he could be relied upon.

The harvest itself went quickly. Shahhat's brother-in-law, Kamil, agreed to help although he feared Sobhy's wrath if he should learn of it. Shahhat hired two more men from El Kom. The cane was cut by whacking it off at the roots with a hoe, and then it was stripped of green leaves and stacked. A new custom had sprung up in the past few years that any man who came and cut cane for a day could take home all the fodder he could load on his donkey in payment. As a result, Shahhat and Kamil, who soon wearied of cutting and would often straighten up, resting their aching backs, were soon shouting to everyone who passed, "Hello, hello, *effendi!* Anyone who wants fodder for his livestock, he can come and cut with us! Oh, men and women, come! If you want to feed your family!"

Kamil's face, though he was merely forty, was as creased and lined as an old man's, and he always went about in a grimy old tunic, his large hands seldom clean. A quiet, taciturn man in the village, he came alive in the fields and was forever exclaiming, "Oh, my God, Allah, help the poor people!" or "This day is black! Oh, Allah, send us a breeze and an army of workers from the sky!" Shahhat sang loudly as he cut, and when Kamil admonished him, saying he should sing religious songs and not those of love, he bellowed at the top of his lungs, "Help us, our God, we are Moslems! Oh, our holy Prophet, be satisfied with us!"

Such noise, accompanied by curses, coarse jokes, and guffaws of laughter, attracted many workers. Kamil would greet each new arrival, "Ah, we have caught another fish in our net! Come and take your share of fodder, neighbor. Did you fall from the sky or did the wind carry you here?"

"Here come some more men."

"You have sharp eyes, Shahhat."

"Wah! Pray to your Prophet! In the house our buffalo fell sick from the Evil Eye. Now you want to make me sick also with your compliments. Then no one will be found in the house or in the field."

"Oh, men, go north to Cairo!" Kamil's voice would rise from the tall cane. "This place is useless for you. Oh, my father, I wish you had not married my mother and brought me into this world because now you see what has become of me and weep in your graves."

Such banter made the time pass so quickly and attracted so many workers that by mid-afternoon the cane was almost half cut. Suleyman, whose cane was next to Shahhat's and whose harvesters had fallen far behind, came to complain, "You sons of dogs are cutting your field quickly. Why, Shahhat and Kamil, when anyone passes do you call, 'Come, come and take fodder!'? You must tell whoever comes now that it is their duty to help me."

This was met with laughter and jeers. But when a young boy arrived to join the workers in Shahhat's field, Suleyman intercepted him, roughly seizing his shoulders. "Come, I hope you eat your father with hot bread, boy! You come to work with me, not here!" The boy squirmed away and joined Shahhat. Shahhat laughed and called to his neighbor, "Oh, Suleyman, see how this boy feels safer here! Not with you!"

"Oh, Suleyman," Kamil joined in, "we are all poor, tired men! Our teeth are falling out from poverty!"

"Be careful, boy!" Suleyman shouted angrily. "That Shahhat is a sodomite!" The workers roared with laughter as Shahhat retorted, "Better that than a catamite like you!" Showered with good-natured jeers and insults, Suleyman retreated to his field, muttering obscene oaths. Then he turned and with his stupid, leering grin called back, "We are all sodomites and catamites!" causing the men to hurl even more abuse at him.

A northerly breeze broke the oppressive heat the next day, and with an even larger number of volunteers, they finished cutting Shahhat's cane by sunset. The luckless Suleyman, whose harvest was not half done, rained them with curses, "Oh, you sons of dogs! Why did you go to Shahhat and not to me?"

"Praise be to God!" Shahhat exclaimed when the last of the cane had been stacked. "If it had not turned cooler today I might have beaten

175

someone. Instead of being happy we have finished, we might have ended with a funeral."

The harvesters laughed. "You are wicked, Shahhat!" one of them said. "You are like a fire that destroys everything in its path!"

"Come, men, let's finish quickly!" Shahhat called. "Everyone wants to go to his house. But you know, men, when I go home from the open fields, I feel I am entering prison." For in truth, Shahhat seldom felt such well-being as when harvesting. The next day the cooling breeze died, and the heat was so oppressive that when he, Kamil, two hired camels, and their drivers finished carrying the cane to the railway tracks, Shahhat was exhausted. Taiyar came by at sunset to tell Shahhat he could pick up a railway wagon the following morning at a railway yard a kilometer south. He would have to bring someone with him to push the wagon back to his fields.

Seeing Shahhat so worn down, Ommohamed too became subdued; she was anxious nothing go wrong until the cane was safely loaded and taken away. Like all the Moslem village women, Ommohamed was observing the spring Christian festival, a week of ancient rites preceeding Easter Sunday. Onions were to be eaten one day, cucumbers the next, lentils cooked and thrown against the house walls to symbolically drive the flies away, and boiled eggs colored with red, blue, and yellow dyes. The day after Easter was considered auspicious for sailing upon the Nile in a *felluca,* and the day after that summer began.

Faruk went with Shahhat to the railway yard at dawn. They found their wagon and were about to push it down the track when a voice called, "Take that wagon!" It was Lamei, the rich landowner. As always, Lamei was accompanied by several of his hired laborers.

As the men pushed them aside to claim the wagon for Lamei, Faruk sputtered indignantly, "How can you take this wagon, you sons of dogs? It's Shahhat's!"

Shahhat, knowing that Lamei feared any involvement with the police or petty government officials, since his wealth invited extortion, exploded as furiously as he could. "All your fathers are dogs!" he shouted. "I drank a bitter cup to take this wagon! Now every dog tries to take it. And I need two cars, not just the one!"

He shoved one of the workers aside and struck another hard on the side of the head, knocking him away from the wagon to show Lamei he would have a fight on his hands.

"I'll kill the first one of you that touches this wagon again!"

176

Shahhat thundered. "There is no government, no law here! Now I must rule by my fists and take twenty-five years in prison if I must kill one of you to take this wagon! But afterward I shall live proudly!"

Lamei, who was not a bad man and just wanted to get his own work done, now turned angrily on his men. "Did I tell you to take Shahhat's car, you fools?" he demanded. "No!" As his men moved back in confusion, Lamei offered Shahhat and Faruk cigarettes to show this test of wills had left him with no hard feelings. Although he was said to profit by ten thousand pounds each cane harvest, Lamei was a simple, industrious man who labored as hard in his fields as any of his hired workers.

Shahhat and Faruk wasted not a moment pushing the wagon out of the yard before someone else tried to claim it. But Faruk, weakened by dissipation and unaccustomed to physical labor, was soon sweating and panting, and wanted to rest.

"Yi lan dinak!" Shahhat cursed him, pushing harder against the heavy wagon than ever. "Your religion is bad!"

"Yi lan dinak abook!" Faruk retorted. "Your father's religion is bad!" He gasped, trying to catch his breath. "I may get ruptured, Shahhat, and you will be to blame!"

Pushing as hard as they could, cursing each other all the while, they were able to move the wagon slowly forward along the track. In the morning stillness, their gasps, grunts, and labored breathing were broken only by a steady exchange of insults.

"You are the son of a bad one, Shahhat."

"Shut up, you donkey!"

"Donkey! Why . . . May Allah smite you to pieces!"

"Go, burn in the fire, Faruk!"

"May your father burn first!"

"Go to hell!"

"Pig!"

"Pimp!"

"Bastard!"

"Christian!"

"Jew!"

"Jew am I?" Shahhat chuckled, gasping for breath from the effort. "Well, Allah must love the Jews for he has given them everything."

In this congenial fashion, strengthened by the rush of adrenalin from their anger, time passed quickly, and before they knew it Shahhat's stacks of cane came in sight. Seeing there was not far to go, Shahhat wanted to rest. Faruk, ready to drop himself, seized this advantage. "We want to arrive, you lazy son of a dog! You are dirty! Your father is dirty!"

At last they reached the cane and released the wagon, letting it slide to a stop. Faruk stumbled down the bank like the survivor of a train wreck and collapsed onto a pile of cane. He wiped his sweaty face with a rag and breathed heavily in and out, gasping for air. Then he began cursing Shahhat.

"May your house fall down! May all your neighbors houses fall down! May all the houses around them fall down! May all the houses in your sight fall down! It's a black day I ever met you, Shahhat! You are a dirty son-of-a-dog! You are a lazy, good-for-nothing, dirty son-of-a-dog! I did not come to push the wagon. You know I have a bad leg. You are no good. You want everything too easily. May your house sink into the mud of the Nile and you with it!"

Shahhat, his temper exploding, squatted in the path and violently scooped up dust with his hands, flinging it at Faruk in the Arab gesture of extreme contempt. "Take this over your head and the head of your father!" he shouted.

Faruk leaped to his feet, seized a cane stalk, and raised it to strike Shahhat. "You dare to insult my father?" Seeing Faruk's face, and that so much blood had rushed to his head he looked purple and veins stood out on his temples, Shahhat burst into laughter. He could not stop but doubled over, the laughter tumbling out until he collapsed in a coughing, choking fit. Faruk also began to laugh as Shahhat managed to say, "What can I do when I see you so respectful to your father, Faruk?" When Shahhat regained control, he kissed the top of Faruk's turban. The two of them set about loading the cane. Before long some of Faruk's men, seeing them from the threshing ground, came to help, and the wagon was soon filled. Half the cane remained on the ground, and Shahhat realized he would need to get a second wagon somehow. It meant more struggles at the railway yard.

Still, with at least half of it ready to be carried to the factory Shahhat felt more lighthearted than he had since the cane harvest began. As he walked home he made up words to a popular old song.

> Why, why, why, why, why, why?
> If you have money your wife respects you
> And says, "You are the beat of my heart, the
>   light of my eyes.

The days without you I go out of my mind."
But if your pocket is empty
The smell of your sweat burns her eyes.
Why, why, why, why, why, why?
Oh, I'll take hashish and opium
And be strong as a bull.
If a woman is satisfied, her words are
      sweet as honey,
But if she is not, they can roast you like an oven.
Oh, I'll take hashish and opium
And be strong as a bull.
At noonday prayers how I'll soar!
But when they pray at Magreb and the sun goes down,
I'll flutter like a limp, wounded bird.
Why, why, why, why, why, why?

Striding along the canal path with the loose-jointed, loping gait that was second nature to him when he felt carefree, Shahhat felt a sudden surge of happiness, such as sometimes overtakes us when we least expect it. He was barefoot, unshaven, clad in his old black tunic, his dusty scarf wound about his head, and his face gritty with dust from the cane. He felt a thorn in his foot, sat down on a rock, dug it out with another thorn, saw a lizard slither into a puddle and threw a stone at it, and was on his way again, singing, "Why, why, why, why, why. . . . "

El Azap was riding on his donkey just ahead, and Shahhat ran to catch up with him. He leaped up behind his friend and feeling a pack of cigarettes in El Azap's pocket, began wrestling him to get it.

"I'll kill you! Stop, Shahhat!"

"Bastard! Give me a cigarette!"

"No! I don't have any! I don't smoke!"

"Wah! Allah is great!"

"You donkey! Here, but take only one!"

Shahhat took two, slipped one behind his ear and lit the other.

"You thief! Allah is angry with you!"

Soon the friends were affably gossiping. El Azap told about meeting Hagg Abd el Mantaleb on the path. Instead of returning his greeting of "Salaam aleikum," Hagg had replied, "Where is the money? You have a big bill at my shop." The youths laughed. No day was complete without its Hagg Abd el Mantaleb story. El Azap also told how Lamei's workers, while burning a stubble cane field, had accidently set a

179

neighbor's unharvested cane on fire. It was a total loss. The man had accepted his loss fatalistically, saying it was Allah's will, but El Azap had heard Lamei had been very angry with his workers and insisted upon making good its value. Shahhat told him about his own encounter with Lamei at the freightyard that morning.

He scarcely slept that night, worrying about how to get another wagon, so that when Faruk rode up well before dawn, reeking of stale liquor and hashish fumes and not having slept all night, Shahhat was ready to go. As they rode through the dark village, Faruk feared they would have another fight on their hands.

"These people are afraid of any really strong person, Shahhat. If there is trouble today, you speak."

"No, no, Faruk, everyone is afraid of you. They say you are crazy and can do anything. Who is not afraid of such a loud voice? You speak."

"By my God, Allah," Faruk exploded, "you are the first person I want to hit with my stick today, Shahhat. There is no one about now. All the village sleeps. Only me and you and Allah. I could break your head open and no one would know. Today you speak."

Despite the early hour more than twenty men were waiting at the freightyard, Taiyar among them. Shahhat saw the factory's engine had left only three wagons during the night.

When Taiyar greeted them, Faruk answered ferociously, "A black morning! We want to finish loading!"

Taiyar chuckled and said affably, "I know your game, Faruk. I can see the birds flying in the sky and tell which is the male, which is the female. There are only three wagons today and sixteen persons wanting them. What can I do? Don't try to frighten me."

Shahhat saw a woman among the crowd; he recognized her as Basita, a widow from El Kom whose sons had run away to Cairo and abandoned her. Taiyar wanted to give her one of the wagons and the others to two men who had not started loading their cane yet. But the other men angrily crowded around him, shouting, "I want to finish!" "The cane dries in the sun!" "Oh, my God, my house is destroyed!"

Basita became hysterical. She threw herself on the ground by one wagon, wrapped her arms about a wheel, and shrieked, "If anyone else takes this wagon I can do anything! I shall kill anyone! If anyone comes near, I'll kill him! This wagon is mine!" Shocked by this spectacle, the men agreed to let her have one. Faruk tried a similar tactic, shouting in

Taiyar's face like a frenzied maniac, "Your father is a dog, Taiyar! I know you! You want a bribe!" But the other men wanted to draw straws. Shahhat lost. Two other losers became so distraught they started to fight, and one knocked the other to the ground with his wooden stave. As Taiyar and the other men lifted him up and started to carry him to El Kom, the man regained consciousness and cursed them all, his head bleeding, before he fainted away again.

"Oh, by God," Shahhat told Faruk as they rode home. "Many necks shall be broken because of this sugar cane. Why can't they provide enough wagons for all?"

"Don't worry, Shahhat," Faruk assured him. "In a day or two they'll want to shut down the factory, and we'll get all the wagons we need."

Shahhat returned home in an ill temper. When Ommohamed complained to him about some trivial household matter, he turned on her, shouting, "Close your mouth, woman! I've told you a million times to keep your tongue in your mouth. You must stay quiet like a blanket on the bed. See and don't talk!"

Hurt and angry, Ommohamed declared she would go off to the house of Ahmed; there she would be treated politely. As she rode off on Shahhat's donkey, Samah urged him, "Run after our mother and apologize. She is going away angry."

"Let her go to hell!" Yet Shahhat watched her go from the window and stood there a long time, brooding. "Don't worry, my sister," he finally told Samah. "I always know that if our mother takes the donkey she will return by sunset so we can take it to load fodder."

Restless and anxious as his cane dried another day in the sun, Shahhat went out to his well sweep to water his clover. He stripped off all his clothes but his white undershorts and had not drawn water long before some short, thickset, foreign men in black business suits approached along the canal path; he recognized them as Russian tourists wandering over from the temple grounds. Embarrassed, his face and back dripping with sweat, Shahhat lowered his copper bucket into the well and lifted and splashed it out with greater speed, all the time singing, *"Yah loblee, yah loblee. . . ."*

The men stopped on the path above him to watch and take photographs. One of them, fatter than the rest, who stood fanning himself with a fly whisk, sighed heavily and said, *"Ploxo, ploxo,"* telling his companions in his own language, "The poor, poor man is barefoot and has no clothes on his back." The Russian dug into his pocket, produced a small pin and handed it to Shahhat, exclaiming in a loud voice, *"Baksheesh!"* As the tourists moved on, Shahhat examined it, and saw the hammer and sickle and the face of a stern-looking, bearded man. He shrugged, handed the pin to the first passing child, and went back to his work.

That evening Kamil came to the house to say that Sobhy had fired him as his share-cropper because he had helped Shahhat harvest his cane. Sobhy had also informed the police that Kamil was illegally growing vegetables on the canal bank; he had been fined eight pounds and would have to sell a sheep.

Kamil was despondent. He told Shahhat, "Sobhy asked me, 'What have you to do with Ommohamed and Shahhat?' I told him, 'My children take many meals at the house of their grandmother. How could I not help Shahhat harvest his sugar?' Sobhy answered, 'All right! Get out! You'll work for me no more!' I told Sobhy, 'You are not God. Allah will provide.' But, Shahhat, why should he speak to me like this? I've worked in his fields all year, and in that time Sobhy has not given me as much as ten pounds. Only fodder for my livestock. Why should he treat me like this?"

Ommohamed, when she returned home and heard Kamil's story, was delighted by this turn of events. "You are a free-loader, you are lazy," she told her son-in-law. "Why can't you earn more for my daughter and her children? They are paying harvesters fifty piastres a day this year."

After Kamil went home Shahhat was angry with her. "Don't speak to Kamil so harshly," he told her.

Ommohamed threw up her hands. "Oh, my God, he is such a weak man and poor provider. It's terrible for me, looking after his children all the time and seeing they are clothed and fed. Tires me out. Why does Kamil take his children everywhere with him? So people will take pity on them and give them a few piastres."

"What are you saying?" Shahhat was angry. "Because Kamil is poor, you speak so. But you always praise your brother, Ahmed, because he has money."

"Kamil is no good. Why should he work for Sobhy without money?"

"If Kamil needs anything," Shahhat said, "I'll give it to him. I love the poor people like Kamil. You are not the head of this household, woman!"

Ommohamed held her tongue. Half the cane was still to be loaded.

But there was no wagons at all at the freightyard the next morning. Taiyar told everyone the inspector had left instructions each was to wait by his cane the following day. Enough wagons would be provided so all could finish loading.

The day was hot, without the slightest breath of air. Shahhat and the other men gathered under the shade of a large acacia tree by the railway track. Their cane had dried in the harsh May sun for three days now. Soon it would be worthless, a whole year's labor come to nothing.

In Egypt there is a mental state called *kaif,* when a man does nothing, says nothing, and thinks nothing. It is a kind of wakeful passivity, a way of turning off one's mind to abate frustration. In their impotence in the face of incompetent authority, Shahhat and his neighbors drifted into it now. From dawn to early afternoon, the men sprawled about under the acacia branches, speaking little, humming, drowsing, lost in private fantasies, a mental languor as oppressive as the drying heaps of cane along the track or the stubble fields which shimmered with heat under the vivid white sun.

Shahhat was awakened from this stupor by Lamei, who also needed a few more wagons to finish his harvest and was waiting for the engine to bring them. Lamei sat down, offered Shahhat a cigarette, and exhaled with a deep sigh. "Well, do you make a living?" Lamei asked.

"*El hamdu li-llah,* praise be to God," Shahhat responded automatically. All about them the sprawling men dozed; smoking in silence, they gazed across the stubble fields to the tree lines where the houses were, and rising above them, the highest temple ramparts, and higher still, the cliffs of the Libyan Desert in the faint blue distance. These cliffs which rose like a wall, for the Nile Valley was really a deep flat-bottomed trough carved into the desert floor, were of a color difficult to describe. Someone painting them might mix white, yellow, ochre, pink, and a touch of brown, perhaps adding a pale blue as shadows appeared from the sun's westward fall. Sweeping in a majestic arch around the fields of the Nile's western bank, they formed such a distinctive natural setting one could see why the pharaohs chose the Theban Plain for their greatest city.

Lamei cleared his throat and spat. "Without *Nitrokima* this land would be nothing now." Dusty, unshaven, a gray stubble on his chin, his eyes wrinkling at the corners as he squinted into the distance, Lamei looked as worn down by the harvest as Shahhat himself. "Our land has been cultivated since ancient times," he continued. "We even use the dust of their old towns for our fertilizer. Every field is filled with bits of pottery and human bones, Shahhat. The earth is old and exhausted."

"It was a great mistake to build the Aswan Dam," Shahhat responded in a weary voice. "The government thought it would get more food. But the soil becomes weak. The cane was not good this year. It was a great mistake to stop the yearly flooding of the Nile." His voice sounded bleak and old beyond his years. "Perhaps they should blow it up and let the river flood again."

Lamei chuckled. "No, no," he said in his calm way. "Now it is good. We cultivate three crops a year and with many things, sugar, beans, peas, clover. Say I had one hundred acres in the past and grew only the old crops, wheat, barley and lentils. I might get a thousand pounds, and if I paid two hundred pounds for the seeds, water and all, my profit was eight hundred. And perhaps from those hundred acres, twenty to thirty per cent was lost to rats and insects. Now, if I grow sugar cane, I can get perhaps fifteen thousand pounds from that hundred acres. Okay, so I must invest half of it. I still make seven, eight thousand pounds. Before the High Dam, the government could not help us much. Now we make two, three times more than before."

"I am only a poor, ignorant man," Shahhat said, thinking that only someone as rich as Lamei could afford to speak so. Lamei predicted that someday, perhaps in another ten or fifteen years, the Nile Valley would no longer produce grain and fodder. He had heard talk of importing sorghum and forage from Sudan and wheat from Iraq and Syria, so that Egypt could grow fruit, vegetables, flowers, and seed to sell in Europe. "We will do what is good for Egypt," Lamei said. "And to make much money. We can do anything once we have the experience."

"No!" Shahhat was roused from his stupor. "We must eat from our own labor and our own hands, Lamei. Never depend on other countries! Can our animals eat flowers? Can our families eat flowers? My buffalo must be fed from my own land. Why should I buy fodder from others? It's not good."

"If the government gave us flour for bread, Shahhat, we can do anything they want."

"Never!" Shahhat's voice rose so loud he woke several of the sleeping men. "The *fellaheen* would never agree! Those officials in Cairo sit in a chair and have no experience. Can a minister take my hoe and cultivate my maize? No, he can only read books." Shahhat's whole being told him man's natural lot was to repeat and preserve; what a man knew was better than what he did not know.

"In Cairo they say . . . "

Shahhat cut Lamei off. "Spare me Cairo. I want the good things here."

Lamei smiled. "We cannot leave the old things easily, can we, Shahhat?" After Lamei went, Shahhat still felt upset. He stared across the stubble fields toward the desert cliffs telling himself that this land was a gift of the Nile, and that without its flood waters and silt it would someday surely die. His thoughts were interrupted by Suleyman's coarse voice, calling drowsily, "Your father is not good for Allah, Shahhat! Why talk so much with Lamei? You tire our heads!"

The afternoon deepened. Shahhat searched the southern horizon for any trace of engine smoke but saw nothing. Restless, seeing the sun moving toward the horizon in the reddening western sky, Shahhat went across the stubble fields to Faruk's threshing ground. Faruk was bent over a brush fire, making tea. They had just begun to drink it when Shahhat, with his remarkable eyesight, saw the first few puffs of smoke. Then came a faint whistle. And, finally, coming around a wide bend below the freightyard, the engine itself. Shahhat counted fifty wagons. He watched transfixed as the engine would advance a distance, then let off some of the cars. Soon it was pulling only twenty-five, then fifteen, then eight. Hundreds of men must be lining the tracks, waiting for wagons, he thought. With intense relief, Shahhat saw Lamei had been allotted only seven so that the eight remaining cars were being left for him and the others by the tree. But there were nine waiting there, counting himself. There were only eight wagons.

"Take care, Faruk," Shahhat exclaimed. "We're going to be one short! It looks like a fight! C'mon, Faruk, let's go and get a wagon!"

"No, my legs and back are sick from last time," Faruk complained. "I can't run."

Shahhat was off, running across the field toward the slowly advancing engine. Seeing him, the men under the tree jumped to their feet and started running up the track. Faruk looked about for his turban and sandals, then noticed Shahhat had stopped and was squatting down. "By my God, Allah," Faruk cursed. "That son of a dog has picked this moment to answer the call of nature!" Faruk did not realize that Shahhat had become so excited his stomach had betrayed him. Faruk, barefoot and bareheaded, was instantly scrambling toward the engine as fast as his legs could carry him, leaping over dikes like a young boy and splashing through canals as if the devil himself were behind him.

Suleyman reached the first wagon and claimed it just as Shahhat

185

came up. Shahhat shouted wildly at him, "Suleyman, it's mine. Yours is the next! Seize it quick! We don't want a fight and there are many wagons!" Suleyman, seeing the second was unclaimed, dashed off to it. Two of Faruk's men, who also came running from the threshing ground, helped Shahhat push his wagon forward. Suleyman and some other men were so excited they rammed their wagon into Shahhat's, forcing him and Faruk's workers to jump down the embankment to avoid getting crushed. Shahhat roared abuse at them, and they let his wagon get ahead. "Push hard, Shahhat!" the man next to him shouted. "We're afraid somebody will try to take this wagon! Let's get it away and loaded quick!"

Faruk, who had found a donkey somewhere, was riding up and down the path below the embankment, shouting orders and abusing everyone. "One for one, men! Each man take only one wagon! Mohammed, your father is a dog! Leave that one for Ala Adeen, you greedy bastard! Suleyman, no one should load his wagon until all are fairly distributed!"

"By my God, Faruk," Suleyman thundered at him savagely, "we shall load our wagon even if all Sombat flows with blood!"

"Take it then, Suleyman! May your house be destroyed!"

A man came running past Shahhat. "Help me, Shahhat!" he cried. "Oh, my God, I must get a wagon for my father-in-law!"

Shahhat did not even look back to see who it was. "I don't care for anyone!" he told the man pushing next to him. "I'll take this wagon to my cane and have done with it!"

When they reached Shahhat's cane, they loaded it quickly as the sun set and darkness fell apace. The others rushed off to load other wagons, Faruk had vanished, and, the work finally done, Shahhat set out for home alone, carrying a ladder he had borrowed in El Kom. He had never felt so tired, and looked at the star-filled sky with an expression of great relief that the cane harvest, thank God, was over for another year. He felt hot and feverish and all his muscles ached. When a passing man greeted him and asked where he was going, Shahhat barely managed his habitual grin and joking reply, "I go to hell!"

After leaving the ladder, he reached home at dark to find Ommohamed standing in the lane, calling and frantically waving her arms. "Shahhat, come quick! My buffalo! Oh, my buffalo!" Gasping for breath and hysterical, she managed to tell him the buffalo had strayed into the temple grounds and fallen into El Mahala, the name the villagers gave to the sacred pond of Ammon-Ra. Ommohamed was terrified, thinking the

186

accident was a judgment against her for once praying there to the ancient god.

Shahhat rushed into the temple and broke through a crowd of villagers gathered around the pond's steep, grassy banks. Down in the black waters, covered with green scum, the buffalo thrashed about, more frightened by the excited crowd than anything, since the pond was quite shallow. Stripping off his tunic and flinging it aside, Shahhat slid down the bank and waded chest deep up to the buffalo, shouting directions to everyone. "Quick, get ropes! Come, men, you stand and watch while my buffalo drowns! Watch those children, don't let them fall in! Oh, Kamil, clear away that grass!" The buffalo became calmer in Shahhat's familiar presence, finding the water refreshing and cool.

In the darkness, everyone was stumbling about and falling on the slippery grass. "Stand back, you children!" Shahhat called. "Don't let anybody get near the water!" He quickly tied ropes around each of the buffalo's legs and looped another under its belly. Kamil cut away the grass to clear a muddy path for the buffalo to be slid up along. Lines of men formed holding ropes, and Shahhat kept shouting directions in a breathless, hoarse voice. "Pull hard, men! Come, men, exert yourselves! Pull!" For a time, despite the shouting, heaving, and groaning, nothing happened. And then with a great splash the buffalo emerged from the water and, making loud frightened snorts, was hauled up the muddy bank. As Shahhat led the buffalo home, everyone stood about reliving the episode in excited voices, speculating on the buffalo's value, observing what Shahhat said and did and how he looked, and enjoying the unexpected evening's entertainment.

Mother and Son

AFTER SUPPER Shahhat had diarrhea. His head was burning. When he saw Samah strike Nubi and Ahmed, he exploded. "Leave them alone! This is the hottest day of the year! They're small boys and are tired!" Samah was angry. "You spoil them," she retorted. "Even if I ask them for a grain of salt or a drop of water, they refuse."

Losing control, Shahhat threw one of his sandals at her, and when she dodged and cursed him, he leaped up with such a terrible expression, Ommohamed cried, "Run, Samah, run!" He regained his temper at once, but Samah stayed angry with him all evening, telling her mother, "Shahhat is crazy."

He felt worse the next morning and vomited twice. But he had promised Faruk he would take two sacks of lentils from the threshing ground to the inspector's office, two miles away on the other side of Sombat. When he got there the office was shut, and a large crowd of men was waiting outside. Shahhat waited until noon, and the inspector, accompanied by Taiyar, finally came. But the inspector refused to take Shahhat's lentils, saying, "If I start taking grain now, I'll be stuck here all afternoon. I have to go and see to the fields. We shall burn all the cane fields in a few days."

To Shahhat, worn out by the heat and his own fever and exhaustion, this was too much. He blew up. "Why won't you take the grain now?" he bellowed at the inspector. "If we don't bring it on time, you fine us! If we bring, you refuse to take it? What are we to do?" The crowd applauded Shahhat, but Taiyar, fearing he would get into trouble, hastened to intervene, pulling Shahhat aside and telling him, "Enough now! Finish! You go home and I'll take care of your lentils."

By the time he got home, Shahhat was reeling. He staggered upstairs and fell into bed, turning his head to the wall. He felt dizzy, hot, nauseated, and his eyes brimmed with tears. Both Shahhat and Ommohamed had an exaggerated terror of all illness. They did not fear death, but it required the merest trifle—an upset stomach, a slight chill—for them to feel they were dying. Above all, they feared fever.

As soon as she felt his forehead, Ommohamed could not do enough for him. She forgot everything else and stayed by his side, begging him to take tea or coffee. Shahhat merely shook his head, made a sound with his tongue like "tssk tssk," and rolled back to face the wall. At supper that evening he managed to down some beans cooked in oil and raw green peppers his mother prepared for him. During the night he dreamed his stomach was swelling up like a giant balloon, and he woke up sweating with fright.

The fever and diarrhea persisted the next day; Shahhat did not stir except to stagger out to the high grass by the temple wall, returning

188

pale and faint. The neighbors, hearing Shahhat was sick, all came to visit in the evening. Each shook his hand and formally greeted him, "*Salaamtek,* good health, Shahhat. Your illness came quickly. I hope it is not serious and will pass with peace."

His friends came to joke. "What, Shahhat? Not dead yet?"

He would manage a wan grin. "You like me to be dead?"

"Yes. Why not? If it is Allah's will." And they would laugh, cheering him up.

Shamsuddin, the student, came, full of his own affairs. His father had told him he could afford no further studies, and after his next examination would have to go into the army. "Well, it is my sacred duty," he told Shahhat. The student could scarcely control his envy; he said Hagg Abd el Mantaleb was sending his oldest son, Ahmed, to the university in Cairo the next year. Shahhat knew Shamsuddin sometimes lied to strangers and told them he studied in Cairo and not just a technical institute in Aswan. Yet Shamsuddin managed to make a pious virtue out of everything he did. When he left he told Shahhat he hoped he would recover in time for the Friday prayers at the mosque as he had been chosen to deliver the sermon on "how to pray."

This cheered up Shahhat more than anything; he could scarcely conceal his amusement. Afterward he told Ommohamed, "What a bunch of hypocrites we have in our village! All the greediest scoundrels like Hagg Ali will go to hear Shamsuddin tell them how to be good Moslems. *El hamdu li-llah!*"

Many of Shahhat's visitors talked about a sudden plague of scorpions; overnight they were to be found everywhere, on the canal path, in the road, even in the houses. Small boys were going about in the dark with lanterns and pails, trying to catch them to sell to the hospital in Luxor. Two small children and an eighteen-year-old boy had been fatally stung in El Kom, and, what seemed worst of all, a woman was stung while she sat wailing among the mourning party at the youth's funeral. Shahhat said that maybe they could blame the Aswan Dam. Before, large numbers of scorpions had drowned in the yearly floodwaters. None of the visitors stayed long although Ommohamed insisted everyone take tea. What with the perpetual clamor, the fumes of cigarette smoke, the gossip, and the noise, Shahhat was left worn out and feeling worse than ever.

The second night of his illness, a hot southerly wind, the dreaded *khamaseen,* arose, so that the air became scorchingly hot and saturated

189

with choking dust. As always happened when it appeared in summer, there were outbreaks of fever and diarrhea all through the village; Ommohamed said that with the hot dusty wind and scorpions everywhere, she could not remember more oppressive days. Ommohamed was forced to shutter the windows and the house became stifling.

Shahhat slept most of the third day, but at sunset he went outside and stood upon the open roof to watch the spectacular red and gold of the dust-filled sky and its reflection in the water of the canal and the windows of the inn—the air around him seemed inexpressibly cool after the stuffy heat of the enclosed house. He brought his bedding outside, but soon the *khamaseen* came up again—he was driven indoors by whirling dust so thick it settled on his face and shoulders like pollen. Even when he pulled a blanket over his head, almost suffocating, the dust still found its way into his eyes and nostrils.

Most villagers recovered from such bouts of fever and diarrhea in a day or two, but on the fourth night of his illness Shahhat took a turn for the worse. His fever rose so high and his skin became so hot and dry he could not sleep, but stared silently at some point on the ceiling as his mind drifted absently about. After her evening prayers, Ommohamed did not leave his side, but sat on the floor beside his bed, clutching his hand from time to time to feel his pulse.

It alarmed her to see him lying there, eyes open, hardly taking a breath, and she asked him, "Shahhat, does your head ache much? It feels very hot?"

He replied, but not at once. "Yes. I keep dreaming."

"What do you dream?"

"All sorts of things." For some time he did not speak again, and then, when she thought he must be sleeping, he startled her by asking, "Mother, if I died right now, the gravedigger would put me in a tomb, would he not? And the angels, Munkar and Nekeer, would come to examine me?"

"Yes, my son."

He spoke in such a faint, weary voice she had to lean forward to follow him. "I do so many bad things. Like drinking and chasing girls and swearing and fighting with you. And I took that twelve pounds you gave me for Faruk. The two angels would not be beautiful, I think. No, they would have ugly, terrible faces. They would take me by force, beating me all the way, down to the seventh hell. And I would stay there until all my sins were gone."

Ommohamed was terrified to hear him speak this way. "*Malesh,*
malesh, never mind," she tried to sooth him, wiping his hot forehead with
a cool, wet cloth. "Perhaps, my son, the angels would take you directly to
Paradise."

Again there was a long pause. "Munkar and Nekeer," he finally
said. "No, no, no, no." He made a sound, a kind whispered chuckle, as
if he were amused. "Not like Shamsuddin. No. They will ask me, 'Do
you sometimes curse your mother?' If I say yes, they will beat me. If I
say no, I become a liar and they must also beat me. Like the headman and
ghaffirs." He stopped speaking, closed his eyes and dozed off again. To
Ommohamed the time dragged agonizingly as if the evening would have
no end.

After it was dark outside and she stood by the window, Ommohamed looked like a silhouettte. She stayed there a long time until Shahhat
again opened his eyes.

"Shall I bring a lamp?" she asked.

He did not answer.

"Does your head ache very badly?"

"Very. I keep dreaming."

She resolved to fetch the doctor at daybreak. Hours went by.
Samah and the two boys came in and silently carried their bedding out
to the rooftop veranda. Ommohamed sat down again on the floor beside
Shahhat's bed. He still wore his old black tunic just as he had when he
returned from the inspector's office; he had refused to change. Once, Samah
crept in and asked her mother in a hushed whisper if there was anything
she could do. Ommohamed could think of nothing but staying by
Shahhat's side. She told Samah, "Life would be nothing to me without
him."

"I know you feel that."

"Nothing." Ommohamed's voice quivered with a sob. "If he . . .
does not recover, Samah, I could not bear it." Samah saw her mother's
face was swollen and streaked with tears, and when she spoke, her voice
broke into little sobs. "When he was born it was I and not his father who
first whispered the call to prayer in his ear. Did I ever tell you that? But,
oh, my God, what is that time compared to now? He is my first son to
live to be a man." Ommohamed muffled her weeping with a cloth so it
would not waken him.

Around ten o'clock a quivering red glow began to fill the room.
Samah came to say the men were burning the cane fields as they did each

year after the harvest. Ommohamed rose and went outside to gaze east-ward where an extraordinary spectacle met her eyes. In a single line, stretching from one end of the eastern horizon to the other, halfway toward the Nile, rose a wall of fire seven to eight feet high which swirled and scattered sparks in all directions like a long series of fountains spray-ing fire. The whole valley seemed to have burst into brilliant flame. She could almost hear the crackling of the fire.

The inspector and his men must have waited for the *khamaseen* to die, but there was still a faint breeze and everything in sight was bathed with the quavering red light. The fire meant all the cane was harvested and loaded and taken to the factory. Though the fire was a long way off, as far as Sombat, it seemed close and threatening to Ommohamed. Black shadows moved over the fields, flocks of birds took flight, and the flames moved high and intense, so white and fiery it seemed as if every blade of grass in the fields was clearly visible. Then slowly the highest flames died, and wisps of smoke began to drift over the village.

Ommohamed went back to sit by Shahhat's side in the darkened room. As some unburnt patch of cane would suddenly flare into flames, its red light filling the door, Ommohamed was reminded of the fires of hell. She shut her eyes and dozed, but even drifting off to sleep, she could still see the fiery light, like the Last Judgment. She found herself in a fearful, flaming landscape where Satan himself—big, black, horned, and hideous—was driving Shahhat into the fire with a long stick, just as he himself chased the boys with a switch if they badly misbehaved. Fright-ened, she jerked herself awake, hastened to feel Shahhat's pulse, watched his chest to see if he still breathed, and broke into tearful prayers to Allah to spare her son.

About two o'clock in the morning, Shahhat began to violently toss and turn, groaning and muttering unintelligible sounds as if in some dreadful nightmare. He had slept restlessly all evening, but now he pulled this way and that as if trying to escape something terrible. His head was burning and he breathed with difficulty. Ommohamed covered her mouth with her hands, unable to tear her eyes from him; she tried to rouse him from his delirium, softly calling in a hushed voice, "Shahhat, Shahhat." He moaned loudly and in such agony that Samah and the boys outside peered into the doorway, scarcely breathing, thinking Shahhat was going to die.

The two young boys were horrified at the thought, felt like crying, and longed to say something kind and comforting to him. Shahhat's hoarse groans became louder and more frequent, and Ommohamed saw his mouth was trying to form the words, *Allahu Akbar, Allahu Akbar.* . . .

Suddenly he opened his eyes, sat bolt upright, and, staring transfixed at some point in the darkness, shouted in a loud, estatic voice, "*Allahu Akbar! Allahu Akbar!* God is most great!"

The children shrank back in terror. Outside, the neighbors called in alarm. Shutters were thrust back and doors opened. Dogs began to howl, babies to cry—Ommohamed rushed to the window, flung back the shutters, and cried, "No, no! Shahhat is very sick and he had a dream! It is nothing!"

When she turned around, Shahhat had fallen back into his pillows and was breathing heavily. Deep sobs shook his body, and he fought for breath. Ommohamed clutched his hand and waited for him to speak. When he did he spoke calmly, in a weak but excited voice, his eyes still focused on something far and distant from the room.

He had dreamed, he said, that he was in a graveyard. He was wandering about in his old, torn black tunic among some tombs. His head hurt; he was being tormented by demons from Satan who were clawing and howling inside his head; he thought it would burst. He was sobbing and crying, and fell against the sharp gravestones, bruising himself. It was like some wild and angry devils, deeply miserable, whirled around inside him with fury, trying to get out.

Then there appeared before him a bearded man in white who was carrying prayer beads. This man called to him in a strange echoing voice, "Who? Who are you, Shahhat? Who are you, oh, Beggar? Come, come! Why do you dress in the black rags of an unclean spirit? Here, enter here!"

And they passed through an enormous gate, and at once the air was cool and inexpressibly pure and filled with such a brilliant, dazzling light Shahhat could scarcely see. It blazed golden like the sun, and from this light emerged a second man, also bearded, but golden shafts of light pierced the space about him in air so swarming with blinding sparks and glittering particles that Shahhat covered his eyes with his hand. And they took his black rags and burnt them. They gave him a gleaming white tunic to wear, and the second man tied a green sash, made of the richest silk, about his waist.

And they led him forward into a great garden with miraculous trees and flowers and fountains and such inutterable beauty it filled Shahhat with a sense of holiness impossible to describe. He held his breath,

193

his heart ceased to beat, and he heard a great chorus of magnificent voices rise in a thunderous shout, magical and estatic in its rapture, "*Allahu Akbar! Allahu Akbar!* God is most Great!" And he, too, joined in the tumultuous cry, shouting into the great garden and running past the flowers and fountains in the golden mist, crying with joy as an inexpressible rapture filled his whole being. . . .

In the torrent of Shahhat's words, in the fire of his eyes, and in all his movements, Ommohamed saw such beauty that she stood transfixed as if rooted to the ground and thought, it is an omen. Now he will be good. For she understood the dream. The first man was the Angel Gabriel and the second the Holy Prophet himself, for only the most blessed were given the highest spiritual pleasure of beholding him. It was he who tied the green sash about Shahhat and exorcised the demons that tormented him by burning his old black garment.

Ommohamed was so ambitious, hoped so fiercely, and yet had never found what she needed to make her happy. Now as Shahhat fell asleep, his skin cool to her touch and his fever gone, she uttered joyous prayers of thanksgiving. Yet even now doubts flickered through her consciousness whether she wanted her son to change.

PART FOUR

The Moving Finger writes; and, having writ,
Moves on: nor all your Piety nor Wit
Shall lure it back to cancel half a Line,
Nor all your Tears wash out a Word of it.

The Rubaiyat of Omar Khayyam

Tragedy and Comedy

IN REAL LIFE the single fortuitous event that happily changes everything is rare, as Ommohamed, for all her romantic imagination, well
knew. Instead, people may be doing the most ordinary thing, for instance,
having a meal around a fire—just having a meal—but at the same time,
and without them thinking about it, their true happiness is being created.
The same is true of tragedy. Few lives are suddenly smashed. Behind the
common run of failure, such as Shahhat's to fully master his condition
and fill the vacuum left by his father's death, lies a whole series of obscure
fatalities and misjudgments, most of them so small as to pass unnoticed
when they happen.

As May turned to June and then July, and the storms of desert
sand and dust turned into persistent scorching heat, the first anniversary
of Abd el Baset's death came and went unobserved, for the family had
no money for the final rites.

During these months, Shahhat, his mother, and her brother,
Ahmed, found themselves drifting into a clash. None of them wanted it.
But, like fish caught in a net, they were all enmeshed in false hopes of
their own making and driven by compulsions for which they could give
no clear account. As in all family quarrels, anger born of thwarted affection made their arguments more random and their words more cruel.

Of the three, Ahmed might believe a man could shape his
own life. To Shahhat and Ommohamed, fate was decided by unpredict-
able outside forces, the good by Allah alone. Yet could not Satan's demons
so poison a man's will he could inflict irreparable damage upon himself
and those he loved best? As in Shahhat's dream, only Allah could save
them.

Once the sesame was sown and the green sprouts of a new cane
crop began to grow, there was little field work—fortunately, as the heat

by noon had grown unbearable. Shahhat, with time to spare, borrowed a hundred pounds from Hagg Abd el Mantaleb. He hoped that if he proved himself as family head and provider, and could pay for his father's last rites, he would be free at last to be himself. He first tried his hand at buying and butchering sheep. When this proved unprofitable, he bought a knife sharpener and went from door to door.

Both enterprises failed. To make matters worse, Ahmed blamed the failures on Shahhat's lack of purpose. He demanded that either Shahhat try harder or give him his new meat cleaver and knife sharpener to sell in town for a profit. Angered, Shahhat spent a night at Abdullahi's. When he came home he was reeling drunk and dazed by hashish. Ommohamed waited until he slept, then took what money remained in his pocket and used it to buy two sacks of flour from Hagg Abd el Mantaleb; at least, she told Shahhat the next day, the family would not starve. Shahhat was left in debt, his capital gone and without the means for earning more.

His mother, torn as always between reality and fantasy, would throw up her hands and cry, "Where shall I find the money to feed my children? Where?" But it would not be long before she spoke grandly of inviting the extraordinary number of two hundred sheikhs to perform the last rites.

This would infuriate Shahhat. "You must go slowly, slowly with the money!" he would explode. "Not spend everything you have on sugar and tea and invite half the village to our house! If we are to afford but ten sheikhs, we should be eating onions and bread!"

"You're not my husband!" she would flare up. "You're not the children's father! What right have you to criticize?"

Shahhat began to drink more. One evening he staggered home from Abdullahi's to find his mother and Ahmed sitting together, and when he entered he saw from the way they exchanged glances they had been discussing him. Some devil prompted him to give them something to talk about. He announced he intended to marry a certain girl who happened to be a cousin of Sobhy and Hagg Ali. No such thing had crossed his mind before. Now he was rewarded by their consternation.

Ommohamed cried out in dismay and Ahmed shouted at him, "Are you not a man? How can you speak of marrying anyone from that family?"

"After one year I shall do it!" Shahhat vowed to them. "And you cannot stop me!"

Soon Ommohamed began suggesting this girl or that from among her own relatives as a suitable bride. Shahhat said they all looked like buffaloes. Ahmed threatened to go to the army and ask that Shahhat be conscripted. He dropped the threat when he saw that Shahhat welcomed the idea.

In the furnace-like summer heat, the crops fared poorly. The inspector failed to provide enough water to the fields at Sombat. The cane fields dried and cracked, and Shahhat's sesame, which had sprung up healthily in May, soon ceased to grow and by July stood stunted under the scorching sun, at last dwindling and yellowing into a barren harvest. "Nothing, *mafeesh!*" Ommohamed wailed when she saw it. "The sesame crop will be nothing." She no longer blamed Faruk, though she described his work as only "'so-so." She complained to Shahhat, "What can Faruk do? There is no water from the government. We spent much for *Nitro-kima,* but there is no water." She still owed the government two hundred pounds and almost a hundred to Hagg Abd el Mantaleb for household provisions. No pension money had yet been paid.

In her anxiety, Ommohamed increasingly sought Ahmed's advice. It seemed to Shahhat she could scarcely speak anymore without an "Ahmed this" or "Ahmed that," which made him all the more resentful. He got back at them by speaking even more determinedly of marrying someone from his father's family. At last Ahmed, apprehensive that Shahhat might be serious, urged Ommohamed to go to court and seek to be made legal guardian of Samah, Nubi, and Ahmed. That way, he argued, if Shahhat made such a marriage and it came to a break, she would still have legal control of four-fifths of the land. Anxious and bewildered, Ommohamed agreed, and a court hearing was set for the second week of August, adding to Shahhat's other humiliations.

And so, as the summer wore on and August began, Ommohamed and Ahmed made demands, Shahhat resisted them, and their relations worsened. Ommohamed was perfectly aware of what would happen if she went too far, and in the depths of his stubborn heart, Shahhat knew also. But they set out to hurt each other in the grip of truths more intense than knowledge.

Two days before the court hearing was to be held, Shahhat picked a quarrel with his mother. He objected that she had sent Samah to the fields to cut grass.

"I've told you a hundred times that Samah must not go by herself to the fields for fodder," he declared. "I will not allow the neighbors to gossip about my sister."

Ommohamed had no intention of being drawn in, yet she could not resist putting on a smile, a distinctly sarcastic smile, and replying, "Yes, my son, if you would only bring us enough, there would be no need for Samah to go."

Wounded, Shahhat cast about for a taunting answer, saying, "I want to sell the buffalo anyway and buy a taxi." He saw the anxiety flash through her eyes; he had hit the mark.

"No! Never!" she cried, genuinely alarmed. "The buffalo was bought by Ahmed for the two boys and Samah. Not you." She added pointedly, "Their father died, and they found a new father in Ahmed."

When Shahhat started to curse Ahmed, she cut him off. "If you don't stop, I'll not stay in this house another minute! I'll take Samah and the boys and go to Ahmed's house! I'll get him to take me to Cairo to see if I can get my widow's pension from the government or not. If I cannot get it, I can wash clothes and scrub floors. Or anything. The children can work as servants also."

Shahhat was shocked. Never had his mother spoken in such a way. "Why?" he roared at her. "You have no home? By God, you can cut off my moustache if you ever get so much as a tenth of a piastre out of the government!" He went on, speaking heedlessly and angrily in the same vein, telling her that if she felt the house was too small for them both, it was he, not she, who would leave. He would go to Cairo. Yes, and he would take the two boys with him. Shahhat called to them, "Nubi! Ahmed! Who agrees to go to Cairo with me?" The boys, who adored Shahhat and did not understand why he and their mother fought so much these days, eagerly agreed.

"You see!" he exclaimed in triumph to Ommohamed. "And you, Samah?"

Samah, having heard enough of this foolish talk, turned angrily on both Shahhat and her mother. "What nonsense you speak! If you all went away, I should never leave my father's house. You both should be ashamed!" This sobered them and ended the quarrel.

When Ahmed came to the house that evening, as had now become his habit nearly every day, Ommohamed told him of Shahhat's threats. "You must speak to him, Ahmed. He wears me out."

"He cannot be serious about selling the buffalo," Ahmed advised her. "It is a small problem and will probably solve itself. Leave it."

"He's always threatening me these days. He says, 'I shall go to Cairo and leave you!' Oh, Ahmed, I don't know where to turn. If I go to you, Shahhat gets angry and says, 'Ahmed shall not set foot in this house any more. Why do you offer him tea? Why do you offer him food?'"

Ahmed was not concerned. "Shahhat does not want you to sell the buffalo, my sister. He just wants to start a fight with you. So he has an excuse to run off to Cairo. To run away from responsibility."

In truth, Ahmed felt as much irritation with his sister as with Shahhat. It was becoming plain to him that Shahhat's relations with Ommohamed were growing worse, and that he himself was partly to blame. Ever since Shahhat had realized he was failing to replace Abd el Baset as head of the household he had become irritable, easily excited, and difficult to be around. At home he told his wife, "I would be much relieved if Shahhat and Ommohamed were reconciled. I want Shahhat to act like a man, to look after his fields and the household and make a suitable marriage. That is all I want."

Ahmed blamed Ommohamed as much as Shahhat. It was she who had plunged the family so badly into debt and who kept on spending as if Abd el Baset were alive and bringing home his earnings from gambling. Ahmed also felt strongly that no woman should interfere with the crops and field work; to him this was the man's province entirely, even if the man was Shahhat. Now he turned harshly upon his sister.

"You are the cause. You do not control your house. You do not control your son. You spend money you do not have. You needlessly make enemies." Then, seeing the tears well up in Ommohamed's eyes, he agreed to speak to Shahhat.

He found him in a shed behind El Azap's house, where Shahhat was helping his friend grease a plow. The youths were grimy, their faces and tunics smeared with black streaks, and El Azap hastened to bring a clean blanket and a bench for Ahmed, who was wearing his immaculate pale yellow *gallabiya*, to sit upon. The uncle remained silent for a time, then cleared his throat and asked Shahhat, "Well, what is it that you want, my nephew?"

"I want to sell the buffalo."

"Why?"

"Just like that. I am going to do it. And not anybody can enter my house and tell me this or that. I shall do what I want. It is like that, Ahmed."

Ahmed saw that Shahhat's stubborn declaration merely con-

Ahmed during a quarrel with Shahhat.

cealed his sense of failure, and he was determined to speak reasonably to him, for Ahmed believed, more than most Moslems, that a man can determine his own character and destiny. Had he not done it himself?

"You are a man," he said in a gentle, reasonable tone. "You have two small brothers and a sister. You must take care of them. How can your mother feed them and get them clothing and shelter without you? She has made many enemies with all her pride and gossip. You are the one who must look after your family now. Instead of your father. Or your mother. Or me."

Moisture welled up in Shahhat's eyes and a lump rose in his throat. Hearing his uncle speak so, he wanted to tell him all that was troubling him. He had never for a moment wanted to sell the buffalo or take a bride from the family of Sobhy and Hagg Ali. What he did want was to be treated like an adult man. Now, hearing Ahmed speak to him as if he were one, he was tempted to pour out his soul. Who can say, if he had done so and Ahmed had listened sympathetically, that Shahhat, as so often had happened in the past, would not have stayed unreconciled? But his character, or the demonic energies sent by Satan to prey upon his soul, or Ahmed's appearance—seated there so handsome, elegant and cold, with his air of worldly success and uncompromising authority—or perhaps all these things, decreed otherwise, so that it did not happen.

"I want to sell the buffalo," Shahhat repeated.

Ahmed showed the dull bewilderment of someone who is beginning to feel offended. His expression of sympathy and reasonableness slowly gave way to anger and indignation. His features became sharper, harder, and more forbidding.

"Look, Shahhat," he said, "the buffalo is not for you and not for me. I had to go through hell to get it for your sister and brothers. If you think that you can sell it now, you do not know your head from your body!"

There was still time for Shahhat to step back. Then his mother appeared in the doorway, and seeing her proud, anxious face, he again repeated, "I want to sell the buffalo."

Ahmed drew back with flashing eyes and said, coarsely forcing out each few words, "Look, Shahhat. Until this moment I have respected you because you are a man. But if you think you can touch that buffalo . . . "

"Nothing in this village or all the villages can change my mind!"

Ahmed was on his feet at once. "Be quiet! I am your father! Do not speak to me like this!" In fury he smashed his fist down on the wooden bench, trembling in his rage.

"My father is one year dead. I have no father. I have no mother also."

"Ekhrus!" Ahmed shrieked at him, in a piercing cry. "May your tongue be cut out so you cannot speak!"

"Malesh, malesh," said El Azap, stepping between them. "Let it be forgiven."

"No!" Shahhat thrust him aside. In fury, uncle and nephew began to curse each other. Face to face they hurled oaths and insults, Ahmed so trembling with anger he reached down to seize one of his sandals and raised it as if to strike Shahhat with it. Never in their lives, even in a frenzy, had they said so much that was cruel and unjust. In both, the selfishness of the unhappy showed itself—Shahhat because he felt himself to be such a failure, Ahmed in his injured pride at not being paid respect. Unhappy men are more selfish and unjust than the comparatively contented; misery does not unite people, as one might imagine, but divides them.

Ahmed, breathing heavily, lost control and hurled his sandal at Shahhat's face with terrific force. It struck with a loud, smacking sound. After a pause, Ahmed's face contracted with horror as if he could not believe what he had done. He relived slapping his wife and causing her lifelong deafness in the same way. He had taken her to doctor after doctor but nothing could be done. Now he had almost injured Shahhat in a like manner. Numbed and sickened he stumbled back to the bench and buried his face in his hands. El Azap took Ommohamed outside.

Shahhat's face bore the red mark of the blow, and in pain he lowered his head and stared at his uncle with that deep, ugly hatred only the grief-stricken can produce when they see someone they have always admired crumble before their eyes.

When he spoke, his voice came in an animal snarl. "If you put your shoes in my mouth, my uncle, I cannot speak. But if I should strike you now, even if you were ten men, I should destroy the ten!"

"Yes, that is right," Ahmed replied in a hollow, dead voice, barely paying attention as if everything was over. "I shall never set foot in this village again. I shall take my sister and Samah and the boys to my house and feed them and clothe them, everything. It is finished between us."

"Take your sister only. Samah is my sister, and Nubi and Ahmed are my brothers. They do not belong to you. They belong to me."

Ahmed went to Ommohamed and told her, "I want you to come and stay in my house. Go and fetch your children and your possessions."

"No, no, no!" she cried, speaking between her sobs. "I shall not leave my husband's house."

"Yes. It is right, my sister."

Ahmed turned and strode down the road, moving rapidly as if eager to leave them behind as quickly as he could. When he reached his house near the Nile, he told his wife, "I shall never return to their village." He repeated everything three times, the Moslem way of expressing irrevocable decision. "Never, never, never! I don't want, I don't want, I don't want!" Ahmed's thoughts were unjust, cruel, and inhuman. He wanted to get a pistol or a knife and go back and kill Shahhat. He passed sentence on both Shahhat and Ommohamed, and his heart ached with his contempt for them. Then, cooling a little, he began to pray, whispering, "I demand help from the God against this dangerous evil. A devil whispered to me to kill Shahhat. Oh, my God, Allah, forgive me!"

When he grew calmer, he told his wife, "I want nothing more to do with them, the son or the mother. I wash my hands of them."

When Shahhat returned home he did not speak to his mother but bathed, changed his tunic, and gathered his few possessions into a small bag. Then he turned to his brothers and said, "Nubi! Ahmed! Tell your mother goodbye. We go to Cairo."

Ommohamed could not believe he was serious. "Yes, go, go!" she mocked him. Calling up all her will and pride she told him haughtily, "Your uncle told me half he possesses is mine. But I told him I shall not leave this house. I said this was not Shahhat's house. It was my husband's house and I shall stay here until I die."

"Take the land also!" Shahhat shouted at her. "I don't want it! I'm not coming back!"

"Hah!" she cried, her voice rising. "You think that without you no one will look after it!" She burst into harsh laughter, her eyes bright with fury, and summoning up all her pride and will, she shrieked at him, "If you found me lying on the railway tracks cut to pieces you would not care! If Ahmed even hears I am weary, he comes to me!"

Shahhat pushed her aside. "If all this house falls about your head, my mother, I will not lift a finger!"

He turned and strode out, the two boys hurrying to catch up. They were barefoot and wearing the grimy cotton tunics they habitually did. Seeing they were really going, Ommohamed pursued them, panting, almost falling, a frantic figure, her veil falling to her shoulders, her hair flying in the wind. "I have no more use for you, Shahhat!" she screamed after him, so that all the neighbors came to their doors and windows. "Go! Go! I have lost all hope of you changing! Never set foot in my house again!" All at once she stopped and began sobbing. Then, summoning up the cruelest thing she could think of, she shrilly screamed, straining her lungs:

"I prefer Ahmed to you!"

These were the last of his mother's words that Shahhat heard. Ommohamed did not realize what she had done. In her furious repudiation—and Shahhat would remember that screamed "I prefer Ahmed to you!" as long as he lived—she had set him free.

Left alone, Ommohamed went up to her bed, fell onto it and sobbed into a pillow. For hours she lay there dressed, staring at the ceiling, telling Samah to send the shocked neighbors away. She felt that the whole room from floor to ceiling was filled with a giant block of iron, and that if the iron were only removed, then all would be well. Then she remembered there was no iron, only Shahhat's departure. Time stretched into eternity. She heard Amr's voice crying the evening call to prayer. Now and then people could be heard speaking downstairs. Her thoughts turned to Nubi and Ahmed. The hearing to make herself the children's legal guardian, rather than leaving it to Shahhat as male head of the family, was just a day away. Suppose Shahhat had not been joking and really meant to take the boys to Cairo with him? He was just vengeful enough to keep them away from the hearing. What would the judge do if they were not present? Alarmed, aroused, and keyed up by the thought, Ommohamed hurried downstairs, looking untidy and unattractive with her swollen face and rumpled clothes. She flung her long black cloak about her, had Samah saddle the donkey, and left the house, riding rapidly toward the Nile. Ahmed was not at home, and his wife had seen nothing of Shahhat or the boys. Distraught, Ommohamed left the donkey there, took the ferry across the river, and hired a carriage to the railway station. They had been seen there buying tickets and boarding the evening train for Cairo. It had gone. Ommohamed returned home in a state of utter despair.

She need not have worried. Since Shahhat did not appear to dispute her request, and indeed proved his irresponsibility by keeping the boys away, the judge awarded her the children's guardianship without difficulty. Ahmed went to court with her. Afterward Ommohamed felt guilty; in her heart she knew Shahhat would never lay claim to the land, even what was his own share by right. He was not a good son to her, but he was very much her son. He had the same fierce pride.

A week went by. If anyone came from Cairo, Ommohamed would come to ask them if Shahhat and the boys had been seen. She feared to go herself; how could she find them in a city of eight million people? When no one knew anything, her heart hardened against Shahhat. She would never forgive him now. "I have decided," she told Samah, "that Shahhat will never again set foot in this house as long as I am alive."

If anyone asked about him, she would reply with wrathful bitterness, "He is dead. He is better dead."

Nine days after the quarrel, Ommohamed was preparing cheese when a neighbor came to the door crying that Nubi and Ahmed were coming up the road. Ommohamed could not believe it. Stunned, she leaped up, spilling the milk, and rushed to the door. The boys turned into the lane, and, seeing them, she was filled with such relief and joy that she rushed out to gather them in her arms, weeping and kissing them over and over. Then she saw how weary and thin they looked, and that they were still wearing the same tunics they had worn when they left home, which were now filthy. Her anger rising, she fiercely questioned them. They said that Shahhat had forced them to return; they did not want to leave him, but there was no more money. He had borrowed two pounds, taken them to the railway station, and left them in the care of a soldier from Qurna who was coming home. He gave the soldier the money, but when the train conductor came, the soldier made them hide under the seats and kept the two pounds himself. He refused to part with a single piastre, and the two boys had gone without eating and had to borrow four piastres from a man from the village they found in the market to pay the ferry boatman. In Cairo they had stayed in the small room of a distant cousin of Abd el Baset, a waiter in a cafe, who fed them morning and evening. Shahhat was gone all day, looking for work. He had found nothing. Nubi was sick; he told his mother he had diarrhea and had vomited on the train.

Tears flowed down Ommohamed's face, and when they completed their story she fell to her knees and began wailing like a woman in mourning. "Come," she cried, "come, Abd el Baset, come to me! Come, Abd el Baset, come to see Nubi and Ahmed! Come, my husband, and see what Shahhat has done!" Su'ad and Batah came from their house, but Ommohamed could not be calmed. "What can I do?" she shrieked. "Nothing!

There is a God, and He can do what satisfies Him!" With sudden violence she ripped off her veil and threw it aside, turned her wet face to the sky, and threw up her arms.

"Oh, my God," she cried in such a terrible voice that all who heard her were chilled. "If I am evil, punish me! But if you find Shahhat has done evil, you must burn my son in the fires of hell!"

Of Fierce Desert Horsemen and Allah's Will

O N THE EIGHTH OF AUGUST, a Friday, Shahhat returned, in time for the Feast of Abu Hagag, the Moslem patron saint of Luxor, which was soon to begin. As Shahhat stepped outside the railway station he saw at the far end of the street near the river that men on long ladders were hanging long strings of lightbulbs—festooning the mosque and tomb of the saint, which was set within the granite walls of the ancient temple of Luxor. He was facing directly into the late, flat, afternoon sun, and great shafts of light pierced through the open spaces between the treetops and minarets and temple pylons. Abu Hagag's tomb rose from a great court built by Ramses II, and against the blinding sun the strings of lights glittered like jewels. Behind the temple was the Nile and the ferry boat that would take him across to the western bank. Ordinarily Shahhat would have hurried there, but now he had no particular destination, and he stood and stared at the bright spectacle for a long time.

The Feast would last ten days and each night would attract tens of thousands of *fellaheen* from all the surrounding villages. They would make pilgrimages to commemorate the holy patron on the site of his life and death.

All through each night thousands of men would gather—as the deep, hoarse voices of poetry singers were amplified to a deafening roar by loudspeakers—to dance themselves into a frenzy of religious ecstasy, swaying and twisting and turning their bodies for hours on end with the utmost violence. The air would be rent with the piercing, joyous ululations of women and the voices of the poetry singers rising ever higher and faster.

Vendors would go about crying, "A grain of salt in the eye of he who doth not bless the Prophet!" and there would be wandering processions of *darweeshes,* twirling wildly about and brandishing long staves with lanterns. Outside the temple walls in a large spacious park would be found bands of musicians with bagpipes, flutes, drums, and cymbals; conjurers, buffoons, jugglers, belly dancers, puppeteers, and wrestlers. On the grass, swings and whirlgigs would be erected for the children and there would be dozens of stalls stocked with coffee and sweetmeats. The villagers would form innumerable circles to perform dances and fight mock battles with wooden staves or twirl about with knives clenched in their teeth, the sharp, pointed blade poised against their inner cheek. Everyone would noisily greet the slightest acquaintances like dearest friends, and great quantities of wine, liquor, beer, and hashish would be consumed. After midnight black-shrouded women could be found in shadowed huddles under the trees willing to give their favors for a price. With the crowds milling about, the blare of the many bands of musicians all playing at once, the hawkers' loud, sobbing cries, the imprecations of the many performers, the beats of drums, the piercing scream of flutes and the gnashing of cymbals, the laughter, screams, and shouts and, rising above it all, the amplified prayers from the tomb, there would be an enormous din. In the daytime, there would be more processions, camels gorgeously caparisoned, gaily decorated carriages full of flowers and children, hordes of barefoot pilgrims waving branches to the chant of Koranic verses, and, as in the days of the pharaohs, *fellucas* at full sail would be borne through the streets on donkey carts.

But all this would be as nothing compared to the appearance on the final night of the Feast, August twentieth, of fierce Bedouin horsemen, brought from the Arabian desert who, brandishing wooden staves over their heads, screaming thrilling cries, and galloping furiously back and forth on a narrow track through the crowd, would commemorate how Islam itself rose out of the sands and rock to proclaim its just God of war

209

and the desert. The rest Shahhat might miss but never these horsemen, who stirred his Bedouin soul to its core.

That night and for days thereafter Shahhat slept at the house of El Azap. He did not stir out during the blistering heat of the day, but after the wind rose from the Libyan Desert each evening, he would climb the cliffs and walk along the ridge above the valley for hours. As the twentieth, when the moon would be full, drew closer, the cliffs and desert were illuminated in pale light, and Shahhat could be seen upon them after dark, a striding, restless figure, his tunic billowing out behind him as he took these solitary walks. When El Azap asked him why he went up to the desert each night, for this faithful friend had a horror of it himself, Shahhat replied he went there to pray. He explained, "Other men may pray for a good harvest or money or a good wife. I ask Allah only that I may die."

Once he passed Ommohamed on the canal path; she turned her head and went quickly by. Almost from the moment he stepped down from the train she had known he was back and could speak of little else. She was wildly inconsistent; one moment she would be cursing Shahhat, and the next she would weep and blame divine providence. Then she would turn contrite. "Because I have been angry with my son, Allah is punishing me and the crops are dying. I want to complain to Allah."

"No!" Samah told her, shocked. Was it not an article of faith to accept the fate that Allah gave one?

Ommohamed would often declare, "I prefer Ahmed. Even if he has not set foot in my house since the day Shahhat left, and has not asked about me, I prefer him. He cannot leave me."

Often in her anguish she blamed herself for having spoken too much. "Shahhat is like his father," she told Samah. "He does not like too much speaking." She went so far as to wish Shahhat had hit her, as Abd el Baset had, and she recalled how her son had saved her that time when Abd el Baset, in a burst of temper, had almost struck her with a hoe.

She deeply missed Shahhat. "When Shahhat worked in the fields, Samah," she would sigh, "I was relieved and happy. Now I am so tired and weary, what can I do? I bought six sacks of *Nitrokima* for the sugar, but now Faruk says we must have two more. Where shall I get it? If Shahhat were here, we could discuss such things and decide upon them together."

Soon she was voicing suspicions that Sobhy and Hagg Ali had bewitched Shahhat. "They think if he goes far from me," she told

Samah, "I shall be at their mercy." This explanation satisfied her need to fix the blame elsewhere, and she consulted Sheikha Daiyi, who agreed Shahhat must have been put under an evil spell. The sorceress filled an empty bowl with water, covered it with a cloth, spun it around as she chanted from the Koran, removed the covering, and peered inside. The water was gone, and in its place she found threads from what she said was one of Shahhat's tunics, fragments of an evil charm, and bits of magic herbs and roots. At her instructions, Ommohamed took them home and burned them. But for once Sheikha Daiyi's magic failed her.

Dismayed when the days passed and Ahmed failed to come, Ommohamed at last went to his house by the Nile. He sent her away at once with harsh words, saying, "If anything happens to me, woman, it is on your head! How can I hold up my head in front of the people? My nephew is not good and you are the cause. I will seek another city to live, far from your house!"

It was then she knew how desperately she wanted Shahhat back. "In the past," she sighed to Samah, her only comforter, "if anyone said the slightest word against me, Shahhat would threaten to kill them. He always gave me his money to keep. He agreed with everything I said. Oh, my God, what have I done?'"

It was not only mother and son who wanted a reconciliation—all the village was concerned. Everyone came to urge Shahhat to go home— Faruk, Sha'atu, old Yusef, and his friends Abd er Rahman, Snake, El Azap, and El Got, even, to Shahhat's surprise, Hagg Abd el Mantaleb himself. "If your uncle saw you working in your fields and that you were good, he would be ashamed," Hagg told him. "Then you would cut all the wagging tongues in the village."

One morning Shahhat went out to the cane fields and spoke with Faruk about the shortage of water. That afternoon, coming to cut grass, Samah found him making mud bricks to mend a broken place in the garden wall; she rushed home to tell Ommohamed.

At last Shahhat gave in and one evening agreed to go with El Azap to see his mother. As they walked through the village he became agitated and nervous, but his friend would not let him turn back. A storm had been blowing in the desert, and now a white, dusty mist hung about the temple walls and the houses and in the open spaces between the trees. No one was about, and seeing the mist-shrouded houses and Sha'atu's shuttered cafe and the empty desert behind it, Shahhat thought the village looked dead and empty, as if in a dream, a deserted ruin like the temple.

211

Up on the desert cliffs the world below had been to him great and mysterious and he himself older and stronger than anyone. Now, going home, it was as if he were descending from one of the furthest unlimited ridges of life.

When they reached the house everything seemed smaller and diminished from the picture Shahhat had been carrying in his mind. Even Ommohamed, waiting in the doorway, seemed shrunken and older, her shoulders bent forward in an unfamiliar way. She was expecting Shahhat to kiss the top of her veil and beg forgiveness. He was expecting her to rush forward to greet him with tears and embraces. Instead neither of them did anything.

Ommohamed had presence, and except for her trembling fingers she was at once harder and colder. She greeted El Azap heartily, "Best arrival to you!" and ignored Shahhat's presence altogether. When she offered El Azap some candy and he joked, "Thanks but I wanted two pieces," she managed a little laugh. Supper had been laid out on a table on the open rooftop terrace: four pigeons stuffed with rice and a large *fatir,* a special favorite of Shahhat's made of flour, onions, chicken soup, and sour cream. El Azap ate greedily with loud smacking noises. Shahhat took nothing but sat as silent and still as a statue, listening to his mother.

For Ommohamed talked without stopping, gossiping in the most lively manner. The family was fine—praise be to God!—but there was still not enough water at Sombat. Abd er Rahman had bought land and not a taxi after all. Sha'atu's wife, Zeyneb, and the wife of Sobhy had both given birth to baby sons, but try as she would she could not remember what names they had been given. "Munkar and Nekeer," El Azap joked, and Ommohamed laughed with gusto. She sat on the floor with three small grandchildren scrambling on and off her lap and tugging at her arms as she spoke, a picture of maternal contentment. Samah brought tea. When Shahhat did not touch his, the embarrassed El Azap quickly drank both glasses and began to perspire for it. Fatih and Namat were divorced, Ommohamed went on in her spirited delivery, but Namat could not re-marry as she was carrying Fatih's child. Suniya was also pregnant again and would soon leave the village to join her husband in Aswan. Batah was to be married in two more days to the Jamasah. Ommohamed's voice fell to a hushed whisper as she said there had been rumours Batah's re-jected cousin, Ali, had run away from the army and had been seen in Luxor, vowing to avenge his family's honor. It could become a blood feud, with killings on both sides. Batah was a bad, shameless, willful girl.

212

Then Hagg Abd el Mantaleb and Salem were feuding again, this time quarreling over the amount of rent Salem was to pay Hagg for some land. That very day Hagg had gone to the police inspector. Old Yusef said, if anyone could believe the old gossipmonger, that . . . Ommohamed went on and on, her voice suiting the episode, now a shocked whisper, an indignant squawk, an amused chuckle, a grim judgment, speaking with relish but keeping an anxious eye on Shahhat. He stared stonily across the rooftops and palm trees. But he listened to his mother's voice and thought how life in the village was a comedy that went endlessly on. Once he would have shared her enjoyment, but now her gay recital filled him with an unutterable sadness.

Outside he told El Azap, "When I entered the house, I felt my chest become narrow. I could not catch my breath. I felt like I was being choked, that some black devil had his hands around my throat." He had not exchanged a word with his mother, nor even a glance. "I'm a man, not a boy. I can find my own place. In a day or two I'll ask the government for papers, and as soon as I can I'll head for Suez. Or maybe even Libya or Saudi Arabia." His voiced lacked conviction. "My father used to bring her much money from gambling. But I can't do that. I'm not my father."

When El Azap let her know the next morning that Shahhat was going away again, Ommohamed at once decided to hold the last rites for Abd el Baset five days after the Feast of Abu Hagag. She knew Shahhat would have to stay for the ceremony; it was the eldest son's duty to serve the sheikhs during a prayer performance. She decided she would invite all two hundred sheikhs from the surrounding villages after all, promising herself it would be her last extravagance. She could slaughter two sheep. Losing no time, she hurried at noon to borrow fifty pounds more from Hagg Abd el Mantaleb. Like Abd el Baset before her, when faced with disaster she had to show everyone, her son not least of all. She refused to believe she had lost him.

Three o'clock in the afternoon. The village lay sleeping and still; life had deserted it. Shahhat was mending the broken garden wall. Ommohamed had been right. As soon as El Azap told him when the last rites would be held, he knew he would have to stay on for them, if only in respect to his father's memory. A solitary black-shrouded figure went by on the road; it was Batah, going from house to house to invite the village women to her wedding. Shahhat admired her courage. Let the villagers condemn her with their gossip. She was not going to let her chance at happiness slip through her fingers the way he had.

He worked only a few minutes more before screams shattered the village quiet, screams such as Shahhat had never heard before. He ran barefoot across the field in the direction of the screams. Some small boys and girls who were playing in the road began to cry and shout. An old woman came rushing toward Shahhat, wailing and wringing her hands. Doors and windows were flung open, and people came running from the nearest houses. Hundreds of pigeons, roused by the disturbance, rose from the temple walls and began to fly high overhead in great, sweeping circles. A crowd was gathering near the edge of the village. Shahhat pushed his way through to the front and stopped. Those from behind ran up, gasping and trembling, jostled those ahead, started to speak, and then they too fell silent like the rest. It was suddenly quiet. No one said a word.

Some distance ahead of them in the road Batah lay unconscious and moaning, her clothes ripped open so that her naked body lay white and exposed in the harsh afternoon sunlight. Her veil had been torn off and her long black hair lay twisted over the pebbles. The sun was so blinding every detail was distinctly visible. Over her crouched a young man in a soldier's uniform. Shahhat recognized him as Hasan's son Ali. He held a military revolver in one hand. He waved it toward them and shouted that he would kill anyone who came closer. There was blood on his hand, and when Shahhat saw the blood between Batah's legs he knew what had happened. In the village a bridegroom broke a virgin's hymen gently, with two fingers, on their wedding night, with her mother present to hold and comfort the girl in her pain. Afterward the mother displayed a bloody cloth to women present at the marriage as proof of her daughter's virginity. The soldier had upheld his family's honor. Batah would not go to her Jamasah a virgin.

No one moved until the soldier stood up, turned away, and ran up the embankment by the temple walls. He soon disappeared into the dunes of the desert. Still the crowd stood stunned. Finally Ommohamed, Su'ad, Bahiya, and some other women rushed forward to gather around the silent girl, shielding her nakedness with their long black garments. Other women fell to the side of the road and sat wailing, as if someone had died. Then they carried Batah to her mother's house.

Shahhat listened to the men's voices around him. He numbly

214

realized their sympathies were with the soldier, not Batah. If I had married Suniya, it came to him, they would have killed me. He stopped listening. Overhead the pigeons, uttering mournful cries, flew swiftly in great circles against the sun. The men began to drift off. Shahhat gasped for breath, so passionate was his desire to go far away.

Shahhat hurriedly climbed the narrow trail which traversed the rocky cliff face, not stopping until he reached the highest ridge above the valley. There he sank down upon some rocks, facing away from the valley toward the empty desert. His muscles ached, sweat ran into his eyes, he breathed heavily, filling his lungs with fresh cool air. All about him was sky, an intense blue above the dusty haze of desert and valley. He wrapped his arms tightly around his chest as if against some inward chill, holding his body tensely, like a beggar hounded from the streets, broken and powerless, or a kicked animal which expects to be kicked again. He sat for a long time this way without moving. He looked like someone lost in space, frozen forever in a pose of despair.

Time passed. The sun began its descent. Soon it sank into a dusty purple mist on the desert's edge. The air grew cold as if to remind him of the narrow limits of man's freedom. Shahhat stirred, knowing he would soon have to return to the valley just to keep warm.

Over and over he asked himself, "What am I going to do?" Like anyone numb and paralyzed with depression, he was unable to think beyond the question to any future. He had spoken of going away, to Suez or other Arab lands, but in his *fellah*'s heart he felt to leave his village was to die. He stared into the desert where nothing but sand dunes stretched to the horizon, and he longed to lose himself forever in such calm emptiness. The rocky cliffs would keep the world away and protect him in boundless space. "The Bedouin lives the best," he thought. "He can take his freedom. When a man lives in a village and becomes a villager, there is always trouble. Two or three Bedouins alone in the desert would take care of each other and love each other much."

Vaguely he imagined himself, a man, a tiny speck, disappearing into this vast, uninhabited solitude. Sand and rock might be his only companions, but he would not fear the emptiness nor the echo that would reverberate with his every footfall. He longed to escape into this free life

215

Shahhat escapes to the hills above the village.

he had never lived. Perhaps he dimly recalled things heard about Arabia long ago. Or he had inherited this vision of a life of freedom along with his flesh and blood from his Bedouin ancestors. He kept his eyes fixed on the desert a long while.

It was getting colder. He climbed up to a rocky out-cropping and looked down the sheer drop of the cliffs to the slopes and valley below. In the fading light the houses and trees, the flat green plain with its broad, winding river, the ruined temples, the canals and roads, were so diminished, and the people, as they moved about, such tiny specks, they seemed

From the rocky cliffs outside Berat Shahhat stares into the desert.

illimitably distant and remote. He could see, strung out a mile from South to north on the slopes just below, the twisting road to the Valley of the Queens, the two crumbling stone giants of the Colossi of Memnon, the Rammuseum to the left, the canyon into the cliffside temple of Hatchepsut, and winding above it, the trail up the ridge and down again to the Valley of the Kings. All these Shahhat had known since childhood. The stone reliefs and hieroglyphics might tell of wars and massacres, but the blood and misery was long past; now they were just pictures on a wall, and the ruins had the same soothing calm of the desert.

It was almost dark, but to the north, around a bend in the river,

Shahhat surveys the Nile valley below.

he could see the white sails of three *fellucas*. To Shahhat, the Nile was
el Bahr, the sea, the giver of life. This was the month, August, when the
river always rose to flood its banks. Now, just since his fifteenth year, the
High Dam at Aswan had held back these waters. The Nile would never
flood again. Shahhat wondered what his life would have been like if the
river had not been tamed. Poorer, but lived in the old natural rhythms
and certainties. For the dam had brought the incessant field work, even in
hottest summer. It had brought the diesel pumps, the fights to load sugar
cane, the feuds and frustrations. It had created the inspectors, the Lameis,

the Faruks, the Hagg Abd el Mantalebs. It had fed his mother's extravagance and fierce expectations. To Shahhat, order and reason were limited and no scientific or technical progress could enlarge them; rather they made life more difficult. For did not hidden demons, blind fate, the solicitations of Satan, the hot fury of one's own blood, await every man in ambush at the crossroads? Why, then, change?

He heard distant sounds of life and listened, straining his ears. He could make out the doleful braying of a donkey. A vendor's familiar wailing cry, "Onions sweet as honey!" A bagpipe playing a wedding tune and the faint wail of mourning women. Someone had married, and someone had died. He thought of his mother the night before, gossiping about the comedy of village life. And of Batah, lying in the road. At once the sense of numb despair returned.

The moon started to rise. It was almost full as tomorrow would be the last day of the Feast of Abu Hagag. The valley grew dark, and around the huddled masses of houses and trees began to flow a sea of thin, moonlit mist, and, what remained long in Shahhat's memory, wisps of vapor, white as ghosts, floated slowly across the open expanse of fields. Near the moon, yellow and enormous as it rose over the curve of the ridge, swarmed transparent patches of cloud. The whole Nile Valley, it seemed, was made of black shadows and wandering wisps of light. At first he saw no sign of life. Then small twinkling yellow glows appeared here and there, village oil lamps, however feebly, reaching even these heights.

And Shahhat felt as if Allah himself were close, looking down, just as he was, from the sky. The star-filled desert sky was so deep and incomprehensible that he imagined it was from here that the angels watched and saw all that was going on below. In the valley Satan and his genii might make men evil and violent. But here at least, high on the desert ridge, all was peaceful, and Allah ruled unchallenged. As he looked down into the shadowed valley, Shahhat remembered Suniya's words that the sunrise was like the land expressing thanks. He had teased her for being *pharaoni,* worshipping the sun. But now he thought perhaps the earth was waiting to emerge into goodness, just as the sun would rise in a few more hours over the Arabian Desert from the night.

Life might seem unrelenting and absurd. But things were what they were, predestined, and part of Allah's plan. That was what human life meant. "Everything is from Allah," he said aloud. "I cannot decide anything. Everything we are is from him."

The path down the cliff face was steep but Shahhat did not think

219

about his strength nor where he put his feet. Sometimes the moon shone in front of him, sometimes behind. As he neared the lower slopes the jackals out on the desert began their hideous, derisive cries. To Shahhat they were like Satan's demons, taunting him with doubts, "See, what will happen, Shahhat, what will happen to you?"

By late afternoon the road to the Nile was full of people, streaming into Luxor for the last night of the Feast. Ommohamed was at home helping to care for Batah, all disapproval for the moment forgotten. She had forbidden Nubi and Ahmed to go to the Feast as Abd el Baset's final rites were still to be held, and the family remained in mourning. But the two boys slipped away and found Shahhat at the ferry landing. He was with El Azap and some friends, and he told the boys to stay close to his side once they entered the crowds on the eastern bank; he would send them home with someone before dark.

His brothers scarcely recognized Shahhat. At El Azap's house he had taken pains to dress for the occasion. Gone were his old black *gallabiya* and gray scarf, the bare feet, and the stubble chin. Instead, bathed, shaven, his moustache trimmed, and wearing a clean white turban and flowing white tunic, evidently new, he had such a handsome, impressive air about him, he seemed quite another person altogether.

A special steamer had been brought from Aswan to handle the large crowds crossing the river; tens of thousands were expected. The boys, rather in awe of Shahhat, were just as glad when he went up to the upper deck to stand alone by the railing. As Shahhat watched the river slide past, the Nile had never looked so beautiful. The late afternoon sun shone blindingly on the water and was reflected in the air itself, which had a golden shimmer and was pure on the river, as it never was in the dusty village. From the deck, the river as it shone in the sun, was of a color impossible to name. It was a tender and soft combination of dark blue, silver, and green; in parts, the water shone copper-like, and in parts, liquid sunshine crossed from shore to shore. And all these seemed to Shahhat to combine in a harmony of greens and blues and silvers to exhale a life-giving warmth. He did not want to leave the river and was sorry when the ferry soon reached the eastern bank and everyone scrambled ashore.

The streets of Luxor were filled with people, and Shahhat, his friends, and the boys at once were swept into a stream of men surging toward the tomb of the saint, which they could see ahead rising above Luxor Temple for it stood in a royal courtyard built by Ramses II, the greatest of all the pharaohs. Slowly, with men pressing about on every side, they advanced from the ferry landing to the police station, then they pushed their way through a narrow lane to the market road, went past a row of shops, and at last turned west to face the river as they were carried in what was now a human sea back toward the Nile. Once inside the temple grounds, great clouds of dust that had been stirred up by the crowd hung over the thousands of turbaned heads, creating a thick, yellow haze. In this unnatural light, they found themselves directly facing the descending sun and had to shade their eyes. Shafts of blinding light pierced the open spaces between the temple pylon, obelisks and colossal statues, the tops of trees, and the saint's tomb. The air swarmed with brilliant particles of dust. Everything appeared as if through bright yellow fog: the tomb festooned with flags, the long glittering loops of naked light bulbs hung between its minarets, the soaring granite pylon, the transparent trees.

With growing excitement, they pressed forward. The way was almost impassable. All about bodies pushed against them. Beads of sweat formed on Shahhat's forehead; he seized the hot, moist hands of the two boys tightly in his own. All about men roared greetings at each other in harsh, excited voices, but nothing could be heard above the general uproar. The heat of the pushing, tightly-packed bodies become suffocating, distorting sight and sound. Shahhat felt his head was swimming. He looked across the turbaned heads, now at the minarets, now at the tomb in its golden haze, and he looked so directly into the sun sparks flew before his eyes. The brilliant dust and the shafts of sunlight that laid swatches of blinding brightness on the white turbans before him affirmed to Shahhat that this golden sight was not mere dust and light but a vision; that this magic spectacle with its fantastic shimmer and roaring multitude before the saint's tomb—which itself expressed the vanity of life and the existence of something higher and eternal—called to him to forget himself, to fade into memories, to die. His past was painful, his future insignificant, and this magic moment, this one moment of life, would soon be past, would have been swept away just like everything else that had ever happened to him. Why, then, live?

"The horses!" someone close to him cried.

He turned and saw them. They came from the left in a roaring fury, as if galloping at full speed over the heads of the crowd itself. There was a thunder of hooves, a cloud of dust, then the heads of the Bedouin riders themselves, thrown back, faces contorted, brown neck muscles straining like ropes, fierce howls and shouts, staves brandished in the air, driving in their spurs, the swish and blow of their crops on the horses' flanks, the horses as wild and frenzied as their riders. Against the blinding sunlight, in the roar and tumult, they were horsemen out of dreams and legends. Shahhat could not imagine anything more magnificent.

He pushed forward, his hands clutching the boys' shoulders, jostling them into position in front of the men so they could see. Policemen, frantically swinging sticks, were trying to push the crowd back and keep a path clear. The horsemen would gallop in one direction, shouting praises of Allah in fierce, thrilling cries, then wheel about and furiously gallop back again, just missing each other and the men lining their way by a hair's breadth. *"Allahu Akbar! Allahu Akbar!"* rose the Islamic war cry. When there was a momentary pause, men would break past the policemen, and heedless of their lives, run across the path in hopes of getting a better look from the other side. Then the horsemen would thunder past again; everyone was caught up in the wild, roaring, passionate frenzy of the Bedouin riders.

Shahhat watched, stunned, amazed, and then overcome with ecstasy. The air's dazzling color—a color he had never seen before—the sky, the minarets, the roar about him, and the riders' frenzied passion filled his being with irresponsible joy and told him he would find himself, that somewhere far away, somewhere in infinite space, he would find deliverance and all he sought in his troubled spirit. When he looked earnestly at the silhouettes of the galloping horsemen, black and rushing against the exploding sparks of the sun, and heard the rapturous roar all about him, he saw himself as in his dream all dressed in gleaming white, his black rags burnt, and running, running, like these wild, frenzied desert riders, running through the wondrous garden of glittering light and tumultuous voices praising God, unhampered, free, himself at last. "It is up to Allah," he whispered.

He rushed forward.

He seemed to safely reach the other side. Still, he hesitated, turned back to face the oncoming horseman with a look of apology on his face. Then the horse was upon him, and he was swept under it.

It seemed as if suddenly there was total silence, but there could not have been for everyone was shouting and screaming at once. It also seemed as if time slowed down so that the horses' plunging hooves and the white tunic and the clouds of thick yellow dust all rolled over and over again together slowly, the white turning red, and the slowly pounding hooves and the yellow dust, rolling over and over again slowly. That is how Shahhat's two younger brothers would remember it: the sudden silence and the hooves rising and falling and the whiteness turning to redness and the dust, rolling over and over and over, all slowly together, slowly.

El Azap reached him first. He fell to his knees and cradled Shahhat's head in his arms. The boys saw the head was bare and hung loosely to one side and that the face was a mask of blood and dust. Then men lifted up the body and carried it into the crowd, and someone roughly grasped their hands and dragged them forward. They saw it was Abd er Rahman and that he was swinging out with his fist and kicking men in front to make way, shouting curses all the while. The crowd seemed to be moving with them, and then through an open space they glimpsed Shahhat's body lying against a wall. Men were bending over it and others stood in front of them with heavy sticks and were flailing out at anyone like madmen, shouting to keep back, keep back. Bodies pushed against them, and for some minutes they could see nothing and scarcely breathe. And then they were being dragged through the crowd again and the boys found themselves being thrust into an open carriage, and there was Shahhat on the seat beside them. He sat bent over, his head resting on an arm. They saw his tunic was torn and bloody, and through the tears his skin also glistened wet and red. Without moving or lifting his head so they could not see his face, but only his curly hair now matted with dust and blood, he spoke to them. They did not know he was in shock and later would not remember ordering them in a harsh, urgent voice to follow El Azap to the ferry, cross the Nile and go to the house of their uncle Ahmed where they would be safe. They heard only a voice so raw and terrible that when the carriage reached the hospital and men carried Shahhat inside the gates, they were glad to get away from this unfamiliar bloody, broken figure now that they understood that Allah had not chosen that Shahhat die after all.

"La ilaha illa-llah! La ilaha illa-llah! Allah! Allah! Allah! Allah! Allah! . . ."

The roar of deep, hoarse voices rose in excitement outside the house, as the ejaculations came faster and more violently. Shahhat waited for his mother to fill another tray with glasses of tea. It was past midnight and the prayers for Abd el Baset's soul were reaching a high pitch of religious frenzy.

Shahhat had been up and about only that day. Although his head was still bandaged and his body stiff and aching, he had insisted upon fulfilling the duties of his father's eldest surviving son. He had been fortunate. A hoof had gashed the side of his right temple, causing heavy bleeding and needing seven stitches. He might always bear the scar. His right leg and arm were still livid with bruises. But they would heal, and the frightening tightness of his breathing the first few days was gone. When the doctor told him he was amazed he had escaped worse injury, Shahhat had said, "Praise be to Allah." He did not speak about the accident. If pressed, he quoted the proverb, "To each the fate that Allah gives him." Interest in the episode soon faded; what mattered to the village was that Shahhat had come home.

The night Shahhat was hurt, waiting at the hospital, Ommohamed had recalled her whole life with him, from beginning to end, in all its details. Then it came to her that her son promised to be an exceptional, a rare—compared with everyone else she knew, even Ahmed—a whole man. And remembering how forgiving Abd el Baset had been with Shahhat and how fond the villagers were of her son, she understood there was good reason to predict for him a satisfying life. With dread she imagined the loneliness of her own future years without his presence in the house. When he came home she had intended to tell him that the past was all a mistake, that they could begin again, that he was at last the adult man she needed, her like, her equal, her son.

But in the few days he had been home Shahhat had said nothing, and Ommohamed lived in dread he planned to go away. She knew she should tell him that everything would begin anew, that she would watch her spending, they would live simply, he would make all the decisions and be the man of the house. But in her pride she could not bring herself to do it.

"*Allah! Allah! Allah! Allah! Allah! . . .*"

The roar of almost two hundred voices rose in deafening persistence. The village had never seen such a *zikr* before even though everyone knew Ommohamed had borrowed from Hagg Abd el Mantaleb to pay for it. Shahhat took the tray from his mother and turned to go.

"Shahhat!" she burst out, at once bringing her hand to her

mouth. She was terrified he would go once the final rites for Abd el Baset were over.

"What do you want?"

Ommohamed could not speak and knew she probably never would. "Peace," she said at last and turned away. She began to cry and pressed a handkerchief to her eyes. She was crying out of sheer agitation with herself, conscious she was close to losing everything.

"Come, stop that," Shahhat said, putting down the tray and reaching out. The shoulders on which his hands rested were warm and heaving. He saw how small and frail she had become and knew her life had already begun to fade and wither. Once he would have resisted her with whatever arguments came into his head. It was clear to him that the most difficult and complicated years with his mother were still ahead. But he did not care. He felt only profound compassion for her. Whatever happened, he told himself, it would be Allah's will. Aware, in his surrender, that he was giving up a freedom he might never find again, he also felt both grief and joy.

Seasons come and go. The winter nights, dark, long, cold, all too quickly become the heat of summer. Then the shadows start to lengthen under the languid, transparent acacia trees along the canal, the harvesters bring home the summer grain, white egrets feed on newly irrigated fields, and it is winter again. Time goes by, and in the course of this time Shahhat does little but go to his fields and return, and it seems to him that he knows every stone, every tree, on the dusty cart road between Sombat and his house. Here is his past and his present, and he can no longer imagine any other future but his fields, the road to the village and back, and again his fields and the house. Soon he is to marry. Ommohamed and Ahmed approve of his bride, a cousin from their family. Shahhat has told El Azap, "This girl is not beautiful or anything like that. But I've watched her and she's a good girl and works hard. She will be good for the house."

Ommohamed has squandered her widow's pension to install electricity, the envy of her neighbors who make do with oil lamps. Hagg Abd el Mantaleb is so enraged he threatens to take her to court unless she repays her old debts, to Bahiya's mortification. If Shahhat rebukes her, Ommohamed replies, "Allah will provide." She still has her heart set on a pilgrimage to Mecca before she dies. The sugar harvests save the family from disaster. Someday the date palms in the garden may even bring a bit of prosperity. Shahhat handles most of the money now; the more independent he is, the more petulant Ommohamed becomes. But if there are quarrels, everyone knows reconciliations will follow. The villagers have grown accustomed to the ways of the son and the mother, just as they have come to tolerate, if not accept, Batah's marriage to a Jamasah. Suniya has left the village for good, and so furtive did they keep their words and glances, no one knows how much Shahhat misses her.

A certain fatalism has overtaken Shahhat, and he no longer thinks about the past. All the wildness of his youth—the fierce hopes and passions—has become vague and formless, like something half-remembered, like a dream. Yet he is as easily amused and quick of comprehension as he ever was. No one tells a better story in Sha'atu's cafe of an evening.

AFTERWORD

*A*s a reporter who writes about peasants, I would like to explain how Shahhat's story was written. Most anthropologists have done field work in villages or in the urban neighborhoods that are their counterpart; my own method begins the same way. That is, when I go to a village I start with its ecological and economic system, or agriculture—the plowing, sowing, weeding, harvesting, and threshing of the basic crops. Since hard physical labor is the central core of life in a traditional village, I also engage in it alongside my peasant subject. This is the quickest way I have found to win a peasant's friendship and acceptance and also get the *feel* of life in any given rural community. If the villagers relax by drinking in the evening, as many do, I join in. I almost always use an interpreter, recruited locally, while also gaining some knowledge of the local language myself. I find the presence of an associate who is part of the local culture provides important moral support. I also make stenographic notes of as much dialogue as I can, preferring the natural unfolding of information through normal conversation to interviews, either written or tape-recorded. Even the best-intentioned interviewer tends to "lead," consciously or unconsciously, a subject along preconceived paths.

In this fashion, a look at agriculture naturally leads to systems of marketing and converting crops to food for the family. From agriculture one also moves into social life and religion. So far the investigation does not differ much from that of an anthropologist. Like the anthropologist, I also have had to study the larger civilization in which a village finds itself—its history, religion, philosophy, art, literature, and present-day politics and economics. Where possible, I also try to interview the peasant's political leadership, in Shahhat's case, President Anwar el-Sadat.

In Shahhat's story, I first moved into the village in 1974, living in the country inn run by his father's cousin, Sobhy. Initially I employed

227

two interpreters, both of them students, one for the morning and another for the afternoon (interpreters tend to tire after five or six hours of steady translation). For a period of three months I studied the village's agriculture and got to know its people. Shahhat and his parents were among my acquaintances; I first met them at the *hafla* described in the story and was present in the village when Shahhat's father, Abd el Baset, died. Soon afterward I returned to Cairo to spend some weeks typing up my notes. When I returned, Shahhat and his mother were in deep mourning; it was as they returned to normal life and once more engaged in village activities that they became my principal subjects. At the same time I obtained the services of a man I came to regard as a peculiarly gifted interpreter, Nubi el Hagag, a petty government official and merchant (he ran a cigarette shop in the evenings) from the town of Luxor, across the Nile some three miles away. This was quite lucky as Nubi came from Luxor's most highly respected family who were generally believed to be direct descendants of the Prophet Mohammed. This gave us great acceptability in the village. Despite his high status among the villagers, Nubi himself was not saintly but enjoyed drinking and carousing as much as the next man; this in turn gave us access to saints and sinners alike.

In each of the dozen peasant studies I have undertaken, there is a certain amount of improvisation and making the best of circumstances. Gradually, a method of work developed that went remarkably well. Shahhat and I arose and went to his fields in early morning; at first he knew no English nor I Arabic. But Shahhat was remarkably quick of comprehension and it was not long before we knew enough of each other's languages to communicate; indeed, today Shahhat speaks English fluently. At mid-day we returned home where Ommohamed had a delicious noon meal prepared which we ate in her comfortable upstairs room and were joined by Nubi, who bicycled from town, his government job completed for the day. For four or five hours each day, while eating and, afterward, over glasses of tea or coffee, Shahhat, his mother, Nubi, and I went over all the events of the previous evening and that morning, reconstructing the dialogue and events which I noted down in a large ledger (eventually these became seven hundred pages of single-spaced typewritten notes). Nubi occasionally stayed on for the evening meal, especially if there were a *hafla* or some other entertainment in the village. During these afternoons, which lasted six or seven months, we also reconstructed the family's past. Rural, half-literate Egyptians, who memorize long passages of the Koran as children, have amazingly clear recall; often Nubi and I

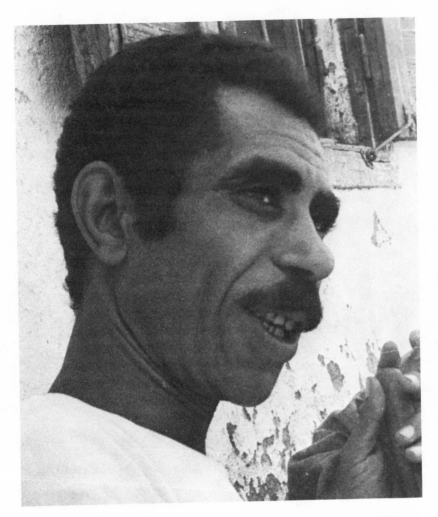

Nubi el Hagag, interpreter.

would interview Ommohamed and Shahhat separately about some past episode; very rarely did their accounts, even of dialogue uttered, ever seriously conflict. The second and third parts of Shahhat's story, ending with his illness and dream of paradise, coincide with this period.

At this point, considering the study over, I returned to Cairo and wrote the first draft from my notes. Shahhat's quarrel with his mother and

Shahhat and Ommohamed look over photographs to illustrate their story.

uncle Ahmed, then, took place while I was not in the village, and these episodes were reconstructed later from separate interviews with the three of them. Advised of the quarrel by Shahhat in Cairo, I returned once more to the village. Hence I was physically present during the more dramatic episodes of the closing section: Shahhat's return home and continued estrangement, the ritual rape of Batah in broad daylight in the village road, Shahhat's flight into the desert, the festival in Luxor (to honor Nubi's ancestor), and the reconciliation. The final, brief paragraphs were written two years later. They represented a denouement I had not antici-

Shahhat, Ommohamed, the author, and a villager. Shahhat and the author worked in the fields each morning and met with Ommohamed and interpreter Nubi el Hagag four or five hours each afternoon to reconstruct events and conversation. Shahhat, who at first spoke only Arabic, gradually learned English.

pated, Shahhat in the original story leaving the village in the final pages. Looking back, I now see the true final resolution was perhaps inevitable.

A reader might have a number of questions about this method and I shall try to anticipate them. Nubi and I tried, as much as we were able, to remain observers and not participants, and I think, in the main, we succeeded, especially because of Nubi's role as a restraining influence. (Shahhat and I were together, virtually every waking hour, for almost a year; several times we had violent, usually drunken, fights, Arab-fashion, coming to blows, once throwing chairs at each other, and sometimes actually knocking each other down. The entire village was always upset over these emotional outbursts and everybody, but especially Nubi, worked for a reconciliation. I rather enjoyed them since they were psychologically satisfying and cleared the air; so did Shahhat.) But when it came to events that represented progress in the story, Nubi and I kept carefully aside.

As a writer I came to feel I knew these people so well it mattered little what came from reconstructions and what was personally observed; nothing, not a word of dialogue, was ever invented by me. The ugly scene when Batah's grandmother fought to save her from a bad marriage, for instance, was observed; Nubi and I stood on the stairway, alarmed, but afraid to intervene, throughout. Again, after Shahhat was hurt at the festival, Nubi and I and other men from the village had to physically fight, swinging fists and kicking, to force the crowd to part so we could get him out; I had to throw a violently hysterical scene at the Luxor hospital to get him treated before he lost any more blood. On the other hand, we were thankfully not present during the scenes of Shahhat's quarrel with his mother; both Nubi and I were relieved to get the versions of the conflicting participants much later when they had calmed down. I was present at Batah's rape and experienced considerable cultural shock, but then, so did Shahhat.

There are many instances in which interior thoughts are described, especially those of Shahhat and his mother; these are based on what they told me they felt at the time. Once our real work began I spent my time constantly with them, eating my meals in their home and occasionally sleeping there, though I preferred to keep my room at the nearby inn as a quiet place to sleep and write. With the possible exception of two other peasant subjects, I doubt if I have ever gotten to know anyone, including members of my own family, as intimately as I grew to know Shahhat.

This method, of deep personal engagement, is of course very different from that of the anthropologist, at least in the technical sense. An anthropologist usually begins such a study with a conceptual model to guide his choice and arrangement of the facts. He is likely to use technical procedures, such as Rorschach tests or Thematic Apperception Tests or any of a wide variety of scientifically accepted psychological tests. He may use questionnaires to gather statistics from a broad sampling of the village's people. Whatever his specific technique, he will follow a path of understanding marked "theoretical," or "scientific," or "scholarly." A journalist,

232

with his different interest, training, and variety of academic attachment, will follow another kind of search for understanding.

In the end, all study of human beings lies in a borderland between science and art and the difference between the journalist and the anthropologist is one of degree; one mixes some science with his art, the other some art with his science. Both the social scientist and the reporter, if they are honest and responsible to the facts, aim to increase understanding with as scientifically acceptable a study or as true a portrait as they are able to perceive and write. "Man will become better when you show him what he is like," runs an entry in Anton Chekhov's notebooks.

This is our common purpose and the reason I have written Shahhat's story, and in the way I did. A real person, his identity and existence are its verification.

Washington, D.C.   RC
Fall 1977

SHAHHAT

An Egyptian

was composed in 11-point Linotype Granjon and leaded two points,
with display type in handset Garamond Old Style,
by Joe Mann Associates, Inc.;
printed on 50-pound Warren Smooth Cream,
Smyth-sewn, and bound over boards in Columbia Bayside Natural,
and also adhesive bound with paper covers,
by Maple-Vail Book Manufacturing Group, Inc.;
and published by

SYRACUSE UNIVERSITY PRESS
Syracuse, New York 13210